THE GOODLY FELLOWSHIP OF THE PROPHETS

THE GOODLY FELLOWSHIP OF THE PROPHETS

STUDIES, HISTORICAL, RELIGIOUS, AND EXPOSITORY IN THE HEBREW PROPHETS

BY

JOHN PATERSON

Professor of Hebrew and Old Testament Exegesis,
Drew Theological Seminary, Madison, N. J.

CHARLES SCRIBNER'S SONS, NEW YORK

L–6.68[V]

Printed in the United States of America

IN
MEMORIAM
PATRIS MEI
VIRI PLENI FIDE
ET SPIRITU SANCTO

FOREWORD

AGE does not wither nor custom stale the infinite variety of the Hebrew Prophets. Though long since dead they continue to speak, and in a day of crisis their word is with power, for they are fearfully modern and strangely relevant. They were "men of the secret" who saw human life in the light of God and spoke of great things yet to come. To us living in a day when it seems we are being afforded the final chance to moralise history and Christianise industry their timeless message has vital reference. To set forth this vital reference is the purpose of this book.

These studies are the outcome of lectures delivered through recent years to theological students, ministerial conferences, and Adult Education groups. The reception accorded them has induced the author to make them available to a wider group; he hopes in this way to mediate to the student of Scripture the sound results of Bible study and, in particular, to show forth the significance for cultural development of those spokesmen of God whom we know as the Prophets of Israel.

The discussion, therefore, is not too technical, though full use has been made of the resources of technical scholarship. The prophets have been studied and interpreted on the basis of the Hebrew Bible, and the oracles, in the main, are rendered directly from the original text. Critical views are not discussed at length, save where questions of interpretation are involved, as, *e.g.*, in the cases of Habakkuk, Nahum, and Ezekiel. The writer has sought rather to sweep into the background the mere "sawdust of criticism," and in questions of Text and Introduction he has been content to set forth generally accepted conclusions. The method adopted in these studies has been to set each prophet in his historical background, relate what is known of him personally, and mark his significance in the history and religion of Israel. Inasmuch, however, as these prophets and spokesmen of God operated with universal ideas and permanently valid principles these ideas and principles are lifted out of their accidental and temporary setting and expounded in their vital reference. The prophets are relevant in our time.

No attempt has been made to reduce the teaching of the prophets to a theological system. Such attempts have been made in the past, and such works are listed in the bibliography. But such a treatment seems questionable in the case of the Hebrew prophets. These inspired personalities are the last men to be compressed within the framework of a system, ecclesiastical or theological. Those "lively oracles" defy such classification, and men whose eyes rolled "with a fine frenzy" are not easily understood or interpreted by our cold logical categories. For the Hebrew "thought with the eye," and the connection of the prophetic oracles is more often *optical* than logical.

Throughout these studies the term Jehovah is employed to render the sacred name: the writer knows well the objections that may be urged against this usage. Undoubtedly it is a mis-formation but it is more euphonious than Yahwe, and as the personal name of Israel's God it has a more personal connotation than *Lord* or the *Eternal*. For these reasons we have retained the familiar term Jehovah.

The thanks of the author are due to Dean Frank Glenn Lankard, of Brothers' College, Drew University, who read the MS and made valuable suggestions; to Professor George W. Frey, Jr., of the Evangelical School of Theology, Reading, Pa., and Assistant Professor F. Heisse Johnson, Brothers' College, Drew University, who both assisted in the preparation of the MS and in the compilation of the bibliography. Thanks are also due to Mrs. F. Heisse Johnson who prepared the Index of Scripture Texts.

Where quotations are made from the Bible they are from the American Standard Version of the Revised Bible, copyrighted by the International Council of Religious Education, and are used by permission.

JOHN PATERSON

Drew Theological Seminary,
Madison, New Jersey
May, 1947

CONTENTS

THE
GOODLY FELLOWSHIP OF
THE
PROPHETS

I

THE GOODLY FELLOWSHIP

IN the goodly fellowship of the prophets we meet with a religious phenomenon unique and without parallel. Here we have to deal with one of the profound movements of the human spirit and with the most significant aspect of Old Testament revelation. Prophets there have been in other religions and in other times, but nowhere do we find a comparable succession of mighty creative personalities who linked the prophetic impulse to spiritual religion and made the religion of Israel a permanent force in the world and a real preparation for the Christian Gospel.

For divination [1] is a perfectly natural human instinct born of man's daily needs and hopes and fears. It is found in all ethnic religions. Soothsayers, seers, mantics, prophets are familiar accompaniments of ancient Oriental cults, and the literature of Greece and Rome has familiarised us with their function in public life. But it is to be noted that the development in Israel was different from that elsewhere. With the development and growth of culture these forms receded to the background and disappeared. State policy ceased to be regulated and directed by them "that chirp and mutter." Such was the general development save in the case of the people Israel, and that is the wonder of the Hebrew prophet and the unique element in Hebrew prophecy. Elsewhere divination is bound by magic and mechanical technique and never emerges from its bonds to become a powerful stimulant of morality or the

[1] Much interesting material on this subject will be found in Alfred Guillaume's *Divination and Prophecy*, 1938, pp. 107 ff.

minister of spiritual religion. But in Israel it did emerge from the chrysalis stage and shone forth with a glory which the passage of time has not dimmed, and for 400 years we have a succession of prophets whose words the world has not been willing to let die.

Nor need we seek to minimise the significance of this fact. For however impressive and imposing the canonical prophets may appear to us it should not be forgotten that the origins of Old Testament prophecy are lowly and obscure. Israel passed through the same stages as Greece and Rome but it passed through them to something nobler and distinct. The boisterous "sons of the prophets," whose ecstatic behavior shocked decent people and made them regard the prophet as a "mad fellow" (II Kings 9:11), are the ancestors of the later classical prophecy, though Amos speaks with scorn of a group that had become professionalised and commercialised (Amos 7:14). But the early crude and crass features were sloughed off by the great prophets, who are not found in gregarious bands like the "sons of the prophets" but appear as lonely souls climbing heights these lesser men could not climb. Many scholars would deny the connection of our canonical prophets with the earlier "ecstatics" and would regard them as religious geniuses. But this is to introduce a thought category which was foreign to the Hebrew way of thinking. The presence of ecstatic elements in the experience of the great prophets may not be denied, though it is less prominent than in the case of their predecessors. The visions of Amos, Isaiah and Jeremiah contain ecstatic elements: Jeremiah cannot be distinguished from the ecstatic Hananiah (Jer. 28), and Ezekiel's book is full of ecstasy. Nor does it seem reasonable to expect it otherwise, for it is the divine method to build by stages and proceed by gradual elevation of existing means and processes. It would seem that there is in the Old Testament a regular and gradual evolution from the crude ebullitions of the sons of the prophets to the inspired statesmanship of Isaiah and the systematic order of Ezekiel. Moreover, despite the crudities of the early prophets it is not to be denied that they were motivated by a flaming zeal for Jehovah, though that zeal might sometimes lack the guidance of adequate knowledge. Though Amos spoke with scorn of the prophets he also regarded prophecy as one of God's signal gifts to the children of Israel (Amos 2:11).

So much it is necessary to state from the historical viewpoint, and what has been said is confirmed by the prophets themselves. There is no instance where the prophets regard themselves as the inspired founders of a new spiritual religion, but everywhere they regard themselves as the restorers and reformers of a religion already in being and known to their auditors. The prophet's appeal is to the knowledge of the people: "Is it not so, O ye sons of Israel?" (Amos 2:11). The complaint of Isaiah is that

"Israel doth not know, My people do not consider" (Is. 1:3)

and the prophet clearly implies that they should have known and that their ignorance is culpable. The religion that had been ethicised at Sinai had become materialised in Canaan, and mechanical relations had been substituted for relations that were originally personal. It was not so in the beginning and it should not be so now. (Jer. 2:2 ff.). The prophets are not founding a new institution or creating a new system; they are pleading for a return to the *status quo ante*. "Return" is the watchword of all; repentance is their common demand.

THE PROPHET'S FUNCTION

The word "prophet" (*Nabi'*) in the Old Testament is derived from a root that means to speak, or better, to *speak by delegated authority.*[2] The *Nabi'* is not one who speaks his own words but the word of one who has authorised and commissioned him to speak. This commission is usually given in the inaugural vision when Jehovah says to his called one:

[2] Cornill, C. H., *The Prophets of Israel,* 1909, pp. 9–10.

"Go, and tell this people" (Is. 6:9)

or

"Go, prophesy to my people Israel" (Amos 7:15).

The prophet speaks because he is commanded to speak, and his word is usually prefaced with "Thus saith Jehovah" or sealed with the phrase, " 'Tis the oracle of Jehovah." The prophet has no option in the matter (Jer. 20:9). This should be emphasised, for there were many in Old Testament times who spoke words without being commissioned by higher authority. "I sent not these prophets," says Jehovah, "yet they ran: I spake not to them, yet they prophesied" (Jer. 23:21). They spoke on their own authority and identified their wishful thinking with the word of Jehovah. They were false, lying prophets. "The prophets are but windbags" is Moffatt's expressive rendering of Jer. 5:13, from which we may gather that the prophet knew well that the unpardonable sin in a preacher is to have nothing to say—and to say it.

This may be further illustrated by the corresponding use of the term *apostle* in the New Testament. This term is derived from the Greek and signifies "one sent, a messenger." Paul speaks of himself on two occasions as an *ambassador* (II Cor. 5:20; Eph. 6:20), and an ambassador does not speak for himself but for the ruler who sent him. There is a profound sense in which the word concerning the Baptist applies to every authentic prophet, apostle, or messenger of God:

"There came a man sent from God whose name was John" (John 1:6). No man may claim kinship with the goodly fellowship of the prophets or the glorious company of the apostles who does not possess this commission from the Great King.

This, moreover, is borne out by the meaning of the English word *prophet,* which is derived from the Greek word *prophētēs.* Liddell and Scott's standard lexicon gives this meaning:

> "strictly *one who speaks for another,* especially one who speaks for a God, and interprets his will to man, a prophet."

The "pro" is the significant part of the word, and at the risk of being elementary we would like to stress this. A prophet is one who speaks on behalf of another and acts as his representative. This precise usage we can observe clearly from the Old Testament itself.

When Moses protests to Jehovah that he is slow of speech and cannot act as spokesman for God at the court of Pharaoh, Jehovah says,

> "See, I have made thee a God (Elohim) to Pharaoh, and Aaron, thy brother, shall be thy prophet (Hebrew, *Nabi';* Greek, *prophētēs*)" (Ex. 7:1).

Ex. 4:16 puts this even more expressively:

> "He (Aaron) shall be thy spokesman (lit. he shall speak for thee) unto the people; and it shall come to pass that he shall be to thee for a mouth, and thou shalt be to him for God (Elohim)."

These early passages make clear what the Hebrew understood by a prophet. A passage from the later period will show the same meaning. In the Maccabean period, when the defiled altar was torn down, the people were at a loss as to what they should do with the stones. The problem seemed incapable of solution because there was no prophet to speak for God and give direction in the matter. They decided, therefore, to wait "until there should arise a prophet (*prophētēs*) to give answer concerning them" (1 Macc. 4:46). To the Hebrew the prophet was one who spoke on behalf of God and interpreted the divine will. His word was not his own: it was the word of Jehovah who called him and gave him the word to speak.

THE PROPHET AND PREDICTION

We have sought in the foregoing to indicate that the prophet spoke for God; here we are concerned with the reference of the spoken word. A common and obstinate error is to think that the prophets were prognosticators and foretellers of the future, writing history in advance and revealing things yet to come. Thus Justin Martyr writes:

> "There were among the Jews certain men who were prophets of God through whom the prophetic spirit published beforehand things that were to come to pass ere ever they happened." [3]

The writer of the Gospel of Matthew also thought thus of prophecy and wrote to show that things happened as they did, "that it might be fulfilled which was spoken by the prophets." But an error is still an error even though it be supported by ancient authorities, and this view is inadequate. It contains a partial truth, for it is not to be denied that the spokesmen for God did frequently predict what would happen in the future, but prediction is not the main element in prophecy. Amos foretold the captivity of Israel, and Jeremiah predicted the fall of Jerusalem; while Isaiah foretold the failure of the Syro-Ephraimite coalition and the failure of Sennacherib to take Jerusalem. Such predictions, and many more, were fulfilled. Men who stood in the Privy Council (Hebrew, sōdh) of Jehovah and knew the divine plan for the world could not fail to predict. But we may not regard this as the main element of prophecy or regard the literal fulfilment of a particular oracle as the test of its value for us. For many predictions were not literally fulfilled. Damascus was not "taken away from being a city," nor did it become "a ruinous heap" (Is. 17:1). Babylon did not suffer as the prophet predicted (Is. 13:15–18) but was taken without a blow being struck, and Jonah saw his prophecy falsified (Jonah 3:4, 10; 4:1). There is profound truth in the word Prof. McCurdy of Toronto was accustomed to say to his classes that "the prophets never meant what they said," *for many things were foretold precisely that they might not come to pass;* they were in the nature of a warning. In that sense all prophecy was contingent and conditional. If we lay stress on the element of prediction we must recognise that

[3] *First Apology,* chap. 31; published in *Douglass Series of Christian Greek and Latin Writers,* Vol. V, 1877.

most of the prophets were left with a considerable weight of unfulfilled predictions. This matter caused many a headache to later writers who viewed prophecy as equivalent to the foretelling and forecasting of events, and it is largely responsible for the development of the Apocalyptic writings.

This emphasis on prediction and its literal fulfilment has been unfortunate in that it has directed and concentrated attention on a secondary element and has substituted a mechanical criterion for a vital standard. The prophet was one who spoke for God and declared the intention of the divine heart; he made plain the purpose of God. That purpose concerned both the present and the future, and in that sense the prophet was both a forth-teller and a fore-teller. The permanent principles of divine sovereignty were set forth in a transient setting; the principles are eternal but the setting is temporal. In those prophets the ethical genius of the original religion attained full maturity and the permanent principles of the divine character were set forth in relation to past, present, and future. History became sacramental, for it was the channel of divine revelation. On this concrete basis of history the prophetic insight operated to set forth the essential truth about God.

This concrete basis and vital reference in all Hebrew thought makes it unnecessary to distinguish between insight and foresight. Insight here implies foresight, for insight into the purposes and plan of God gives men knowledge of what God will do. The secret (Hebrew, sōdh) of Jehovah is with them; they share his counsels and are on most intimate terms of fellowship with him. They are in tune with the Infinite, and "Jehovah will do nothing except he reveal his secret unto his servants the prophets" (Amos 3:7).

The prophets thus speak the revealed will of Jehovah as it concerns the life of the nation and the wider world. They are the interpreters of events. Things did not simply happen but all that happened was part of the divine plan. It might be a famine or a plague of locusts (Joel), or it might be the emergence of some great military colossus (Jer. 25:9; Is. 45:1; Hab. 1:6), or the general state of the nation. In each situation the prophet spoke the word as God gave it to him to speak. God "uncovered their ear" (1 Sam. 9:15) or put his words in their mouth (Jer. 1:9) or caused them to see (Amos 7:11). Prophecy was inevitable.

"Jehovah God hath spoken:
Who can but prophesy?" (Amos 3:8)

THE MESSAGE OF PROPHECY

The fundamental belief of the prophets is their belief in the living God, and to make the living God visible to their people is the purpose of their preaching. Not that they are innovators here but only reformers. God to them was personal, and the relations with his people are wholly personal. The entry into Canaan with its system of Baals and Nature worship had obscured the real nature of Jehovah and brought confusion into his worship. The prophets here assail the worship of Canaan, and recall the people to their first love (Is. 1:2 ff.; Jer. 2:2 ff.). Jehovah is supreme. Nature is interpreted as the minister of God and through its phenomena his moral and spiritual power is revealed. Natural disasters, such as drought, famine, earthquake, are the instruments of his judgment, and through these he speaks to men to recall them to the way of righteousness (Amos 4:6 ff.).

This God, too, is holy and righteous altogether. He demands righteousness and justice from his people. Evil, cruelty, and oppression he abhors, and he is deeply concerned for the sufferings of the poor and needy.

> "Nowhere else as in the prophets has social and humanitarian preoccupation been placed at the center of religion." [4]

Here is expressed a flaming passion against all forms of social injustice, and from those prophets social reformers have never

[4] Causse, A., *Les Prophètes d'Israël*, 1913, p. 83.

ceased to draw strength and inspiration. The prophets are not concerned to found or form new institutions, but every existing institution they examine in the light of the divine righteousness. Righteousness to them is not only a divine attribute; it is a human duty.

For that reason the prophets appear mainly as the fierce critics of the ecclesiastical institution. The dynamic prophet stands over against the static priest, for the dream of a purified world and a holy people surrendered to God can never find satisfaction in the maintenance of the *status quo*. The hierarchy and the monarchy worked together for their own vested interests, but the prophets were fired with the theocratic principle and would acknowledge no authority but the divine. Samuel, Elijah, Nathan, and Jeremiah will rebuke kings to their faces, as did their like-minded successors John Knox and Martin Luther, and the rude shepherd of Tekoa will speak things at Bethel which the high-priest little likes to hear. For to those prophets *life is a unity,* and it must be moralised through and through. Morality may not be divorced from religion, but all life must be flooded with the divine holiness. This wider view of religion and its sphere needs to be emphasised to-day when many seek to separate various human activities, such as Social Service and Education, from the sphere and influence of religion, and would reduce religion again to the barren ecclesiasticism against which the prophets fought continually. Life to them was a unity, and every thought and every activity had to be brought into subjection to God. The prophets, in this sense, stood for religious integrity and the "sole sovereign sway and masterdom of God." They sought a religion that was internalised and personalised, and they denounced the priestly system that stood for a religion mechanised and externalised.

The prophets spoke of judgment and therein they did predict. But they spoke of judgment that they might move the nation to repent and return, that the final triumph might be with divine mercy. In this sense all prophecy was contingent and conditional. But without exception the great pre-exilic prophets proclaim judgment, the reaction of a holy righteous God against human wickedness. God is of purer eyes than to behold iniquity and he cannot look on uncleanness (Hab. 1:13).

That the great prophets also prophesied of restoration and retrieval is also true. Isaiah (7:3) with his thought of the Remnant, Hosea (2:15) and his thought of "the valley of Achor for a door of hope", and the plaintive pleading Jeremiah (33:23 ff.) see beyond judgment, and predict restoration on the ground of their own knowledge of the eternal principles by which God acts. It may be that at times we are conscious of certain tensions and stresses within the prophetic theology, but life is more than logic, and the prophetic mind was large enough to hold together the thought of divine sovereignity and human freedom as well as the thought of judgment and grace. There are oppositions in thought which can be overcome in living experience.

We may now proceed to examine in detail the particular message of each of these spokesmen for God, and Amos will first occupy our attention.

2

AMOS: PROPHET OF RIGHTEOUSNESS

THE name Amos is unique in the Old Testament, and as is his name so is the man. In a history that abounds in striking figures and memorable personalities there is none more striking and memorable than the shepherd of Tekoa. Like a bolt from the blue he steps into the moving scene of Israel's history and as quickly he moves from the stage. His is the briefest of all recorded ministries: according to one scholar his ministry did not last more than thirty minutes.[1] This may be an over-statement, but surely never has so much momentous history been packed into such a brief space of time. From the obscurity he comes and to obscurity he returns, but in that brief interval he kindled a fire that could not be put out. The big words that were as "half battles," to which Amos gave utterance, made an unforgettable impression. Though he founded no church or political institution, and apparently had no disciples, he liberated a spiritual force that abides to this day. Amos is the first of the great writing prophets; he is the first of the goodly fellowship.

There had been prophets before Amos but though he bears the name prophet (*Nabi'*) he represents something new and unique. He repudiates connection with the prophets of his day (7:14) and if he must be called by that name (*Nabi'*) the term must be given a new and higher significance (7:15).

[1] Morgenstern, Julian, *Amos Studies,* Parts 1, 2, 3; 1941, p. 11.

He has all the marks and tokens of the pioneer: he marks the close of an era and the beginning of a new time. He is the father of written prophecy, and his book is probably the earliest book of our Old Testament.

PERSONAL HISTORY

Amos tells us he was a shepherd, and this would seem to imply that he was a simple working man. Some scholars have thought of him as a sheepmaster like Mesha, king of Moab (II Kings 3:4), or Nabal (I Sam. 25:2 ff.), but while the Hebrew text of chapter 7:14—though not the Greek version—affords ground for this assumption the general impression conveyed by his book is that he was the hired servant of an employer. This is confirmed by the fact that he lists as a secondary occupation the dressing or "pinching" of sycomore trees to speed their ripening fruit (7:14). No objection need be made on the ground that a person of such low degree could not be expected to utter thoughts so lofty. Neither in ancient nor modern times has culture been the monopoly of the wealthy classes; the reverse has been more frequently true.

Tekoa lay southeast of Bethlehem and is mentioned in II Samuel 14:2 as the home of the wise woman whose services Joab enlisted to achieve his purpose with David. It was fortified by Rehoboam (I Chron. 2:24; II Chron. 11:5, 6), and lying where it did it was sufficiently removed from the contaminating influence of the neighboring civilisations of Philistia and Canaan. Here the faith of the fathers remained in something of its pristine purity and simplicity. The place was austere and its dwellers likewise. It is to be noted how frequently great prophets like Elijah and Amos emerge from the edge of the desert to strike into the life of Canaan. The significance of this will become clear as we study Amos.

Attempts have been made to show that Amos was not a Judean but a native of north Israel. There is no real reason to think so. Sycomores may not have grown on the height at Tekoa but they could be found lower down on the Shephēlā or on the slopes down to Engedi, and the work would entail only a few hours' journey for the hardy Amos. Amos was a member of the southern kingdom, and his home was in Tekoa of Judea.

THE MAN AND HIS THOUGHT

It is easy to understand how such an environment would affect the prophet's thought. Most of us owe much to our surroundings, and environment has much to do with the molding of character. Amos was rooted in the desert and Amos is as stern and rugged as the desert and its bare surroundings. The wide open spaces in which he lived are reflected in the amplitude of his spiritual vision: the mountains of Moab over which the sunrise broke in glory for him gave a shining clear quality to his expression of divine truth. All his similes and metaphors reflect the bare gaunt background of the desert. His task, too, was his teacher. For the shepherd must know his way about in the desert. He must be quick to detect the rustle of the gliding snake and know the way of the lion and the bear. Every sound in the desert is significant, and the shepherd must know its meaning. He must have sense to put two and two together and know what's what. The desert was the school of Amos, and in that school his powers of observation were developed and his faculties sharpened in high degree. He knew well what the lion's roar meant and what the struggle of the twittering bird conveyed. The way of the eagle in the air and the way of the serpent on a rock were not hidden from him.

Does a lion roar in the jungle and have no prey?
Or a young lion let out his voice except he have captured?
Falls a bird to the ground and no noose be upon it?
Or a snare spring up from the ground without catching?
(Amos 3:4)

There is an orderly sequence in all the phenomena of natural life: cause is followed by effect. Amos learned that in the desert. His varied experiences were related and co-ordinated so that they yielded experience, wisdom, maturity. From those accumulated observations and deductions Amos proceeded to draw wider inferences. Though Amos lived long before Aristotle and knew nothing of Greek philosophy he has been well called "the prophet of causation." Amos saw that one thing led to another in the natural world, and he judged rightly that it was not otherwise in the moral and spiritual realm. For Amos knew both the laws of Nature and the law of God.

This training in the desert developed in him an uncanny insight which enabled him to see to the center of things. To the desert also he owes his direct and vigorous approach in dealing with things. Piercing insight and brutal directness are the characteristics of Amos and all his spiritual sons. John the Baptist is another such desert dweller, and the Baptist did not mince his words. Oliver Cromwell was a humble farmer in the eastern wolds of England until God called him to the task of routing a king and ruling a nation. Such men may often offend with their brusqueness. Amos will speak of society women as "fat cows of Bashan" (4:1), while John will castigate his contemporaries as "a generation of vipers" (Matt. 3:7) and Oliver Cromwell will compound his speech of both as he loftily says, "Take away that bauble." But we cannot miss the contribution such men make to history. "Into politics such men bring facts: into religion they bring vision." [2] Such men see to the roots and realities of things, and they will not be gainsaid.

Amos' thought, then, runs in the category of law, and it so runs whether he be judging physical or moral matters. One thing leads to another; every effect has its antecedent cause. When Amos goes on his business journeys to sell the fleeces of his ugly little sheep he will not leave his wits at home with

[2] Smith, George Adam, *The Book of the Twelve Prophets,* 1928, Vol. I, p. 83.

the sheep. Amos is no hayseed blown in by the east wind to Bethel or Samaria; he is a man with a mission. It may be primarily a business mission, but it is religious also. He is a man with all his wits about him and all his faculties awake and alert to register.

THE HISTORICAL BACKGROUND

There was much to register. The date of Amos is shortly after 760 B.C. Morgenstern [3] would fix his date precisely at New Year's Day of 751 B.C. when Amos delivered his address at Bethel. But there is no reason to limit Amos' activity to this one appearance, and it seems more probable that the date is nearer 760 B.C. At this time Jeroboam II (787–747 B.C.) was king in Israel and Uzziah ruled in Judah (785–747 B.C.). These were both great kings, and their time was one of splendor and achievement. Things flourished as they had flourished in the days of David. Commerce expanded and military enterprises met with success. The ancient foe, Syria, had been subdued and the stolen territories in Gilead were retaken (6:13, 14). People felt comfortable and secure in Zion and Samaria (6:1). Danger seemed very far off. But an Amos is not deceived by the seeming; he sees the real, and beneath all that glitter he could have said with Carlyle, another Amos of another day, "To me through these cobwebs Death and Eternity sat glaring." The social problem had sharpened itself to an intolerable point of agony; wealth had been concentrated into the hands of rich grandees, while the unprivileged were being exploited and sold into slavery. The sturdy yeoman class, once the pride and strength of Israel, was passing out of existence. The rich were building summer houses and winter houses (3:15) and reclining on couches inlaid with ivory (6:4), while their womanfolk gave themselves with unholy abandon to all forms of intemperance (4:1). Those grandees drank their wine from large sacrificial bowls (6:6) and

[3] *Op. cit.*, p. 177.

anointed themselves with the premier ointments, but never a thought had they for communal welfare:

"they are not grieved for the hurt of Joseph" (6:6).

The poor were sold for a pair of shoes, and the peasant found himself and his family sold into servitude through the corruption of justice (5:12). Men grudged the coming of the Sabbath that halted their eager pursuit of nefarious gains; they longed—

"that it might be gone, that they might set forth wheat, even the refuse of the wheat, making the ephah small and the shekel great" (8:5).

Adulteration of food, falsification of weights and measures, venality of justice—all were here in full measure. Life in Israel under Jeroboam II was not unlike life in the last days of the Roman Empire, or in France before the Revolution.

On that hard pagan world disgust
And secret loathing fell:
Deep weariness and sated lust
Made human life a hell.[4]

Pride and fulness of bread—and a famine of the spirit, these are the signs of decay and approaching death. Within a generation Israel was gone. Amos saw the coming of the end. With his sense of law and order there could be no other issue in a world ruled by a righteous God. Men do not gather grapes from thistles or figs from thorns, or as Amos says:

"Shall horses run upon the rock?
Can one plow the sea with an ox?" (6:12, emended text).

THE MINISTRY OF AMOS

With such a background of life and thought Amos was called to exercise his ministry. To such a civilization he was called to speak the divine word. For such diseases he was called to diagnose, and he was called of God. Amos did not

[4] Arnold, Matthew, "Obermann Once More."

take up this work of his own choice. He was called of God and necessity was laid upon him.

> "No prophet was I nor son of a prophet . . . but Jehovah took me as I followed the flock, and Jehovah said to me, Go, be a prophet to my people Israel" (7:14).

The prophet is, in truth, "a man apprehended of God" and he has no option in the matter.

> "Jehovah has spoken: who can but prophesy?" (3:8).

It is not otherwise when Paul says,

> "Woe is me if I preach not the Gospel" (1 Cor. 9:16).

Neither prophet nor apostle had any choice in the matter.

The fact that Amos was an outsider and not a native of the northern kingdom conferred certain advantages. It saved him from the drugging influence of familiarity and from the numbing sense of inevitable complicity in the evils he sees so clearly. His detached attitude made possible a disinterested judgment. But the impartial spectator may lack sympathy, and he will certainly not speak with the passion of Hosea or Jeremiah. It might even be questioned whether a man has the right to pronounce doom on a people for whom he has not agonized in intercession. Amos is the first prophet of doom to Israel and he seems to deliver his message without a quiver in his voice. Such a message will break the heart of Hosea and melt the tender Jeremiah in a flood of tears. Amos is "an hard man." No sobs shake his rugged frame and no tears stain the page as in the book of Hosea. But we may not be less than just to this inflexible man of God. Twice, indeed, we find a brief word of intercession, as if the pastoral heart of the shepherd were strangely moved.

> "I said, Jehovah, pardon: how shall Jacob rise again? For he is small." (7:2).

This note recurs once again (7:4, 5) and then is heard no more. Amos' head did not have to struggle with his heart; his sense of law and order is rooted too deep, and he moves forward as one whose watchword is:

> "Justice, justice shalt thou pursue" (Deut. 16:20).

How the call came to Amos we are not informed; he tells us he was called (7:14) but, unlike Isaiah or Jeremiah, he gives no details. It has been suggested that the call came to him in the midst of a thunderstorm and that echoes of this may be heard in 3:8. Be that as it may, when the call comes to Amos he stays not to confer with flesh and blood, but straight to the head and front of all the offending thing he goes, to the royal sanctuary at Bethel, the Canterbury of ancient Israel. Bethel was but ten miles from Jerusalem, and Tekoa was only twelve miles southeast of Jerusalem. Gilgal lay seven miles north of Bethel and Samaria twenty miles north of Gilgal. From Samaria to Tekoa was not more than two days' journey.

As to when and where Amos delivered the various addresses contained in his book we are not informed. Morgenstern[5] holds that only one address was delivered, and it was delivered at Bethel. There Amos sang the death-song of Israel.

> She is fallen to rise no more,
> the Virgin of Israel:
> Cast down upon her land
> none to upraise her (5:2).

If Amos sang that song, as Morgenstern has suggested, in the gray dawn of New Year's Day 751 B.C. such a message must have fallen upon the heart of his hearers with a sound like that of clods falling upon coffins. Morgenstern may be correct in thinking Amos spoke only at Bethel and that the address did not take more than thirty minutes. In that case Amos will have composed his book and inserted these addresses after his retiral from his mission. But there are addresses in the book that have the appearance of having been delivered to those to whom they are addressed. The speeches in 3:9 ff.; 4:1 ff.; 6:1 ff. are too vital and vigorous to be regarded as merely literary compositions; they were surely spoken to the people of

[5] *Ibid.*, p. 10.

Samaria, and spoken by Amos with his eye upon the object. The series of opening oracles against the nations (1:13–3:2) may well have been delivered in the capital on the occasion of a military review after such military victories as Lo-debar and Karnaim (6:13). Amos had an eye for time and place. The fact, too, that in 7:17 the words of Amos are already known to Amaziah and that the court is not unconscious of a certain furor caused by the prophet from Judea would seem to indicate a ministry extending over a period of time, some months at least.

The interview with Amaziah at Bethel (7:10–17) is highly interesting. The presence of this historical section in its present position raises questions which we need not discuss here. But it does tell us not only of Amos' call but of the effect of his ministry and how that ministry was brought to an abrupt conclusion. A dynasty that had been set upon the throne amid blood and massacre and, at the instigation of the prophet Elisha, might well fear a prophet speaking such words as Amos spoke. As Amaziah says of those words:

"the land is not able to bear them" (7:10).

Something had to be done, and we see how it was done. Here we have one of the great interviews of history comparable to those between Athanasius and Arius, or John Knox and Queen Mary, or Luther and his foes at the Diet of Worms. Divine truth is challenged in the name of the law and human authority seeks to control the oracle of God. The procedure is familiar enough and the results are always the same. History continues to repeat itself.

There is something almost shrewish in the high-pitched tones of Amaziah as he faces the rude shepherd of Tekoa.

"O thou gazer, go, flee thee away into the land of Judah, and there eat thy bread, and prophesy there; but prophesy not again at Bethel: for it is the king's chapel and it is the royal court" (7:12, 13).

The King James version is much too polite here and does more than justice to Amaziah. The high ecclesiastical dignitary was positively rude. "Get out," he screams, "preach elsewhere where you really belong." Amaziah classes Amos with people with whom Amos refused to be classed, the professional preachers of that time whose only thought was cheap notoriety and the fee they expected to receive. We may feel glad that Amos was not Jeremiah, for Jeremiah would meekly take all this like a lamb and go home to pray over it. Not so Amos: Amos will give as he gets, and a Roland will be exchanged for an Oliver.

> "Thou sayest, preach not against Israel, and drip not thy word against the house of Isaac. Therefore thus saith Jehovah, thy wife shall be an harlot in the city, and thy sons and daughters shall die by the sword, and thy land shall be divided by line; and thou shalt die in an unclean land, and Israel shall surely go forth into captivity from his land" (7:16–17).

There was nothing for Amos but to go. Amaziah remained, as always remain those Amaziahs and Pashurs and Caiaphases, "clothed with a little brief authority." They belong to time and are remembered solely because for one brief moment they crossed the path of those who belong to the ages. Amos will go back to Tekoa and Pastor Niemöller to the concentration camp and Christ to Calvary, but the truth which they embody and represent cannot be arrested. For it is truth eternal.

So Amos entered on his ministry, and so he laid it down again. Back to his shepherding in the South and his work among the sycomores [6]—and to the writing of his book.

THE TEACHING OF AMOS

Caution must be used in any approach to the teaching of the prophets, for they were not primarily concerned to

[6] This is not our sycamore but a kind of fig-mulberry tree. Its fruit was infested with an insect (*Sycophaga crassipes*), and until the eye or top was punctured, so that the insects might escape, it was not eatable. Amos' work as "a dresser of sycomore-trees" would appear to have consisted of puncturing or 'pinching' the figs.

formulate doctrine or institute systems. Most of all is this true in the case of Amos who stands at the head of the prophetic movement. For Amos built better than he knew, and he started trains of thought which he could not follow to the end. That is true of all the prophets. Their insights were partial and broken and they were unable to compass the full orb of divine truth. They were but points of light which later were to be gathered into the full light of Christ. Stresses and tensions characterize Old Testament theology and apparent antinomies abound but these are finally resolved in the light of full revelation. It has pleased God to speak "at sundry times and in diverse manners" (Heb. 1:1): we receive one word from this prophet and another word from that.

"The words of Amos" can be understood only in the light of his *social, economic, and historical background*. For Amos is a representative of the Aramaic tradition as opposed to the Canaanite tradition. He represents the nomad or semi-nomad as opposed to the agricultural civilization. There is involved here a real *Kulturkampf*, an aspect of that strife of cultures which assumed various forms in antiquity. It is in this light we must study Amos. There is a socio-economic as well as a religious and theological message, and the two may not be separated.

The desert and the sown land represent two permanent factors in the life of Israel and their continued presence is responsible for the modern, as for the ancient, situation in Palestine. The way of the desert is not the way of the sown land; the *mishpat* (way, manner or custom) of the nomad differs from the *mishpat* of the peasant, and all the elements of cultural conflict lie here. Thus T. H. Robinson writes:

> "the history of Israel, then, is the record of the interaction of these two orders of society, or rather of the spiritual principles which they embodied." [7]

The conceptions of sexual morality prevailing among nomads,

[7] Oesterley, W. O. E., and Robinson, T. H., *History of Israel*, 1934, Vol. I, p. 49.

their lofty sense of personal values as over against property values, their steadfast belief in life, liberty, and the pursuit of happiness, and the idea that all men were created equal—all such strong democratic ideas were native to the desert but clean contrary to the theory and practice of those who lived under organized forms of monarchy. These ideas constitute the essence of the Aramaic tradition and it is such ideas that impel Nathan to denounce David's sin (II Sam. 12) and make Elijah confront Ahab with his social injustice to Naboth (I Kings 21:17 ff.). The two fundamental institutions of desert life, the law of blood revenge and the law of hospitality, are grounded in the thought of tribal brotherhood and the profound sense of personal values.

The agricultural civilization was wholly other. The *mishpat* of the sown land displaced the *mishpat* of the desert, and property values became paramount. What that means can be seen and felt all through the Old Testament. It means the monarchy, the ecclesiastical institution, the hierarchy, and the elaborate ritual of the temple. It means slavery and serfdom and that men are no longer treated as ends in themselves but as means to ends. Property is valued above personality and "the poor are sold for a pair of shoes" (Amos 2:6). The church itself becomes involved in the sorry scheme of things and is bound hand and foot with the ruthless exploiting system. The very institution whose purpose and aim should have been to create and develop personality became an active agent in its denial and suppression. It became a great organization informed only with material principles and oblivious of its spiritual function.

Such a conflict is clear throughout the Old Testament, and it passes over into the New Testament. It seems a never-ending conflict. But though the church is set *in the world* it need not be *of the world,* and it is that conviction that gives rise to the goodly fellowship of the prophets, the glorious company of the apostles, and the noble army of martyrs. It brings Elijah from the desert and it sends Amos to Bethel; these temporal incidents are but instances of an eternal conflict. For the Aramaic tradition must always be at war with the heresy of Canaan.

To understand Amos, then, it is necessary to think of others who represent this tradition, though their approach to the cultural problem involved was wholly negative. Those others are the Rechabites and Nazirites (Amos 2:11), and our information concerning the former is fuller than that concerning the latter. The Rechabites were desert-dwellers who refused to give up nomad life and adopt the agricultural civilization, and in this they followed the command of their founder, Jonadab ben Rechab.

> "Ye shall drink no wine, neither ye nor your sons forever: neither shall ye build house, nor sow seed, nor plant vineyard, nor have any; but all your days ye shall dwell in tents" (Jer. 35:6,7).

The Rechabites were fierce devotees of Jehovah, not unlike the Wahabis in Islam, and the revolution that set Jehu on the throne was carried through with their support (II Kings 10:5 ff.). Amaziah and Jeroboam II might well fear the appearance of one who resembled those fiery devotees from the desert, for those who made kings might well unmake them. They stood for a desert God and a simple faith. They held civilization to be a profound mistake, and believed that Israel's only hope lay in a return to the nomad life and the simple desert cult. For all Israel's social and political ills they had but one cure—a tent in the desert.

The fundamental fallacy of such a solution is easy to see. It makes God dependent on a particular form of social organization and limits him to one sphere—the desert. It makes it impossible for man to meet God where he most needs him, in the busy city street. Thus while Jeremiah applauds the fidelity of the Rechabites he refuses to accept their austere creed (Jer. 35). Jeremiah knows that the God who revealed himself at Sinai as *I will be what I will be* has an amplitude in his nature and character that makes him adequate for every developing civilization. Many scholars believe there is a strong Rechabite strain in the prophets, and particularly in Amos, but Amos had something more than the Rechabite faith. That something more made him the prophet Amos.

Amos will not deny progress or condemn civilization. He will stand for the Aramaic tradition in so far as it is spiritual. He will not condemn the Israelites for becoming farmers or engaging in commerce, but he will condemn them for doing those things and thinking God had nothing to do with them. Amos will bring all such matters within the sweep and scope of God. For Amos faced a civilization that had developed strongly on the material side and failed to keep the pace spiritually. The body politic had waxed fat and sleek, but the national soul was miserably thin and emaciated. That is no novel situation. The prophet's message is here set in a transient setting but it has permanent significance. Nations may learn to fly and yet forget to walk in the path of God's commandments. That is why Amos is so relevant to life. He passes beyond accidentals to essentials. Civilization need not go back to the desert, as the Rechabites assert, nor need we return to the "horse and buggy days," or ply the spinning wheel and wear a loin cloth like Gandhi. Life must progress, but its progress can be guaranteed only as the civilization which emerges is informed and inspired with a deep permanent spiritual principle. Amos knows that it is the business of religion to shape and mold a satisfying culture whether men live in an agricultural civilization or a machine age. That culture can never be fixed and final, as the Rechabites thought, but will vary according to time and clime. But every civilization must be built on moral and spiritual foundations; without such basis, Amos says, it will fall as Israel fell.

> "Except the Lord do build the city they labor in vain that build" (Ps. 127).

Thus Amos is speaking to a concrete situation and he speaks simply. He speaks of God and his demands, of Israel and its relation to God, of wider human relationships among men and God's interest therein. And because those relations, as he sees them, are fundamentally rotten and unsound, he pronounces judgment final and absolute.

THE GOD OF RIGHTEOUSNESS

The people to whom Amos spoke were not irreligious. On the contrary, all the evidence shows that the sanctuaries were crowded and that the altars reeked continually with the smoke of sacrifice. The people were oozing and dripping with religion—of a kind. But it was all hot, feverish, and sensual. Such religiosity could not deceive the sharp eyes of Amos.

> Go to Bethel and transgress,
> To Gilgal and increase transgression;
> Bring sacrifices every morning
> And tithes every three days;
> Burn thank offerings of that which is unleavened,
> And proclaim aloud your free-will offerings,
> For thus ye like it, O Children of Israel.
> 'Tis the oracle of Jehovah Sabaoth (4:4, 5).

Such worship is a profane travesty for it was the act of men and women morally unclean and unwilling to submit themselves to the searching discipline of God. The ethic of the thing done had been substituted for the ethic of the clean heart: religion had become externalized and materialized. The prophet will have it internalized and moralized. Not that Amos is to be regarded as a moralist and nothing more. Amos does not identify morality with religion but he will not accept a religion that excludes morality. Nor is Amos an innovator or schismatic. He is a reformer and all his words plainly attest that he is not introducing new ideas but reiterating the original teaching as proclaimed by Moses and accepted by the people. Amos does not use the term "knowledge of God," which is Hosea's favorite term, but Amos does reckon with the presence of this knowledge in the minds of the people. He appeals to a knowledge which is shared by both them and himself. Amos does not deal with the bull calves or the Baals as Hosea does. What concerns Amos is Israel's thought of God and his demands, and if Amos has little to say about Baal it is because he has so much to say about Jehovah.

For the worship of a people will be determined by its thought of their God, his character and his demands. To Amos God is the God of the Decalogue who gave the Law amid the thunder of Sinai while his people stood in awe and worshipped in lowly reverence. Jehovah was the God who made a covenant with Israel and called them to be his people on terms of his holy, sovereign, righteous will. He revealed himself in their national history and raised up faithful servants to direct them in the way they should go.

> I destroyed the Amorites before you
> Whose height was as that of cedars,
> Whose strength was as the oak:
> I destroyed his fruit from above
> And his roots from beneath.
> And I brought you up from the land of Egypt,
> And led you in the wilderness forty years.
> From your sons I raised up prophets,
> And from your young men Nazirites;
> But ye gave wine to the Nazirites,
> And said to the prophets, Prophesy not.
> Is it not so, O house of Israel?
> 'Tis the oracle of Jehovah (2:9–12).

The whole center of gravity in religion had been changed. The institution of the monarchy, the growth and expansion of the ecclesiastical organization, and the environment of Canaan had combined to destroy the profound sense of awe and reverence that first informed the religion and constituted its vital spirit. Religion had assumed the form of a commercial racket, and men sought to control the Deity in terms of a *quid pro quo* arrangement. The high and holy One of Israel had been reduced to the level of a Canaanite deity, and men thought of God as altogether one of themselves. The thought of divine sovereignty had given place to the thought of human control, and the ritual had supplanted the moral.

We must be careful here to understand Amos and the great prophets Isaiah and Jeremiah. Many scholars assume that these prophets are advocating a system of religion without ritual or sacrifice. This seems quite impossible. The great prophets are united in their denial of the efficacy of mere ritual and in their demand for moral and spiritual relations between the people and God. All are equally emphatic on the point that the original center of gravity in religion has been shifted and that it must be restored. But neither Amos nor Isaiah nor Jeremiah would deny a place to sacrifice. When Amos asks:

> "Did ye bring unto me sacrifices and offerings in the wilderness forty years, O house of Israel?" (5:25)

he plainly expects a negative answer. But Amos refers elsewhere (8:5) to the new moon and the Sabbath as institutions that have a rightful place in the communal life. Obviously we must interpret his words in their full context. The truth is that the fault does not lie with Amos but with the Hebrew language, which had such a scarcity of adverbs and adjectives that it could not easily qualify or modify. The difficulty is inherent in the Hebrew genius whose main mark and token is intensity. The Hebrew knew black and white but it knew nothing of neutral gray. It could say "either . . . or" but not "both . . . and." Amos is perhaps making a preacher's emphasis but he makes it in the only way open to a Hebrew. The modern preacher would say sacrifice occupied a relatively unimportant place in the beginning; Amos says the same by saying it was not there at all. Jeremiah 7:22 puts the matter in another light when he says:

> "I spake not to your fathers, nor commanded them in the day that I brought them out of Egypt, concerning burnt-offerings and sacrifices."

Jeremiah is here denying that sacrifice was instituted by Jehovah, and is suggesting that the ritual is really the pagan element in Israel's religion. It is a survival from the pre-Mosaic period or something that has been incorporated later in Canaan. It was not ordained of Jehovah.

Amos seeks to set the center of gravity in religion where it was originally. In that sense Amos is not innovator but reformer. This he does by setting forth the essential character of God. God, he says, is *not concerned with doing but with being;* God is primarily concerned with his people being like himself. He is the God of Moses who slew the Egyptian who maltreated the poor Israelite (Ex. 2:11); he is the God who heard Israel's cry in Egypt and redeemed them with his strong right hand and brought them out of the house of bondage. He is the God of the commandments: his requirements are few and simple, but they cut clean across the ingrained selfishness of the human heart. He is a God of righteousness, and righteousness is not a national or local concept; it is universal. *Right and not rites* he demands, and he demands it everywhere.

I hate, I despise your feasts,
And will not smell your solemn assemblies;
Yea, though ye bring burnt-offerings and meal-offerings
I will not delight in them. . . .
Take away from me the noise of your songs;
I will not listen to the melody of your viols.
But let justice roll down as waters,
And righteousness as a never-ending stream (5:21–25).

Thus Amos opens his book with a series of oracles against the nations (1:3–2:15). There are seven such oracles but there is reason to doubt the authenticity of some of these. Nonetheless when such additions are expunged there remains a group of oracles in which the divine judgment is denounced against the surrounding nations for various forms of inhumanity. "Man's inhumanity to man makes countless thousands mourn," but it does not escape the all-seeing eye of the

God of righteousness. These nations are condemned not for disobedience to the Jewish law but for breaches of the natural laws of piety written in the heart and conscience of men. These elementary laws are older than the Law given at Sinai; they are as old as humanity itself and they are engraven on the human heart everywhere. It is the possession of such elements of conscience that lifts man above the beast and keeps him on the human level. "The lesser breeds without the Law" are not unconscious of this elementary chivalry and sense of fair play. Here is the very basis of human life; where this is lost the world returns to a condition of moral chaos. The divine righteousness is here revealed reacting against a cruelty that ignores human rights, denies pity, and makes human relations like those of wild beasts. When God, who is the God of all good order, reveals himself in righteousness all that will vanish like smoke before his advent. For he is essentially righteous and full of pity.

> For three transgressions of Damascus,
> Yea, for four I will not turn *it* back,
> Because they threshed Gilead with iron harrows (1:3).

Wherever the prophet looked he found this lack of pity, whole villages sold into slavery (1:6), pregnant women ripped up (1:13), the bones of the dead burned to lime to gratify revenge (2:1), until men seem to delight in cruelty for its own sake. Nor is it otherwise with Israel.

> For three transgressions of Israel,
> Yea, for four I will not turn *it* back;
> Because they have sold the righteous for silver
> And the needy for a pair of shoes,
> And they trample the head of the poor
> And thrust them out of the way.
> Father and son share a harlot
> To desecrate my holy name
> While they spread out pawned garments
> Beside every altar,

And the wine of the condemned they drink
In the house of their god (2:6–8).

There is something eerie and awesome about that "it." What is it? "It" is the reaction of the divine righteousness, the coming of him who is to judge all men, of him who is not only the God of Israel but the God of humanity.

AMOS AND MONOTHEISM

The question whether Amos, or even Moses, was a monotheist is largely an academic question. More important is the question of the character of the deity, and this has been set forth in the previous section. The truth would seem to be that Amos did not think any of those matters through to their logical conclusion. Of theoretical monotheism there is no trace either in Amos or Moses, but of practical monotheism there is a good deal. It was left to Deutero-Isaiah, who is more of a religious philosopher than a prophet, to give us a full-blown theoretical or philosophical monotheism. Amos stands at the head of a line that was to grow and develop.

But it is clear from the opening chapters with his thought of the essentially ethical quality of righteousness Amos is dealing with something more than a national or nature god. Amos does not use the phrase *God of Israel;* his God is a world God interested in all nations and their national movements. He is the efficient cause of those movements.

Are ye not unto me as the Cushites, O sons of Israel?
Did not I bring Israel from Egypt
And the Philistines from Capthor
And the Syrians from Kir? (9:7)

It is not difficult to see how far men's thoughts have moved if we recall an earlier incident in the history of Israel. The Ammonites had attacked Gilead at an earlier time and Jephthah reasons with them on the basis of a nationalistic thought of God.

"Shall ye not possess what your god gives you, while we possess what our God has given us?" (Judg. 11:24)

To Jephthah Jehovah had no concern with the Ammonites but cared only for his own people. But Amos thought in a larger way. To him there was a purpose running through history and that purpose was the purpose of Jehovah. The world of Amos may not have been very large but it was controlled and ordered in detail by Jehovah. The Syrians and Philistines might not interpret history thus: they did not know the purpose of Jehovah. But Israel knew that purpose, for God had sent prophets to Israel though he had not sent them to the nations. And when Jehovah comes to judge he will judge the world by standards of humanity, but he will judge Israel according to the fuller revelation it had received. As Israel had sinned against the fuller light so shall its judgment be more sure and strict.

THE SIN OF ISRAEL

Amos recognizes a peculiar relation between Israel and Jehovah. Israel was the elect nation. But great privilege implies great responsibility.

"You only have I known of all the families of the earth.
Therefore will I punish you for your misdeeds" (3:2).

The word *known* here implies a profound affective content, and it might well be translated *loved* or *elected*. This oracle must have sounded hard to those who were at ease in Samaria and who regarded themselves as the darlings of Jehovah. They were highly conscious of their privilege and prided themselves upon it. Had not the divine favor been revealed to them in their recent military victories? Was not Jehovah obligated to continue his favor to a people who were so assiduous in the discharge of their obligations to him? Did not the altars reek continually with the smoke of sacrifice? Israel was confident and assured. They were not as the other nations. With things as they were they could only look to the future with a large measure of hope. The great day was coming when the world would see *Israel über alles*. That was the popular expectation though it was not shared by Amos. To Amos the relation between Israel and Jehovah was wholly personal and spiritual; mechanical and material relations, such as those implied in the ritual cult, were irrelevant and misleading. From the prophet's viewpoint there could be nothing but a certain fearful looking forward to judgment.

> Woe to those who long for the day of Jehovah!
> Wherefore would ye have the day of Jehovah?
> For it is indeed darkness and not light.
> As if a man were to flee from a lion
> And a bear met him;
> As if he entered the house
> And leaned his hand on the wall
> And a serpent bit him.
> Surely dark is the day of Jehovah and not light,
> Darkness without one gleam of light (5:18–20).

It is necessary to consider the significance of this idea of election in the religious thought of the Old Testament. It goes back to Abraham and the covenant made with him:

> "in thy seed shall all the nations of the earth be blessed" (Gen. 22:18).

The call of the individual patriarch had cosmic significance, and Israel was elected to a missionary vocation. This thought is never lost sight of throughout the record and it emerges again very clearly in Deutero-Isaiah. But the popular view of Israel was narrower than that of the original revelation, and the cosmic viewpoints had been replaced by a narrow nationalism that left the world outside. It emerges in its original sense again in Amos in his judgment upon the nations and in his judgment here upon Israel. To whom much is given of him will much be required.

Israel's sin is against light and against love. For all her

history has been the sphere of divine revelation. Alike by natural calamities and national disasters Jehovah has sought to discipline his people for his great purpose (4:7 ff.) but they refused to learn. The divine righteousness and fidelity had been revealed in the conquest of the land (Judg. 5:11), and the divine love had raised up prophets and Nazirites to point the people to the stars (2:11), but Israel had closed the mouths of the prophets as Amaziah closed the mouth of Amos (7:16). They forgot the mighty redemptive act of God that brought them from Egypt (2:9 ff) and made them a nation; they departed from their covenant loyalty and were disobedient and unfaithful.

Sellin [8] lists five forms of Israel's sin as denounced by Amos. First is exploitation of the poor and oppression of the needy (2:6 ff; 3:10; 4:1; 5:11; 8.4–6). All this is radically opposed to Jehovah's will and revealed character. Jehovah is the protector of the poor and they are his peculiar care. Secondly there is the crying lack of even-handed justice, the partiality of judges who respect persons and forget that justice is the essential being of Jehovah. The springs of communal well-being are poisoned at the source (5:7).

> I know how manifold are your transgressions
> And how mighty your sins:
> Ye that afflict the just, that takes bribes,
> That turn aside the needy in the gate (5:12).

Thirdly there is the flaunting flamboyant luxury of the rich and the bacchanalian orgies of debauched men and women who forget the simple pieties and elementary decencies of life. They have their winter houses and their summer houses but never a thought of God and their fellow-men. Gluttonous wine-bibbers, they devour the lambs of the flock and calves out of the midst of the stall; they sing idle songs to the sound

[8] Sellin, Ernst, *Kommentar zum Alten Testament XII; Das Zwölfprophetenbuch, Erste Hälfte*, 1929, p. 184.

of the viol, and fashion for themselves instruments of music, like David, but unlike David "they are not grieved for the hurt of Joseph" (6:4–6). Fourthly there is the substitution of mechanical and magical relations for the personal relations that must prevail between a people and its God. They seek to constrain by cult mechanism a deity whose essence is holiness and righteousness (4:4 ff; 5:5 ff; 6:3; 8:14). Finally there is that *hybris* or arrogance that dares to pride itself upon its peculiar privilege and fondly imagines no evil will come nigh it.

> Jehovah God hath sworn by his holiness
> Lo, the day will come for you
> When you will be taken away with hooks
> And your remnant with fish-hooks,
> From your stalls will ye be swept away . . .
> And cast beyond Hermon (4:2).

In all this Amos is concrete and atomistic. The deeper analysis was left for Hosea to make, and Hosea will speak of *sin* where Amos speaks of *sins*. But Amos is moving along a line which was to develop more fully. Here we see a thought taking shape in the mind of the prophet; it is the thought of a whole world lying in iniquity and requiring cosmic redemption. Israel is not better than the other nations (9:7); she does not stand in proud isolation over against the heathen—as national religion thought—but is involved with them and exposed to the universal judgment of a righteous God. Here we move on a parallel line of thought that dwells no longer on the idea of Israel's Jehovah but rather on Jehovah's Israel, no longer on the group's god but on the thought of the god and a new group. Here we approach Jeremiah's thought of the new covenant (Jer. 31:31 ff) and the thought of *"an Israel after the spirit and not after the flesh."* Amos did not think this out to the end, but in his treatment of Israel's election he is laying the basis of Paul's doctrine in the New Testament.

THE COMING JUDGMENT

For all this Amos sees nothing but judgment complete and final. The righteousness of God is revealed in holy wrath against Israel. Was there no place found for repentance? The first four visions, which seem to have preceded the active ministry of Amos, appear to indicate a measure of hope. It would seem inconceivable that a prophet would begin his ministry knowing that it should be in vain. In the first two visions (7:1–3; 4–6) Amos makes a brief pointed intercession for Israel, but in the third and fourth visions (7:7–9; 8:1–3) the situation appears more hopeless, and Jehovah says:

"I will not again pass by them any more" (7:8; 8:2).

The day of opportunity has passed; corruption is too deep-seated and radical to offer any possibility of escape. The fifth vision may have come to Amos at Bethel though it was not narrated until after his expulsion from the royal chapel.

> I saw Jehovah standing beside the altar, and he said:
> I will smite the chapiters that the thresholds may shake,
> And break them in pieces on the head of all of them;
> And I will slay with the sword those who survive:
> Not one fugitive shall escape and none shall get away.
> Though they dig through to Sheol
> My hand shall take them thence;
> Though they climb up to heaven
> From there will I bring them down.
> If they hide on Carmel's top
> I will search them out and get them;
> If they hide from my sight at the bottom of the sea
> I will command the serpent to bite them:
> If they go into captivity before their foes
> I will command the sword to kill them.
> I set my eyes upon them for evil and not for good.
> (9:1–4)

Is Amos, then, a prophet of doom and nothing more? Is Duhm correct in saying that here we have the ethical without the teleological, and that "the ethical without the teleological remains unfruitful." [9] Is judgment the final word, and is there no mercy mingled with judgment? Here we are dealing with one of those stresses and tensions that characterizes Old Testament theology. Isaiah inherited the thought of Amos and he resolved the tension by his thought of the Remnant whereby the divine righteousness is vindicated upon the nation, but grace reigns through the survival of a remnant, a holy seed, and the promises and purpose of God to the world remain unbroken. The thought of the remnant occurs in Amos, but Amos uses it apparently only to set forth the magnitude of the national disaster.

> "As a shepherd rescues from the mouth of a lion two legs or a piece of an ear, so shall the sons of Israel be rescued that sit in Samaria . . ." (3:12).

This might seem small enough but it is worth remembering that Elijah had thought of himself as the sole remnant of the faithful (1 Kings 19:14). Jeremiah, too, seems to believe that the whole cause of Jehovah in the world hung on his individual life. The Suffering Servant (Isaiah 53) may be the sole remnant of the true Israel, but he suffices for the divine purpose. May not Amos have had such a thought? It is true that the thought of judgment seems to fill the mind of the prophet to the exclusion of all else, but it is the way of the divine revelation to emphasize one word at a time. Hosea is the necessary complement to Amos, and both Amos and Hosea find their fuller explication in Isaiah, while Micah will synthesize the doctrine of all three (Micah 6:8). The revelation comes "line upon line, precept upon precept, here a little, there a little."

If we could, with Sellin and Kittel, regard the epilogue (9:11 ff) as from Amos' hand, Duhm's objection would be fully overcome. But few scholars accept this as genuine: it has been added by a later hand who sought to soften the asperity of Amos' words. The verdict of Wellhausen [10] is justified. Amos

[9] Duhm, Bernhard, *Die Theologie der Propheten,* 1875, p. 120 ff.
[10] Wellhausen, J., *Skizzen und Vorarbeiten,* Berlin 1892, p. 94.

was not the man to mingle "lavender and roses with blood and iron." Lods [11] rightly remarks,

> "If this appendix were authentic it would reduce the daring denunciations of Amos to the proportions of a village squabble."

Amos cannot be reduced to that low level. Amos was and remains the prophet of righteousness.

[11] Lods, Adolphe, *The Prophets and the Rise of Judaism,* translated by S. H. Hooke, London 1937, p. 85.

3

HOSEA: PROPHET OF GRACE

THE name Hosea signifies "salvation" and in this instance it is a name well bestowed. The Hebrew intended something very definite by a name as is clearly seen in the case of Hosea's greater successor.

> "Thou shalt call his name Jesus: for it is he that shall save his people from their sins" (Matt. 1:21).

Jesus is just the Greek form of the Hebrew Joshua, and all those names are derived from the Hebrew root which means salvation.

The date of the prophet's birth is not known but his period of activity falls somewhere between 750 B.C. and the fall of Samaria in 722 B.C. George Adam Smith doubts whether he lived after 732 B.C. on the ground that the prophet seems to know nothing of the loss of Gilead and Galilee to Tiglath-pileser in that year. This view, however, does not seem probable, and the text of the prophecies in 5:8–8: 6 would seem to imply the conquest of these regions by the Assyrian. This assumption would explain the repeated use of Ephraim for Israel in the latter part of the book, for Israel was then limited to the central highlands and might more properly be designated Ephraim. This view is taken by Alt and Hölscher and is followed by Sellin.

The home of the prophet seems to have been in the hill country between Bethel and Jerusalem. Diblaim or Diblathayim, on the other hand, suggests that his original habitation was east of the Jordan. This would explain, in some measure, his religious conservatism, for the religion of Jehovah kept its pristine purity on the borders of the wilderness and in the desert. His later connection with Benjamin would explain his profound influence upon Jeremiah. It is significant that so many of those early prophets—Elijah, Elisha, Amos and Hosea—come from the edge of the desert.

That he was called to be a prophet at some particular point in time is indicated clearly by the text though scholars differ as to the precise point of time. The matter of his call will occupy our attention later and meantime we may pause to ask what Hosea was before he entered upon the prophetic vocation. Various conjectures and surmises have been made as to his early occupation. From the frequent references in his book to baking and ovens some have deduced that he was a baker, but it is questionable whether there is anything in these references (7:6–8) that a plain intelligent layman might not express. It seems more probable that he was a peasant farmer, for his speech smacks most frequently of the soil. Plowing and reaping are familiar enough to him, and the common chores, such as picking up the stones and piling them in a heap and setting up a fence, are known to him (2:6; 12:11). He knows how to hold the plow and drive the oxen (4:16; 10:11) and how the farmer must keep his eye upon the weather (6:4) and struggle with the weeds that grow faster than the crops (8:7). The harvest, too, he knows though there is nothing here of the harvest joy, and the threshing that follows harvesting (9:1; 10:11) when the corn is separated from the chaff (13:3). He knows also how the corn is ground and kneaded into dough (7:4–8), and how the baking proceeds apace, and the baker must quickly turn his cakes lest they be burned black and hard on one side (7:8). Flax and all the processes connected therewith (2:5–9), the shearing of sheep and dressing of wool, which the industrious housewife turns to clothing for the family (2:5)—these things Hosea knows and knows well. Grapes, figs and olives (7:14; 9:2) are familiar sights to him and he tells us how they must be tended if the wayfarer would find a quencher for his thirst (9:10) and olive oil wherewith to anoint himself (2:5, 8).

It seems probable, then, that Hosea, like Elisha, was a farmer. Nevertheless, there is a surprising element here, for this dweller in the sown land seems to glorify the desert life. This, as already indicated in the case of Amos, is a not uncommon feature in the prophets, and here they display affinity with the Rechabites. But Hosea is no Rechabite; both Jeremiah and Hosea reveal the spirit of these ascetics, but they eschew their formal practices. Hosea loves the soil of the sown-land and regards Jehovah as the God of the farmer (2:8, 9). Hosea knows, too, that Jehovah is the God of the emergent cultures and that successive civilizations must be the sphere of his revelation. Elijah may journey to Horeb to find Jehovah (1 Kings 19) but Hosea will meet God in his own shattered home in the sown land. For Jehovah is not bound to Horeb or to the desert.

Hosea does not love the desert for its own sake. He knows well its dangers and disasters. In the desert men die of thirst (2:3; 13:5). From the desert comes the hot blasting sirocco (12:1); the lion and the panther dwell there and thence they come to ravage the flocks and devour vines and figs (5:14; 2:12). Men left the desert and pressed into the *Sown* because life in the desert was unkind and cruel. The desert was the fruitful mother of men but she was a stern nurse. It was not the desert Hosea cared for but rather the experience that once was Israel's in the desert, and which might be Israel's again in the *Sown*. To "recapture that first fine careless rapture" depended not on forms or localities but on spiritual attitudes which once were found in Israel and now were found no more. For Israel had proved faithless and had apostatized.

One word more may be said in regard to the prophet and his background. It has been mentioned already in our study of Amos but it may be repeated here. The life of the peasant, the sturdy yeoman on the land, does not preclude a fair degree of culture. "No man of the common people speaks as he does," [1] says Sellin, and he holds that Hosea left his farming

[1] *Kommentar zum Alten Testament,* XII; *Das Zwölfprophetenbuch,* Erste Hälfte, p. 6.

and joined one of the prophetic guilds or schools of the prophets. But as we saw in the case of Amos the shepherd or peasant is little likely to be a rustic boor. Grace and "gumption" can constitute quite a large intelligence and

> "to associate inferior culture with the simplicity and poverty of pastoral life is totally to mistake the conditions of Eastern society. . . . Among the Hebrews, as in the Arabian desert, knowledge and oratory were not affairs of professional education or dependent for their cultivation on wealth and social status." [2]

By nature, as by grace, Hosea, like Amos, was fitted to become the spokesman of God. In neither case need we predicate extraneous influence or adventitious aids in the making of these men of God.

AMOS AND HOSEA

Amos fills a great place in his blunt statement of things as they are and as they ought to be. But Amos is not enough and he must be supplemented. Amos' eye is fixed upon the outward conduct of life, but Hosea centers upon the inward springs of character. Amos is the voice of conscience, but Hosea travels the way of emotion and mysticism. Amos is overwhelmed by the thought of the divine righteousness while Hosea is subdued and awed by the vision of the divine love. Hosea scales heights that are inaccessible to Amos, and stands amid the central fire while Amos lingers on the circumference Amos is to Hosea as John the Baptist is to Jesus, and as G. A Smith finely observes:

> "A preacher to the conscience is not necessarily a preacher of repentance." [3]

Amos has no hope, but Hosea finds a moral basis for hope in the love of God and the repentance of the people. Amos and John the Baptist and Jonathan Edwards represent one aspect

[2] Smith, W. Robertson, *The Prophets of Israel,* 1912, p. 126.
[3] *The Book of the Twelve Prophets,* 1928, p. 237.

of truth which we are in danger of forgetting to-day. But something more is required than these preachers offer, and that something more is found in Hosea. It is easy to make a generalization here and say Amos represents law while Hosea speaks of grace, that the moralism of the Tekoan was succeeded by the evangelism of Hosea, but that would not be just. Hosea knows law and righteousness while Amos is not ignorant of mercy and grace. They differ profoundly on the point of emphasis. Thus Amos' censure is evoked by man's inhumanity to man while Hosea's passion is kindled by Israel's infidelity to God. Amos will relax the bonds that bind Israel to God and see Israel, together with the whole world, as lying in iniquity, but Hosea will regard those bonds as close and intimate ties, and he shows no interest in the world outside Israel. To Amos judgment is irrevocable and the day of grace has passed; to Hosea mercy finally triumphs and love wins the final victory. To Amos love was exhausted, but to Hosea it was inexhaustible. Hosea sounded depths which Amos could never fathom; in a most intimate fashion the word of Jehovah came to Hosea through a tragedy in his own home. Like Job he utters "words that breathe and thoughts that burn," for his words are struck out on the anvil of a suffering human heart. His short staccato sentences palpitate with emotion, and it would seem at times—so difficult is the text—as if the page were bedewed with tears. We may sum up the contrast in the words of Lods:

> "Amos had widened the national religion of the people until, in principle, it embraced all peoples. Hosea deepened it by making it consist solely of an interchange of love between the nation and its God. With a greater aptitude than Amos had for probing to the heart of things he is not contented with external rules of conduct: he must search out the secret feelings by which actions are prompted." [4]

Amos, we might say is extensive; Hosea is intensive.

[4] *The Prophets and the Rise of Judaism,* p. 89.

THE STORY OF THE FAITHLESS WIFE

"Jehovah said unto Hosea, Go, take unto thee a wife of whoredom and children of whoredom; for the land doth commit great whoredom, *departing* from Jehovah. So he went and took Gomer the daughter of Diblaim; and she conceived and bare him a son. And Jehovah said unto him, Call his name Jezreel; for yet a little while, and I will avenge the blood of Jezreel upon the house of Jehu, and will cause the kingdom of the house of Israel to cease. . . . And she conceived again, and bare a daughter. And Jehovah said unto him, Call her name Lo-ruhamah; for I will no more have mercy upon the house of Israel, that I shall in any wise pardon them. . . . Now when she had weaned Lo-ruhamah, she conceived, and bare a son. And Jehovah said, Call his name Lo-ammi; for ye are not my people, and I will not be your *God*" (Hos. 1:2–4, 6, 8).

In these simple words the tragic story of Hosea is told in the third person. The story is told again in chapter 3 in the first person, and though a great deal of discussion has centered around these two versions the most reasonable interpretation is that they both recount the same story. Such is the traditional interpretation, and it still seems the most satisfactory reading of the situation. We refrain from discussing other theories and content ourselves with indicating the position adopted with reference to these two accounts.

Many scholars have regarded the story as an allegory, mainly on the ground that such a command could not proceed from a holy God, but the general consensus of opinion is that here we are dealing with an actual fact and that in some way Hosea's domestic experience was bound up with his prophetic mission to Israel. All the passion and pathos of evangel were born of a desolating experience that came to him in his own home. It has been suggested that Gomer was a temple prostitute when Hosea married her,[5] but it seems preferable to hold here to the older interpretation which regards her as pure and chaste before her marriage to the prophet. As to when Hosea became conscious of her infidelity various opinions are held, but that question is not of main importance. It makes the teaching of the prophet in regard to Israel's relation to God more obvious if we assume Gomer's corruption to be subsequent to her marriage. There is nothing in the record to forbid this assumption, and it is widely supported by authority.

With reference to the divine command and the difficulty felt in regard to this it should be observed that it is a common usage of the Hebrew language and thought to represent as purpose that which we would naturally describe as result. The Hebrew believed so strongly in the divine sovereignty that he found no place for secondary causes. Everything that came to pass—good or evil—he regarded as part and parcel of the divine purpose.

> Shall there be evil in the city
> And Jehovah not have done it? (Amos 3:6).

Thus when Isaiah sees the result of his ministry to be a hardening of men's hearts and a closing of eyes and ears he reads this back into the original call and expresses the final result as the initial purpose of God (Is. 6:9, 10). Would Isaiah have proceeded on his way if he had seen this sorrowful issue from the beginning? Would Hosea have entered upon this marriage with Gomer bath Diblaim if he had known how fraught with heartbreaks that experience must be? The prophet in each case is looking back and interpreting experience: he is expressing that which finally eventuated as the original purpose and plan of the Almighty. Thus we have the record in its present form and we learn how, to put it in modern terms, human experience became here the channel of divine revelation. Through this tragic reality Hosea learned that all our

[5] Robinson, T. H., *Prophecy and the Prophets,* 1925, pp. 75–6.

love is but a spark of the eternal flame in the heart of God himself. God hid a Gospel in the heart of Hosea's suffering and made his surpassing sorrow the root of his deepest and most abiding joy. Pain turned at last to peace and the ultimate secret of life was revealed. One of the old Scottish theologians, Erskine of Linlathen, observes, "there is nothing so sad as a great sorrow lost." Hosea's sorrow was not lost; out of it blossomed and grew his evangel. In one of his beautiful little poems Dean Plumptre (who takes the view that Gomer was unchaste before her marriage and that Hosea married her in the hope of reforming her; this view does not affect the relevance of the poem) writes with rare insight:

> And yet through all the mystery of my years
> There runs a purpose which forbids that wail
> Of passionate despair. I have not lived
> At random, as a soul whom God forsakes,
> But evermore His spirit led me on,
> Prompted each purpose, taught my lips to speak,
> Stirred up within me that deep love, and now
> Reveals the inner secret.[6]

SOCIAL AND POLITICAL BACKGROUND

This does not differ greatly from the time of Amos. It may be that a gradual worsening is here, for the great Jeroboam II soon passed and was succeeded by a group of weaklings whose reigns vary only in their brevity. Man-made and man-murdered, they come and they go, and a general instability appears. Decay, moral and political, sets in and the eagles gather to the prey. But the nation is blinded and fails to discern the signs of the times.

> "Gray hairs are here and there upon him, but he knoweth it not" (7:9).

Israel has despised his birthright and soiled himself beyond all cleansing by his careless intercourse with the nations.

[6] Collected under the title *Lazarus and Other Poems.*

"Ephraim hath mixed himself among the nations,
Ephraim is a cake not turned." (7:8)

It would do no violence to the text if we rendered it,

"Ephraim is a half-baked scone."

The expression mingles scorn with heartbroken love. For—

"Sorrow's crown of sorrow is remembering happier things." [7]

Crassly and crudely the nation goes unheeding towards its doom. The priests rejoice in the sins of the people and the ecclesiastical institution waxes rich on ill-gotten revenues (4:8); yea, the priest turns robber on his own account (6:9), and religion becomes a large-scale racket.

"There is no truth and no mercy and no knowledge of God in the land" (4:1).

Totally lacking are those motives and principles that make men good or evil: truth, the self-consistency of moral purpose; mercy or loving-kindness (Hebrew *Chesed,* Hosea's peculiar and characteristic word) which signifies the fundamental quality of soul that serves as spring and motive of all right action in personal relationships; and, finally, knowledge of God, that loving intimacy with him with which the good man stands related to God.

"Nothing but swearing and breaking forth
And killing and stealing and committing adultery;
They break out and one deed of blood follows another." (4:2)

The very foundation of the national life, the Law of Moses, has been subverted; the national heritage has been bartered for a mess of international pottage, and God's chosen people, whom he redeemed by his strong right hand from Egypt, has become no better than a vile strumpet. The people who were intended to be a creative factor in the world are turned to moral jellyfish without power to make any impress on the world. Character has gone and ruin approaches fast.

[7] Alfred Lord Tennyson, *Locksley Hall.*

HOSEA AS MORAL ANALYST

The word *religion* does not occur in the Old Testament but the idea is expressed in various ways. *The fear of Jehovah* is frequently used throughout the Old Testament to express what we call religion. Hosea uses a more intimate expression and in his book he calls religion *knowledge of God*. This is what we should expect from an emotional and mystical nature such as Hosea was. In Hebrew psychology the heart is the organ of intellection and the word *knowledge* always has a large affective and emotional content. It may almost be equated with the term *love* (Amos 3:2), and is commonly used throughout the record of a man's most intimate converse with those he loves (Gen. 4:1). This affective content is present almost invariably in Scripture, and as George Adam Smith remarks:

> "the word *to know* almost invariably starts a moral echo whose very sound is haunted by sympathy and duty. It is knowledge, not as an effort of, so much as an effect upon the mind. It is not to know so as to see the fact of, but to know so as to feel the force of: knowledge not as an acquisition but as an impression. To quote Paul's distinction it is not so much the apprehending as the being apprehended." [8]

This emotional stress can be perceived and felt in the reading of Hosea's book.

> "My people perish for lack of knowledge" (4:6). "They know not Jehovah" (5:4). "They knew not that I healed them" (11:3). "Because thou hast rejected knowledge I will reject thee" (4:6).

The remedial purpose of judgment is to bring about repentance, and the result will be newness of life that consists of knowledge of God.

> "I will betrothe thee to me in faithfulness and thou shalt know Jehovah" (2:20).

[8] *Book of the Twelve Prophets,* p. 351.

Israel's ills are due to his failure to understand the real character of his God. This failure to understand has issued in wrong attitudes and evil conduct. Amos did not analyse thus but Amos did not get the insight that came to Hosea through tragic experience. Why did Gomer not know? Why was Hosea misunderstood? And why did Israel not know?

There could be few natures so rich in affection as Hosea whose love became a symbol of the divine love. And yet Hosea was misunderstood: there was profound failure here on the part of Gomer bath Diblaim. "She did not know" (2:8) is true of Gomer, and it is true of Israel. The nation had known, or, to use the language of Paul, had been known of, God in the person of its ancestor Jacob, and the same God of their fathers declared himself and revealed his character to Moses. The God who redeemed them from Egypt by his strong right hand and revealed his grace, truth, and covenant loyalty in all their subsequent history—why was there no knowledge of him in the land?

"Wine and harlotry steal away the wits" (4:11).

So it had come to pass, and men failed to put two and two together so that out of experiences they might harvest experience. This is the prophet's agony and he must bear it:

"Ephraim is a silly dove without heart" (7:11).

So the Authorized Version reads, but if the Hebrews had had a word for brain—as they had not—they might have rendered it:

"Ephraim is a brainless idiot,"

though that rendering would have imported a degree of harshness alien to the heart of Hosea.

It had not always been thus with Israel. It need not continue thus. Such is the message of the prophet. To Hosea, as to his great successor Jeremiah, the period of the nation's youth was the ideal time (2:14–16). The declension set in when Israel entered Canaan. Hosea is unique in many of his thoughts, and not least so in his treatment of the national history.

I found Israel like grapes in the wilderness:
Like the first-ripe fig on the fig tree in its first season,
I saw your fathers.
But they came to Baal-poor
And dedicated themselves to the shameful thing,
And became abominable as the object of their love. (9:10)

The prophet in his analysis finds three main misdeeds in the national history. These have brought Israel to her present sorry state. They are the main elements in Israel's sin against love.

In the first place Hosea castigates the haste and flurry of the national politics that seeks security in arms and alliances.

"They call to Egypt, they go to Assyria." (7:11)

and they fail to understand that Jehovah himself is the Savior of his people. Hosea's position is similar to that of Isaiah (Is. 7:9; 31:3); both hold that the arm of flesh is vain, and that faith alone can save. Lods[9] probably reads too much into the prophet when he asserts that Hosea is condemning material weapons in the name of spiritual forces, for though Hosea has some unique insights it is questionable if he had attained such a level of idealistic thought. The prophet here is against entangling alliances because they imply a distrust of Israel's God.

The second misdeed indicated by the prophet may seem striking and strange. Hosea seems to be opposed to the institution of the monarchy. According to the Old Testament records there were two schools of thought in regard to the institution of the Kingdom (1 Sam. 8 and 9), and the character of succeeding monarchs seems to have accentuated this division of opinion as to the value of the institution. There can be little doubt that it worked out in many ways to the detriment of religion, and Hosea shares this opinion. For almost inevitably it came about that where the king was regarded as the Anointed (Messiah) of Jehovah dynastic interests were identified with the divine purpose, and a theory of the divine right

[9] *The Prophets and the Rise of Judaism*, p. 92.

of kings emerged. Some scholars have thought that Hosea is merely objecting to certain individual kings, and certainly the bloody deed, instigated by Elisha, that set Jehu on the throne is roundly denounced by Hosea (1:4). But there are other passages (3:3–5; 13:9–11) that seem clearly directed against the institution itself, and Hosea seems to protest against the very principle of monarchy (9:15; 10:3, 9). We need not stop to ask what Hosea would have set in its place, for the prophets were not concerned to found or establish institutions. They were concerned, however, to denounce institutions that seemed to come between the people and their God. To Hosea the monarchy was such an institution.

Hosea's third charge of capital misdeed is Israel's idolatry. The nation that in its youth walked in the wilderness as the bride of Jehovah is now filled with "a spirit of whoredom" (5:4). They have forsaken Jehovah and gone after other gods that are impotent to save. Ephraim is wedded to idols (4:17), and Hosea's scorn for those idols is matched only by that of Deutero-Isaiah.

> Thy bull I loathe, O Samaria,
> Kindled is my anger against it. . . .
> A mechanic made it: it is not God.
> Splinters shall it become—Samaria's bull. (8:5, 6)

The reasons for this national apostasy are mainly to be found in the change of environment that came to Israel when it passed from the desert to the sown-land, from nomad life to that of the agricultural civilization. The institution of the monarchy and the development of the hierarchy are related to each other; their emergence was inevitable in the sown-land. The presence of Rechabites and Nazirites might serve to keep alive the memory of an earlier time, but all the efforts of the prophets could not arrest the process of assimilation to Canaanite practice. At Rome people will do as the Romans do. But all this was essentially a failure to know the real character of Israel's God. Jehovah was not merely a desert God, as the ascetics maintained, nor did Jehovah object to their becoming farmers. But he did object strongly to their becoming farmers and forgetting him who gave them power to become farmers and gave the farmer the reward of his labor.

For she did not know
That it was I who gave her
The grain and wine and oil
And the silver which I multiplied for her;
And the gold which they prepared for Baal. (2:8)

They took his gifts and gave thanks for them to other gods, and the life which he had given them in moral austerity and purity they soiled in physical debauchery at the shrines of Baal.

But I am Jehovah thy God
From the land of Egypt;
Another God beside me ye knew not,
And there is no Savior but me.
I fed you in the wilderness
In the land of drought,
But the more they fed the fatter they grew,
And their heart became arrogant,
And thus they forgot me. (13:4–6)

Relations that once had been ethicized and spiritualized were now materialized and most grossly naturalized. Men who had once heard the voice of the living God were now busy kissing calves! (13:2). The marriage bond that had been forged in the fires of Sinai was broken and defiled by Israel. Hosea's favorite word, *Chesed,* means much more than loving-kindness or mercy as it is usually translated. It is a word with many shades and difficult to render in English. George Adam Smith translates it as *leal love,* and that may convey in some measure its emotional content. It is as comprehensive as the Latin *pietas,* and it signifies good faith and loyalty. It denotes the relation between the faithful God and his trusting people, as also the relation of the believer to God, and also that of man to man in a godly and sound society. It includes the thought of justice and righteousness and it enriches both these ideas with a wealth of love and high regard. It denotes the loyalty of a man to his wife, of a master to his slave, of a patron to his client. "It is," say Oesterley and Robinson:

> "a fundamental quality of soul which serves as a spring and motive for all right action in personal relationships." [10]

In its later usage it becomes almost equivalent to grace or love in the New Testament sense. It is that quality in God to which man may appeal when he dare not call upon the divine righteousness. It represents the very essence of the divine being, for God's heart is a heart of love. Man is likest God when he has *Chesed* in his heart and reveals it in his relations with his fellows.

Thus Hosea will take an attitude to the cult similar to that of Amos:

> "For I delight in *Chesed,* not sacrifice; and in knowledge of God more than burnt-offerings." (6:6)

"All the blood of beasts on Jewish altars slain" will not avail if *Chesed* is lacking. No amount of zeal or outward show can replace the broken marriage bond. The whole ritual is irrelevant and impertinent here. All God requires is the complete answering trust and faithfulness of his bride and the surrender of her heart's love to himself. The relation that was personal in the beginning must become personal again. To know God in personal relations means the abandonment of the mechanical cult; it means what the New Testament means by repentance, *Metanoia,* change of mind and a new fronting to reality. Then Israel will cease to say *Baali* (my Baal) and will say *Ishi* (my husband).

> For I will take away the names of the Baalim from her mouth,
> And they shall be remembered no more by their names. . . .
> I will betrothe thee unto me for ever,

[10] Oesterley, W. O. E., and Robinson, T. H., *An Introduction to the Books of the Old Testament,* 1934, p. 353.

I will betrothe you unto me with righteousness and justice
And with *Chesed* and mercy.
I will betrothe you unto me with truth
And thou shalt know Jehovah. (2:17, 19, 20)

Sellin speaks of Hosea as veritably Johannine, *ein richtige Johannesnatur,* and in this thought of knowledge Hosea is strongly akin to the Evangelist. The thought recurs again and again in John and not infrequently with the same tragic emphasis as in Hosea. "If thou knewest . . ." (John 4:10) emphasises the prophetic teaching that lack of knowledge puts life in jeopardy. Men may err fatally for lack of such knowledge of God and his ways. Ralph Waldo Emerson, most prophetic of American writers, expresses the same idea in his poem on "the Hypocritic Days."

Daughters of time, the hypocritic days,
Muffled and dumb like barefoot dervishes,
And marching single in an endless file,
Bring diadems and faggots in their hands.
To each they offer gifts after his will,
Bread, kingdoms, stars and sky that holds them all.
I, in my pleachèd garden, watched the pomp,
Forgot my morning wishes, hastily
Took a few herbs and apples, and the Day
Turned and departed silent. I, too late,
Under her solemn fillet saw the scorn.

Men fail to discern the signs of the times and discover the meaning of the days. That is lack of knowledge, and for lack of that knowledge Israel perished.

But something more follows from this. Hosea is operating with a seminal thought that interprets the experience of men and nations. For clearly there is involved here the question of historical sense: because that sense of history was lacking there was failure in love and gratitude. "They forgot me" (13:6); "Israel hath forgotten his maker" (8:14). Israel failed to remember what her God had been and done for her: the happy days of her espousals were forgotten in the riot and revelry of the Baal orgies (9:10). History had been the sphere of revelation to Israel, and that history still could be a veritable sacrament of the love and grace of her God. But memory failed to function and its gracious ministry was repudiated. There was no knowledge of God in the land.

Here Hosea lays hold of something vital and permanent. This is confirmed by what we read of Hosea's greater successor. For on that night in which he was betrayed we read that Jesus called his disciples to the last supper, and as he dispensed it he spoke the words, "This do in remembrance of me." The Lord of men knew well the passion of Hosea and he knew, too, how easy it is for men to forget their best friends and forgive their worst enemies. And he did what he did that memory might abide as the basis of gratitude, and that men might not sin against love. But men still forget, and because the sense of history is deficient there is no answering love.

It may seem a far cry from Hosea to the Russian novelists but they are the best commentators on this matter. There are few moral analysts to equal those Russian writers, and they are unexcelled in their uncanny power to lay bare the workings of the human spirit. In the present instance we can call upon Turgeniev to interpret the experience of Hosea. In one of his little poems he tells how the human graces and virtues were once invited to a banquet with the gods. Here is what transpired at the heavenly feast:

> They talked and chatted o'er the meal,
> They even laughed with temperate glee,
> And each one knew the other well
> And all were good as good could be.[11]

But there was a fly in the ointment, and a discord in the heavenly symphony, for, as the writer goes on to say,

[11] Turgeniev, *Novels and Stories,* Vol. XVI, p. 358, Scribners, N. Y., 1922. Quoted by Turgeniev from an unknown source.

Benevolence and Gratitude
Alone of all seemed strangers yet;
They stared when they were introduced,
On earth they never once had met.

Perhaps the Russian is unduly hard on human nature, harder than Hosea or Jesus. The Gospels contain an interesting story (Luke 17:11 ff.) that should be set alongside Turgeniev as a corrective. It is the story of ten lepers who were cleansed and of one who returned to say "Thank you." Benevolence and gratitude can and do sometimes meet, though the question must often arise "Where are the nine?" The failure of memory is culpable and from its failure comes the sin against love.

THE SIN AGAINST LOVE

Thus we come to Hosea's deepest thought. Israel's sin, like that of Gomer, is the sin against love. There is something here that breaks the heart and sharpens agony to the point of crucifixion. It is love outraged, grace spat upon and despised. It is not only a forgetting or lack of knowledge: it is something more positive and aggressive. It is the doing despite to grace, the trampling underfoot of love, the profaning of the holy marriage bond. With many a tender similitude does the prophet set forth God's gracious love.

"I taught Ephraim to walk, I took them on my arms, But they knew not it was I who healed them" (11:3).

In the prophet's wealth of affection the similes become mixed and there is a passion in the language which no translation can obscure.

"I drew them with cords of a man, with bands of love:
I was to them as they that lift the yoke from off their jaws,
I bent down and fed them." (11:4)

To Hosea God is love, holy righteous love. The God of Amos is law incarnate, but the God of Hosea was born in the heart and mind of a man whose love the cruelest wrong could not quench. Retribution is the watchword of Amos but Hosea proclaims redemption. Faith in God's undying love is his theme, and in the might of his love Hosea travels farther than Amos. Amos stands on the outside, but Hosea agonizes as he stands at the center of sinful involvement and seems to carry it all upon his heart vicariously. With Amos thought controls emotion, but for Hosea "the heart has reasons that the reason cannot know." Outraged love will smite harder than offended righteousness, but its smitings are remedial and redemptive: its purpose is not to satisfy justice but to bring back the wanderer even when, like Gomer, the wanderer has made her bed in hell. All the passion of outraged love and all the assurance of the evangel is in these words:

> How shall I give thee up, Ephraim?
> *How* shall I cast thee off, Israel?
> How shall I make thee as Admah?
> *How* shall I set thee as Zeboiim?
> My heart is turned within me,
> My compassions are kindled together.
> I will not execute the fierceness of mine anger,
> I will not return to destroy Ephraim:
> For I am God, and not man,
> The Holy One in the midst of thee. (11:8, 9)

The name Ephraim occurs thirty-seven times in these prophecies, as if the very word were music to the prophet's soul. It was surely graven on his heart as it was upon the heart of God. For God's last word is not judgment but mercy. Judgment is his "strange work, but mercy is his delight."

DOCTRINE OF REPENTANCE

Thus Hosea moves beyond Amos. With an equally strong belief in the divine righteousness Hosea combined a belief in the divine compassion. Hence to him judgment is disciplinary, not retributive. And precisely because Hosea has such a full thought of God he has such a profound doctrine of repentance.

It is worthy of note in this connection that when the prophet buys back Gomer he does not forthwith restore her to her first status: he sets her in a separate place and waits for her return to sanity and purity (3:2). For the sinner must become conscious of sin and conscious of the love that redeems from sin. The prophet knows that forgiveness cannot be thrown at the sinner as one throws a bone to a dog. Forgiveness costs, and costs tremendously; it is purchased with great expense of spirit, both to the giver and the receiver. There can be a forgiveness that is as the casting of pearls before swine, but the prophet knows only a forgiveness that is related to penitence, an act in which all moral and spiritual values are vindicated and upheld.

> "I said unto her, thou shalt abide for me many days: thou shalt not play the harlot, and thou shalt not be any man's wife; so will I be toward thee." (3:3)

No cheap and easy handling of this moral tragedy may be allowed; no empty slushy sentiment can be permitted to do violence to moral realities.

> Lord, who shall stand, if thou, O God,
> should'st mark iniquity?
> But yet with thee forgiveness is,
> that fear'd thou mayest be.
>
> . . . .
>
> And plenteous redemption
> is ever found with him.
> And from all his iniquities
> he Isr'el shall redeem.
>
> (Ps. 130:3, 7, 8; metrical version)

Forgiveness is a reality that awes the soul and subdues the heart that receives it. Its only answer can be in reverence and adoration. Israel will learn in the iron discipline of the Exile the greatness of her God and the wonder of his love. Judgment will finally be swallowed up of mercy, and the final triumph will be with love.

Behold I will allure her
And bring her to the wilderness
And speak to her heart.
Then will I give her vineyards there
And the valley of Achor for a door of hope.
And she shall respond as in the days of her youth,
When she came from the land of Egypt.
And it shall be in that day, saith Jehovah,
That thou shalt call me Ishi [my husband]
And no more shalt thou call me Baali [my Baal] . . .
And I will betrothe thee unto me for ever;
Yea, I will betrothe thee unto me with righteousness and justice,
And with loving-kindness and compassion.
And I will betrothe thee unto me with faithfulness,
And thou shalt know Jehovah. (2:15, 16, 19, 20)

We can sum up the matter in the words of Cornill, who represents the soundest and sanest Old Testament scholarship.

> "When we consider that those thoughts in which humanity has been educated, and which have consoled it for nearly 3000 years, were first spoken by Hosea, we must reckon him among the greatest religious geniuses which the world has ever produced. It is not too much to say that the entire faith and theology of later Israel grew out of Hosea, that all its characteristic views and ideas are to be first found in his book.[12]

These are large words, but not too large; for they are true.

[12] Cornill, C. H., *The Prophets of Israel,* 1895, p. 50.

4

ISAIAH: PROPHET OF FAITH

TRADITION has it that Isaiah was of royal blood but there is no exact evidence for this tradition. Probably too much has been made of it. That he was "a man of quality" may be inferred not so much from the nobility of his style or from his easy relations with the great as from his aristocratic horror of any unheaval in the existing order of society; that "the base" should attack the honorable (3:5) seems to him the last word in political indecency. Isaiah was a born aristocrat and could visualize no society without aristocrats in the seats of the mighty.

But whatever may have been his lineage according to the flesh, there is no doubt as to his rank in the spiritual order. In some respects he is excelled by others who overshadow him in this excellence or in that, for "one star differs from another in glory," but for all-round excellence and distinction Isaiah is outstanding. Himself his own parallel, he stands without a peer and overtops all by the force of his personality, the wisdom of his statesmanship, the power of his oratory, and the far-reaching results of his ministry.

THE CALL OF ISAIAH

> "In the year that king Uzziah died I saw the Lord sitting upon a throne, high and lifted up; and his train filled the temple." (Is. 6:1)

The prophets rarely use the first personal pronoun in their writings. This is the more remarkable inasmuch as extant

Babylonian and Egyptian documents reveal the fact that such reserve and such self-effacement were not usual. Those foreign kings proudly recorded their conquests with great detail and with abundant use of the first personal pronoun. The inscribed monuments reveal an inordinate egoism.

> "The land of Beth-Omri and the whole of its inhabitants I carried away to Assyria. Pekah their king I slew. . . . Hoshea I appointed to rule over them . . . ten talents of gold, 1000 talents of silver I received from them as tribute." [1]

In Egypt it was customary for individuals to have their record written and inscribed upon the walls of their tomb. There may have been as much—or as little—truth in those tomb inscriptions as in modern epitaphs, but the itch for fame seems to haunt men in every time and clime.

All this makes it the more remarkable that the prophetic writings should be marked by this personal reserve and modesty. This self-effacement is without parallel in contemporary documents or later literary forms. These prophets "bravely did their deed and scorned to blot it with a name." The subject falls into the background and the experience is set forth to the glory of God and for the good of men. They see no man, not even themselves: they see only God, and they record what they have seen and heard with his eye upon them. Thus the stamp of a noble authenticity and intrinsic genuineness adheres to the record.

Moreover, the prophets seldom deal with external matters, such as wars and conquests and tribute. They deal with spiritual experience. That is the mark and token of the great writing prophets, though it is not true of the earlier records which deal mainly with outward action and its results. The later style is a new creation in literature: it comes in with the writing prophets, and it finds its consummation in Jeremiah.

"In the year that king Uzziah died I saw the Lord." That

[1] Schrader, Eberhard, *The Cuneiform Inscriptions and the Old Testament;* translated by O. C. Whitehouse, 1885, Vol. I, p. 251.

is not just a date in Hebrew history; it marks the birthday of a prophetic soul, and it marks the end of a spiritual pilgrimage. Julian Morgernstern [2] thinks this date can be fixed precisely:

> "In a very interesting passage the Talmud (Jer. Erubin V.22c) records the surprising fact that the temple at Jerusalem was so located and built that on the two equinoctial days of the year the first rays of the rising sun would shine directly through the Eastern gate." [2]

This gate was closed through the remainder of the year but was opened on the equinoctial days. The autumnal equinox was celebrated in ancient Israel as New Year's Day, the day when Jehovah was thought to sit in the heavenly court and decide the destinies of Israel for the coming year. As the rays of the rising sun streamed through that Eastern gate, shining through the four doors, set in ascending order, right into the inmost shrine, that might well appear as the coming of the glory of the God of Israel (kebod elohē Yisra'el). The origin of such a structural plan in the building of the temple does not concern us here; from later abuses (Ezek. 8:16) we might infer it had some relation to an earlier worship of the sun. But if this were the autumnal equinox, then Isaiah will have received his vision on New Year's Day of 747 B.C.

Morgenstern's suggestion may seem fanciful, but such a background would explain the attendant circumstances of the vision. The blaze of morning glory flooding the shrine with unearthly brilliance, and the fulness of light that dazzles the eyes of the seer, would afford rare opportunity to a mystic soul and conduce to spiritual elevation. The brazen serpent beside the altar, gleaming in that radiance, might well suggest the titanic forms of the seraphim. But we need not try to be wise above what is written. When all is said and done the prophetic experience is something that defies analysis. But it may reward us to look at some of the details of this most "numinous" chapter of the Old Testament.

[2] Hebrew Union College *Annual,* 1926, Vol. V, p. 45.

It may have been that the prophet's heart was sorrowful and pained, and, like the singer of Psalm 73, he had gone to the house of God. It may have been sheer regret and grief at the passing of the great king Uzziah, for, as he marked the royal obsequies, he felt as if the sun would never shine again. The nation had basked so long in the sunshine of Uzziah's glory that it seemed as if it would never end—and now the king is gone, the great Uzziah is dead.

> Imperious Caesar, dead and turn'd to clay,
> Might stop a hole to keep the wind away.[3]

Isaiah had known no other king: this was the end of an epoch, and dark clouds were gathering on the horizon. The brilliant past had faded into nothingness, and the future—could there be a future?

It may have been such a mood that drove Isaiah to the temple. Or, because the workings of the human mind are generally complex, there may have been a mingling of feelings and emotions. Was he already, like Saul, feeling an inward discontent? Was he questioning the validity of the religious ceremonial, and wondering whether the ritual was but a vain pomp and show? Could it be that in God's house "wickedness and worship" could abide? Faint stirrings and restless questionings filled the mind of the son of Amoz in the year that king Uzziah died.

On that day, and in that place, Isaiah saw the Lord. Perhaps the crowd had gone, and the prophet was left alone, wondering what it all means, if it means anything. Suddenly the walls seem to fall away, and everything assumes giant proportions. The throne is elevated, and beside it stand those gigantic figures full of worship and ready for service. Every detail is impressed on the prophet's wondering gaze.

> "Above him stood the seraphim: each one had six wings; with twain he covered his face, and with twain he covered his feet, and with twain he did fly" (6:2).

[3] Shakespeare, *Hamlet,* Act V, Sc. 1.

Whereon one of the old commentators remarks:

> "With twain he covered his face, lest he might look on God, and with twain he covered his feet, lest his uncomely parts should be seen of God."

It is worthy of note here that four wings were used for reverence and adoration, while two were employed for service. This would seem to say that the strength of our service depends upon the measure of our worship and adoration. The depth of our devotion and reverence will measure our real accomplishments for God.

Devotion, too, is expressed vocally, and at the mighty music of the seraphim singing the Trisagion the foundations tremble and the house is filled with smoke. Smoke is the usual accompaniment of the divine appearance, or theophany, but it means more in this present instance. Smoke is that which arises when the divine holiness and human sin come into collision. For God is of purer eyes than to behold iniquity, and he cannot look on any unclean thing. Here we have visualized the divine reaction against human wickedness.

This chapter, as already stated, is the *numinous* in the Old Testament. That is to say, it is charged with the sense of God, and nowhere do we find the "otherness" of God so clearly set forth. Nowhere else do we feel so strongly the presence and the pressure of God. Sight and sound combined to emphasise the ineffable, all-embracing holiness. The ideal is before the prophet's eyes, though soon the vision and sight of the sordid real will mar its splendor. We must continually pray in the words of the Lord's prayer, "Hallowed be thy name," for the process of hallowing is slow and tedious. In the vision of the ideal everything was "holy, holy, holy": all had been hallowed and the ideal was made real. When John glimpsed the New Jerusalem he says, "I saw no temple therein." The Holy City needs no temple, for it is all temple: church and community had become identical terms, and the holiness of God flooded every nook and corner of that city. Isaiah knew, as we know, that there remains much to be done ere the unredeemed tracts of life and experience are brought under the rule and sovereignty of God.

In the vision of the exalted Lord, and in the blaze of unutterable holiness, Isaiah sees himself as he really is. In the fierce light that beats upon the throne he can only say,

"Woe is me, for a man of unclean lips am I,
And I dwell in the midst of a people of unclean lips:
For the King, Jehovah Sabaoth, my eyes have seen" (6:5).

When Amos received his vision he looked out on an unrighteous world: Hosea looked upon a faithless spouse, but Isaiah looked within. Social regeneration must begin with inward cleansing.

> "Then flew unto me one of the Seraphim with a live coal in his hand which he had taken with tongs from off the altar; with this he touched my mouth and said: Lo, this hath touched thy lips; thy guilt is gone, thy sin forgiven" (Isaiah 6:6–7).

Here Grace specialises. The prophet is referring to a common usage both of the sanctuary and of domestic life. Stones were made red-hot at the central fire and lifted with tongs and applied to any object it was required to heat. The method is similar to that employed by the workman or housewife who heats an old-fashioned ironing bolt in the fire. There may be a further meaning here. It would seem to have been the custom that when a man desired to present a gift to God, which, though of costly material, might be ritually unclean, he brought his gift to the priest who made it to "pass through the fire" (Num. 31:22 ff.). Not that he would burn the costly vessel but in symbolic fashion the priest would touch it with a hot stone from off the altar and it would then be rendered ritually clean and dedicated to the service of God. No priest would willingly destroy a gold chalice or silver paten that might be made fit for service in the sanctuary. The original rite was later modified by symbolism in the same manner as we employ sprinkling in infant baptism where total immersion might endanger life.

Fire burns and fire purifies. Fire expands and fire transforms. The old capacities are sublimated and life receives a new orientation. The living imagination of John Bunyan that found expression in cursing and swearing is not destroyed at his conversion; it is turned into a new channel, and that same colorful imagination that expended itself in oaths and curses now expresses itself in the glorious allegory of the *Pilgrim's Progress*. No man can see God and live. That is the expression of primitive superstition but it represents a real spiritual fact. Isaiah saw God and died; he died and rose again. He put off the old man: he became a new creation by the power of divine grace. Isaiah belongs to the class of twice-born men.

Thus the prophet is ready for the vision of duty. There is strange compression in the recital here. Eleven words in the Hebrew represent the challenge and its acceptance:

> And I heard the voice of Jehovah say,
> Whom shall I send?
> And who will go for us?
> And I said, Here am I: send me (6:8).

Truly "Esaias is very bold." Yea, he is bolder than we appreciate. For if this was New Year's Day then, according to Jewish ideas, it was judgment day, and Jehovah has come to his temple to judge his people and announce their destiny. Who shall be God's agent in this high matter? There is no shrinking on the part of Isaiah. Unlike Moses, and unlike Jeremiah, Isaiah is bold and resolute to undertake the task. God's call has come and God's man stands ready. Eyes that have seen the King will not quail nor quiver before aught human. But what a task is this!

> And he said, Go speak to this people,
> Hear on—but perceive not!
> See on—but understand not!
> Coarsen this people's heart,
> Make their ears dull, their eyes heavy;

Lest they see with their eyes, and hear
with their ears,
And their heart understand, and health be restored
to them (6:9–10).

This may have been the commission given to Isaiah at the beginning, and the prophet may have been summoned to be God's doomster to Israel. On this interpretation Isaiah would be Amos *redivivus,* and this may indeed be so, for in the earlier part of his ministry Isaiah seems to be re-echoing the shepherd of Tekoa. But it may also be—and the present writer thinks so in company with many others—that this story was written long after the event and that Isaiah is "reading back" his later experiences. As we have already pointed out in the case of Hosea, the Hebrew, by his overwhelming thought of the sovereignty of God, tended to express as purpose that which we would call consequence. Isaiah is here reading back into the original call all that eventuated in his subsequent ministry. Would Isaiah have undertaken a ministry that was to end in total futility? Would Hosea have made such a marriage had he known at the beginning what tragedy was involved? Isaiah was to find in course of time that it is one of life's deepest tragedies that the Gospel may be "a savor of death unto death." The human soul becomes calloused, and people become Gospel-hardened, and a moral obfuscation creeps over the soul, and the last state of that man is worse than the first. Let Savonarola testify here, and Savonarola stands in the prophetic succession:

"Preach to those as one may, they have the habit of listening well and yet acting ill; the habit hath become a second nature and they continue to listen without obeying."

Or listen further to the Florentine as he renews the experience of Isaiah in the popular reaction of the populace.

"Thou wilt be as a rook on a steeple that at the first stroke of the church bell takes alarm and hath fear, but then, when accustomed to the sound, percheth quietly on the bell, however loudly it rings." [4]

The sin of the people is against light clear and full. But the thought of the end—or is there any end?—overpowers the prophet, and the inhibitions of affection and patriotism plead somewhat tremblingly in the spirit of the tender Hosea:

"How long, O Lord, how long?"

And he said:

> Until there be laid waste
> Cities without dwellers, and houses without men,
> And the land be left desolate,
> And Jehovah have exiled men afar,
> And desert places spread throughout the land:
> And if a tenth be still in it
> This again must be consumed,
> Like the terebinth and oak
> Of which, after felling, a stump remains (6:11–13).

Destruction complete and final: is there no hope? A later writer felt the poignancy of all this and added a word that might soften the oracle, just as this was done at the close of the book of Amos: "A holy seed is the stock thereof."

But that word is not in the Greek version and it must be presumed that it was not in the text when the translation was made from Hebrew to Greek sometime in the second century B.C. But the hope was certainly in the prophet's heart, and very soon he will set it before men's eyes in the strange symbolic figure of his son Shear-jashub (a remnant will return, i.e., to God). For though there is throughout the Old Testament a continual tension between righteousness and grace, as there is also tension between divine sovereignty and human freedom, the prophet is certain that grace reigns and will triumph ultimately. Isaiah is the prophet of faith.

[4] Villari, Pasquale, *Life and Times of Girolamo Savonarola*, 1888, Vol. II, p. 126.

THE FAITH OF ISAIAH

We have already stated, in our study of Amos, that the insights of the great prophets were broken and fractional. They seldom compass the full measure of divine truth or unfold the full revelation. Fuller understanding comes to them with growing experience, but frequently it was left to later writers to unfold the full significance of the original vision. Isaiah gets a vision of the exalted Lord and his world purpose, yet somehow we are conscious of traits of narrow nationalism adhering to his utterances. His God is *the Holy One of Israel* and Zion is his seat, and while this "domesticating of the Deity" gives intensity to religion it also has obvious disadvantages, though these disadvantages are not too prominently revealed in Isaiah's preaching. Jeremiah, again, has insight to see the human heart as the seat of religion and propounds his doctrine of the New Covenant (Jer. 31:31 ff.) which makes religion a world affair, the concern of every human being. Here Jeremiah soars to the empyrean, but by a strange juxtaposition we find him in the next chapter (32) engaged in a real-estate transaction, and Jerusalem is made integral to the future hope. Job (19:25 ff.) gets a momentary glimpse of life beyond the veil and then seems to return to his wrangling with the three friends. Paul is rapt into the third heaven (II Cor. 12:2) but Paul cannot relate what he has seen and heard. We can only account for this by saying that a limitation adheres to the best of human faculties, and the finite must always have difficulty in describing the infinite. Isaiah was a Jerusalem man, out and out, and he turns constantly to the life of that city. He has seen things as they ought to be, and he looks on things as they are, and his heart is pained by what he sees. His moral sense is offended. But the prophet has faith that judgment will not be the final end of things; he believes in God, and Jehovah is the God of the promises. In his view Israel is indispensable to God, and Jerusalem is inviolable. In this faith was born the doctrine of the Remnant. It may not be expressed in chapter

6 but it must have been forming in his mind when he met Ahaz by the waterworks (Chap. 7). Shear-jashub was more eloquent than words; the lad was a walking parable. The prophet here comes in by the eye-gate and uses an expressive symbolism. In the overwhelming experience of his call God had done something for Isaiah which Isaiah knew God could do for the nation and for every individual therein. The prophet's faith is the victory that will overcome the world. He knows, if we may put it so, that he has a God big enough to remake the world and good enough to make it a Christian world. The term "Christian" may be anticipative here but it is what Isaiah meant. The prophet knew the way might be long and the going hard but the end is sure.

It takes a soul
To move a body; it takes a high-souled man
To move the masses even to a cleaner sty;
It takes the ideal to blow a hair's breadth off
The dust of the actual.[5]

That ancient civilisation had advanced in manifold ways of evil. The task might well daunt a high-souled man. The first chapter may have been written late in the prophet's life—though many judge it early—but it represents the prevailing state of affairs.

Hear, O heavens, and give ear, O earth,
For Jehovah speaks.
Sons have I nourished and raised
but they have rebelled against me.
The ox knoweth his owner,
and the ass his master's crib,
But Israel is without knowledge,
my people without insight.
Ah, sinful nation,
guilt-laden folk,

[5] Browning, E. B., *Aurora Leigh.*

Miscreant race,
children degenerate,
Wherefore will ye be smitten further,
wherefore aggravate defection?
The whole head is sick,
the whole heart diseased;
From sole of foot to head
no soundness is therein,
Naught but bruises and wales
and fresh wounds—
Unpressed, unbandaged,
not softened with oil.
Your land—a desolation;
your cities—a conflagration,
Your tillage before your eyes—
strangers consume it:
And the daughter of Zion is left
like a booth in a vineyard,
Like a lodge in a cucumber-field,
like a walled watch-tower.
Except Jehovah Sabaoth
had left us a remnant,
We had been as Sodom,
had matched Gomorrah (1:2–10).

Everything here was radically wrong, and all was wrong because the stability and good order that come from faith in God and knowledge of his will were totally absent. Here was a people cut loose from its moorings, without moral and spiritual ballast.

THE WORLD AND THE WORD

Into such a world steps the prophet, the spokesman for God, and he does precisely what the Reformers did in the sixteenth century. The word of God has to be set in its rightful place, and effete and decadent institutions must be swept away. The mechanism of ritual must give place to spontaneity of worship, and the right of the believing soul must be vindicated. It is of considerable significance that when the Reformers abolished the Mass they set the Protestant sermon in its place, in the very place that the central act of the Mass had occupied. By that act they declared that the word of God is the central thing in worship. For the word of God searches the heart, illumines the conscience, and edifies the whole man. Preaching, when it is prophetic, makes God visible so that people "taste the powers of the world to come" (Heb. 6:5; Moffatt version) God is made visible in his holiness as the prophet had seen him, and the prophet will have his experience become the experience of all men. In the light of that vision the people knew themselves—as Isaiah knew himself—for what they really were, and they also saw what, by God's grace, they might become. Religion becomes fused with morality: the service of God becomes reasonable and intelligent, no longer static and formal but dynamic and inspired.

> Come now, let us reason together, saith Jehovah:
> Though your sins be as scarlet,
> they shall be as white as snow;
> Though they be red like crimson,
> they shall be as wool (1:18).

Commentators have found difficulty with this evangelical statement. It seems to make religion unduly simple. But there are *some things too good not to be true.* Isaiah had proved that in his own person. Divine grace does answer man's cry of distress, and it answers without delay. The soul can deal directly with God, and it needs no intermediary. Religion is not concerned so much with doing as with being, being cleansed and renewed by living contact with the living God.

Thus we turn from the foul, sensual, reeking atmosphere of ritual worship in the first chapter, and enter the spacious prospect of the second. For these chapters represent well the constant oscillations between the ideal and the real. In the opening verses of this second chapter Isaiah sees Jerusalem as it may be when God's grace has had its perfect work. It matters little whether Isaiah himself composed this song, which is found again in Micah 4:1–4, or whether both prophets are here making use of the work of an earlier writer. Some scholars hold that the passage has been inserted in both books by a late editor, but this seems less probable than the supposition that it was ready to the hand of Isaiah and Micah. In these words Isaiah expressed his faith. He may be expressing that faith in the words of an older hymn, as we ourselves do in worship, but the faith is the faith of Isaiah.

Behold the mountain of the Lord
  In latter days shall rise
On mountain tops above the hills
  And draw the wond'ring eyes.

To this the joyful nations round
  All tribes and tongues shall flow;
Up to the hill of God, they'll say,
  And to his house we'll go.

The beam that shines from Zion hill
  Shall lighten every land;
The King who reigns in Salem's tow'rs
  Shall all the world command.

Among the nations he shall judge,
  His judgments truth shall guide:
His sceptre shall protect the just,
  And quell the sinners' pride.

No strife shall rage, nor hostile feuds
  Disturb those peaceful years;
To ploughshares men shall beat their swords,
  To pruning-hooks their spears.

No longer hosts encount'ring hosts
Shall crowds of slain deplore;
They hang the trumpet in the hall,
And study war no more.

Come then, O house of Jacob, come
To worship at his shrine;
And walking in the light of God
With holy beauties shine.[6]

"Castles must first be built in the air before cottages can be built on the ground." So wrote David Livingstone from darkest Africa to his sister Janet in Blantyre, Scotland. The dream must first haunt the heart of the visionary before it can become the deed of hand. Isaiah dreamed the dream and built the castle in the air. Later workmen gave it real form. There may be features in this dream that appear less than Christian. Isaiah here thinks proudly of Jerusalem and of other nations being drawn to it in the day of its exaltation. There is no thought here, as in Deutero-Isaiah, of missionary outgoing and sacrificial service. Isaiah's universalism maintains itself beside his nationalism.

Isaiah has his feet rooted in the past, and for him that past is not too distant. Amos and Hosea go back to Moses but Isaiah finds the real beginning of things in the glories of David's reign. He is essentially patrician and his ideal reflects the pride of birth. Micah from the western plains will give us a democratic ideal of the golden age, but Isaiah cannot forget his preference for "blue blood." Micah is a commoner, but Isaiah is an aristocrat. As we have already indicated the great prophets had their limitations and this should not be forgotten. Human prejudices as well as inherited tendencies color their oracles. There is an earthly element adhering to all our heavenly dreams, and our ideals betray their point of origin.

[6] Is. 2:1-5; Scots Paraphrase version.

FAITH AND THE IDEAL

The main interest here is that we have those predictions of the ideal. In this matter Isaiah is essentially the prophet of faith, and by faith, as the New Testament says, we "are convinced of what we do not see" (Hebrews 11:1; Moffatt version). Amos and Hosea have an ascetic element that finds its hope in a return to the past; Elijah flees to Horeb, but Isaiah resolutely sets his face forward. Hope takes the place of regret, progress supplants conservation, and the whole face of the world is changed. He thinks long, long thoughts, for he has a great view of God. It may be that he builded better than he knew, but it is his attitude that is significant and momentous. It marks the opening of a new epoch in the spiritual pilgrimage of men. It is faith laying hold of the promises and unfolding their undreamed wealth of blessing. Isaiah sowed seed which bore fruit an hundredfold, and though it is difficult to say that Isaiah wrote all those passages which are found in his book it would be true to say that he is the spiritual father of them all. The kingdom of God is like leaven, and leaven exerts a progressive influence. Others may walk in a clearer light, but it was Isaiah who first kindled a fire that could not be put out. Deutero-Isaiah, Ezekiel, Zechariah, Daniel, Enoch will take up the tale and point us onward and upward until a whole nation is standing on tiptoe "waiting for Him who is to come." The impulse that started all this train of idealistic thought is faith in a God highly exalted, who is Lord of Nature and Lord of History. The dream takes different forms at different times, but at bottom it is the same: when Christ comes he comes to "execute the offices of a prophet, of a priest and of a king." The great river finds its source in some tiny upland stream, and, as it flows from its point of origin to the sea, it is enriched by many tributaries. Thus "all the hopes of all the years" find their consummation in him, in the King whose kingdom is not of this world, in the Prophet rejected by the Jews and crucified by the Romans, whose memory makes the scene of his martyrdom a sacred city for all the nations, in the great High Priest whose spirit guides and sanctifies the church which he founded that it may be a true theocracy. Isaiah dreamed dreams and saw visions which only the Christian church could interpret fully.

THE MESSIANIC THOUGHT

Isaiah is the most messianic of the prophets. Passages like those of the ninth and eleventh chapters are graven on our minds and hearts through the music of the great oratorios.

For unto us a child is born,
To us has been given a son;
And dominion is upon his shoulder:
And his name has been called

Wonderful Counsellor,
Hero divine,
A father for ever,
Prince of Peace.

Great is his dominion
And unending the peace
Upon the throne of David
And throughout his kingdom;

To establish it and support it
In justice and righteousness—
From now and for ever
The zeal of Jehovah will do this.[7]

"Man's reach exceeds his grasp, else what's a heaven for?" Men did not cease to dream. A great God means a great hope, and here we have the hope of a warless world under the

[7] Is. 9:5, 6.

leadership of a king, who shall be a counsellor more wonderful than Solomon, a friend and father more devoted than David, a Prince of Peace who shall seek the good of his subjects and inspire them to live in peace. Outward aggression and domestic treason shall find no place in the ideal community and the Golden Age.

But even further did the prophet travel on wings of faith, and the eleventh chapter shows us something larger, the cosmic significance of the divine redemption. Scholars are less inclined to attribute this to Isaiah, but if he did not himself write it his was the faith that inspired it.

And a shoot shall come forth from the stock of Jesse
And a scion from his roots shall bear fruit;

And upon him shall rest the spirit of Jehovah,
A spirit of wisdom and discernment,
A spirit of counsel and might,
A spirit of knowledge and of the fear of Jehovah.

He shall not judge by what his eyes see,
Nor will he decide by what his ears hear;
But he will judge the needy with righteousness,
And decide with equity for the poor of the land.

He will smite the tyrant with the rod of his mouth,
And with the breath of his lips will he slay the godless.
Righteousness will be the girdle of his loins
And faithfulness the belt about his waist.

And the wolf shall dwell as guest with the lamb,
And the leopard shall couch with the kid;
And the lion shall eat straw like the ox,
And the calf and the lion cub will graze together;
And a little child shall be their leader.

And the cow and the bear shall be friends,
They shall lie down together;
And the suckling shall play over the hole of the asp,
And over the viper's dwelling the weaned child shall trip about.[8]

Isaiah is here looking back to Creation as it came from the hand of God, to that time when men lived at peace with the animals. But man sinned, and man's sin had cosmic effects. All Nature was infected and poisoned by man's sin, and the whole natural order was disrupted and broken. Isaiah looks forward to a time when salvation will be total and cosmic, and wild beasts will have laid aside their wildness because man will have laid aside his sin. The world will then be as God intended it to be. Not without reason does Mark record the significant fact that the wild beasts were concerned with the Temptation of Jesus. "The wild beasts were with him" (Mark 1:13). As Paul says, "The whole creation groaneth and travaileth in pain together until now" (Rom. 8:22). When that day comes, to which both prophet and apostle looked forward, it will have cosmic significance in the region of redemption. In the thought of the prophet there may be present elements that are local and temporal; the kingdom is of this world, and much that is purely physical adheres to it. But the whole conception of salvation in the Old Testament has large material content. Even in the New Testament such material elements are still present. Centuries were to pass before men could hear those "words of grace and beauty" and recognise a kingdom that was not of this world. Coming events cast their shadows before, and all those are part of the *praeparatio evangelica* in the Old Testament.

Again in 32:1–20 we see the prophet returning to this subject and reiterating the hope which the world has never been willing to let die. For it is not a hope that springs from individual or national temperament: it is a hope that is

[8] Is. 11:1-8.

sheerly objective and depends on God alone. It does not depend on man's endeavor or accomplishment. God inspires the hope and God himself is its final end.

The hope here seems to run in molds that seem indispensable to Isaiah. Micah's Messiah is a working-man, but Micah is thoroughly democratic and Isaiah is patrician. There is much here to remind us of Plato's ideal in the *Republic,* but whether a man be Socialist, Democrat or Republican what we long to see is an aristocracy of character ruling in God's name and by divine grace, an aristocracy that shall make righteousness and justice visible and eloquent in all speech and action. For justice seeks the full life for all, and when justice is enthroned among men all Nature will be renewed, and the very "stones of the field will be in league with man" (Job 5:23).

The permanent message is here set in a transient setting which we may easily enough neglect. But the message remains. Democracy that is to endure must rest on the twin pillars of freedom and justice, truth and brotherhood.

> "There is no wealth but life, life including all its powers of love, of joy, of admiration. That country is the richest which nourishes the greatest number of noble and happy human beings." [9]

We still dream our dreams and see our visions, but we are building on the prophetic foundations.

THE STATESMANSHIP OF FAITH

It is not only in these visions of the future, of a world redeemed and humanity renewed, that the prophet's faith is revealed. That faith showed itself also in practical action in his dealings with the history of Judah. Here we see the statesmanship of faith. The prophets, be it said, were not generally qualified to dabble in affairs of state, and when they did, as

[9] Ruskin, John, *Unto This Last,* Sect. 77.

in the case of Elisha, the results were likely to be disastrous and regrettable (Hos. 1:4; 8:4). Men who are given to ecstasy—and that in such degree that it was not easy to distinguish them from madmen—are little likely to possess that nice sense of judgment and poise that is required in all decisions of national importance. For that reason the Hebrew prophets have been well called "the storm petrels of Hebrew history" (Wellhausen). The great writing prophets rarely played any part in politics, but Isaiah is the exception that proves the rule. He was peculiarly qualified in this respect. The friend of kings and princes, with ready access to the great of the land, he could easily learn all that was transpiring. He was possessed of remarkable poise and sanity, and the ecstatic element is less prominent in Isaiah than in others. Indeed he seems the least ecstatic of all the prophets. He is always master of himself and of every situation and circumstance that emerges. Moreover he has seen King, the Lord of Hosts, and he views things from above. He sees all movements, national and international, in the light of God's world purpose. His God is in control of nature and history. "The whole earth is the fulness of his glory" (6:3). He knows what Jehovah is about to do, for he stands in the counsel of the Almighty. The secret of the Lord is with him. His faith enables him to see all things in their proper perspective. Ahaz and his advisers may pride themselves on their *Realpolitik* but they are merely cheap politicians with their eye on the main chance. Isaiah is a statesman who sees beoynd what is in front of him to the final and distant issue; he understands the real significance of every detail.

If we wish a definition of a statesman as opposed to a politician let us ask Demosthenes about it. It is the statesman's business, he says,

> "to discern events in their beginnings, to be beforehand in the detection of movements and tendencies, and to forewarn his countrymen accordingly; to fight against the political vices, from which no state is free, of pro-

crastination, supineness, ignorance, and party jealousy; to impress upon all the paramount importance of unity and friendly feeling, and the duty of providing promptly for the country's needs."[10]

And it is because Isaiah is a statesman of this caliber that he goes down to where the king is supervising preparations to withstand invasion (chap. 7). Isaiah would find no fault with Ahaz for doing that, but he did find fault with Ahaz because he failed to see that the country's real need was its need of God. It had a God who was able to keep it and deliver it. Isaiah does not object to Ahaz giving heed to material things but he does object to Ahaz thinking that material things are the only things. Ahaz, in doing what he did, was adopting counsels of expediency that might avail for the moment but would mean final disaster to the nation. Opening the door to Assyria was to purchase immediate release but in the long run it fatally compromised Judah. Through that opened door came "the overflowing scourge" that was to destroy them. As he stands with his little son, Shear-jashub, whose very name was a prophecy, he hurls his words at Ahaz. Put not your trust in alliances with men, but make your alliance with God. Salvation is of the Lord. "If ye will not believe, surely ye shall not be established" (7:9). What Isaiah said was more pointed than the English version suggests. Luther gets it better with *"Glaübt ihr nicht, so bleibt ihr nicht,"* and perhaps we could render the word-play better by "If ye will not confide, ye shall not abide," or more briefly, "No faith, no fixity." Here we are dealing with the view from above and the view from below. One is reckoning with material realities, the other with spiritual certainties. Facts are real, says Ahaz, and politics must be of the same quality. Faith is insubstantial and intangible, and all kings need is "a big stick to beat them with." So the *Realpolitik* expert says, and so speaks Ahaz. Ahaz's limited view, confined to material things, filled him with fear that is half-sister to cowardice. But faith "tastes the powers of the

[10] Demosthenes, *De Corona,* No. 246.

age to come," and is enlightened as to the proper objects of fear and dread.

"Jehovah of Hosts, him shall ye sanctify;
And let him be your object of fear and dread." (8:13)

Realpolitik touches life only on the outside. It makes physical readjustments and fixes frontiers and "liquidates" the masses. We are very familiar with its procedures. It thinks materially and acts physically. But so often in history we see the outworking of something that is inward and spiritual. So often God chooses "the weak things of the world to confound the things that are mighty" (1 Cor. 1:27), and might is overthrown by right. Faith triumphs. God's winds blew and the great Spanish Armada was broken: Cromwell put his trust in God and kept his powder dry. The bayonets of Garibaldi had "ideas on their points", and Mazzini was animated by unquenchable faith. The final word is not with chariots and horses, tanks and bombs; it is with the side that believes in God and his purpose for the world when everything seems to contradict that faith.

"The Egyptians are men, and not God,
And their horses are flesh, and not spirit." (31:3)

That is the fundamental difference, and it is fundamental. There lies the difference between Ahaz and his like on the one hand and the prophet on the other. That is the faith that overcomes the world. "Not by might, nor by power, but by my Spirit, saith the Lord of Hosts" (Zech. 4:6).

It matters little where we look at this matter. Isaiah is piercing to the roots and realities of things; he sees right to the center. He knows God is wise. God has a plan and a purpose, and that plan and purpose concern the whole world. The Assyrian may come down like a wolf on the fold, but he will not take Jerusalem, for it is guarded by Jehovah. Here perhaps we see a limitation in the prophet's view: in his adherence to the local and temporal he was undoubtedly the child of his age. Later prophets will maintain the same purpose of God, and will hold that God is strong enough to achieve his purpose even without Israel or Jerusalem. Jeremiah will take a stand exactly opposite to that of Isaiah. But Isaiah knew that Assyria was but the instrument of God for Judah's chastisement, and when God is through with his instrument he will dispense with it. The axe may not boast itself against him who uses it, nor the saw against him who wields it (10:15). Assyria may presume—and did presume—but God is mighty, and she shall be broken. And so in the wonderful story of Sennacherib's attack (701 B.C.) the prophet's faith was signally vindicated and Zion was delivered (37:1 ff.).

THE FELLOWSHIP OF FAITH

Not only is Isaiah the prophet of faith; he is the founder of the faithful community (8:16). With that overwhelming sense of God's purpose he sets himself to create a community or church that shall work together with God towards the establishment of his kingdom. Round him gather a band of disciples, as Jesus gathered around himself a group of men whom he might send forth to teach and to preach, and Isaiah himself proceeds to form the holy remnant. He first makes that separation between church and state which represents the essential freedom of the sons of God and is vital to all true democracy.

> "Till then no one had dreamed of a fellowship of faith disassociated from all national forms, maintained without the exercise of ritual services, bound together by faith in the divine word alone. It was the birth of a new era in Old Testament religion, for it was the birth of the concept of the church, the first step in the emancipation of spiritual religion from the forms of political life—a step not less significant that all its consequences were not seen till centuries had passed away. The community of true religion and the political community of Israel had never before been separated in thought; now they stood side by side, conscious of their mutual antagonism, and never again fully to fall back into their old identity." [11]

[11] Smith, W. R., *The Prophets of Israel,* 1912, p. 274.

5

MICAH: PROPHET OF DEMOCRACY

MICAH of Moresheth-Gath is dignified with no long pedigree. The prophet of democracy makes no boast of his ancestry, and from his book few personal details can be gathered. His name signifies "Who is like Jah [Jehovah]?" and might well suggest a man like Elijah, "Very zealous for the Lord God of hosts." The lack of a fuller description here may indicate a plain man sprung from the common folk, or it may be evidence of that humility which effaces self. Micah was both poor and humble.

His home-town or village, according to the best evidence, was Moresheth, a small village on the Israelite border close to the Philistine city of Gath. It lay about 1000 feet above sea level on the gently descending terraced land that ran down from the hills of Judea to the Maritime Plain. It is but seventeen miles away from the home of Amos on the other side of the watershed, but whereas Amos looked out upon the bleak mountains of Moab and down to the dense Jordan jungle Micah's view was towards the fertile plains and the Great Sea beyond. Amos lived in the lonely wilds but to Micah "the lines were fallen in pleasant places and a goodly heritage was his"; he lived in a district rich in agriculture and among good, sturdy independent yeomen. Here there was food sufficient for man and beast, and while the great world did not thrust itself upon those dwellers in the countryside they were close enough to the main highways to feel the pulse of the larger life of the big world.

Life on the border of Judah and Philistia was not unlike

life on the border of Scotland and England about the fifteenth century. Raids and forays were frequent, and in many a local "scrap" the Hebrews were toughened and hardened; there must have been incidents like that recited in II Samuel 23:11–12:

> "And after him was Shammah the son of Agee a Hararite. And the Philistines were gathered together into a troop, where was a plot of ground full of lentils; and the people fled from the Philistines.
> "But he stood in the midst of the plot and defended it, and slew the Philistines, and Jehovah wrought a great victory."

Such an environment was likely to produce strong men of independent spirit, and Micah shows the influence of his environment.

THE HISTORICAL BACKGROUND

Micah prophesied in the days of Jotham, Ahaz and Hezekiah, and in those years stirring events took place. In 735 B.C. Ahaz was threatened by a Syro-Ephraimite coalition that sought to raise a front against Assyria. Ahaz refused the proffered advice of the prophet Isaiah, became tributary to Assyria, and thus initiated the connection of Assyria and Judah. The northern kingdom was stripped of its might, and in 722 B. C. Samaria was forced to surrender after a heroic struggle. The other tributary states, Philistia, Phoenicia, Ammon, Moab, together with Judah, continued to be restive under the galling yoke of the oppressor; and in 720 B.C. Sargon had to suppress revolts in points as far apart as Hamath and Gaza. Again in 711 B.C. he had to deal with another such revolt in which the revolting states were supported by Egypt. Ashdod was conquered and its population deported in accord with Assyrian methods, and an alien group set in their stead. It seems probable that Gath also suffered a similar fate at this time. The death of Sargon in 705 B.C. was the signal for renewed rebellion, and to this period belongs the siege of Jerusalem by Sennacherib in 701 B.C. As Sennacherib claims in this campaign to have taken forty-six of the cities of Judah, we can understand the sore pressure to which the inhabitants of the open countryside were exposed. It is largely this situation that lies back of Micah's prophecies and gives rise to the problems with which he deals.

MICAH THE CONTEMPORARY OF ISAIAH

The period of Micah coincides generally with that of Isaiah of Jerusalem (740–701 B.C.). Though they exercised their ministry at the same period of history there is no record of any personal contact, nor may we infer from their books that they ever met. Calvin refers to Micah as "Isaiah's friend, and, as it were, colleague," but this seems scarcely correct. Nor is there reason to think with Hans Schmidt [1] that Micah was a disciple of Isaiah. Sellin thinks the influence of Isaiah is to be seen in Micah's expression of Messianic ideals (chaps. 4, 5), but this is doubtful. Micah seems to be too independent to be in debt to anyone.

These two prophets represent two different social levels, and their viewpoints diverge. We have here two separate approaches, and though they are one in their fundamental faith they are certainly not one in the interpretation of the faith and its application to life. Isaiah is an aristocrat; Micah is a democrat. Isaiah is the friend and confidant of kings and princes, but Micah associates only with the common people. Isaiah lives in Jerusalem and regards the capital as the hub of the universe; Micah lives on the land and has as little regard for Jerusalem as the Western farmer has for Washington. Isaiah is concerned mainly with politics and international affairs, but Micah does not pass beyond ethical and religious considerations.

In the course of time and the passing of the centuries

[1] *Die Schriften des Alten Testaments,* II, 2, p. 130.

Micah may seem to have suffered in comparison with his great contemporary. That may be due to the fact that we are generally more interested in capitals and kings than in the countryside and its humble dwellers. That, again, may be charged to a general failing on the part of human nature: we tend to "worship bigness" and fail to assess the real value of men and things. We despise "the day of small things." The little man, who by his wisdom saved a city, is forgotten, while the worthless king, who thoughtlessly brought the city to ruin, is remembered (Eccl. 9:13 ff.). That is how the preacher saw the matter, and he was wonderfully modern in his insight. And if Micah had not preached in the country we would not have had the golden book of Jeremiah (p. 151).

THE BOOK OF MICAH

The book of Micah falls into three sections, (a) chapters 1–3, (b) chapters 4–5, (c) chapters 6–7. The first of these sections is ascribed with almost unanimity to Micah. Concerning the second there is a variety of opinion, and many scholars would deny these to Micah. There may be certain additions here but, by and large, we agree with Sellin and Schmidt, who attribute them to Micah. It has been objected that Micah was too much occupied with pressing social ills to have any time for visionary speculations, but one might well ask in this connection whether any social reformer could persist in his social task without the vision of humanity redeemed. Nor is there any real reason to think that the early prophets prophesied nothing but doom; that simple criterion is now abandoned by most competent scholars. The third section bears a closer resemblance to the oracles of the first section and there is no reason to doubt that here we have the genuine oracles of Micah. Eissfeldt [2] would regard 7:7–20 as a later addition, and this is admitted by most scholars. With these reservations

[2] Eissfeldt, Otto, *Einleitung in das Alte Testament,* 1934, p. 457.

we are prepared to regard the book as proceeding from the prophet whose name it bears.

INFLUENCE OF MICAH

That the influence of this prophet was considerable and enduring is made clear by a citation of his prophecy as to the destruction of Zion (3:12) a hundred years later when Jeremiah had spoken similar words (Jer. 26:18). Jeremiah would certainly have fallen a victim to popular fury had it not been for those grave and reverend elders from the countryside who recalled the words that Micah had spoken a century before. It is to be observed that after the lapse of one hundred years the words of a *minor* prophet were still fresh in men's minds while nothing is said of his great contemporary Isaiah. We may be grateful to Micah not only for his native worth and dignity but also for the fact that when he was dead and gone his living words availed for a deliverance of one who was the most Christ-like of all the prophets.

That thought on his enduring influence leads to a further reflection on what is involved in this connection. For the fortunes of this great country of America are largely decided by what goes on in the minds of farmers in the West and the "deep South." It is true that those dwellers in the wide open spaces pay as little regard to the capital as Micah did to Jerusalem. For while Jerusalem and Washington represent their respective countries to the outside world, that which primarily matters in any country is the tiller of the soil, the humble farmer who works upon the soil. The landlords and the politicians, the mortgagors and bankers belong to the capital and the great cities, but that on which they ultimately depend is the labor of the farmer, who, amid his unremitting toil, has little or no time to intermeddle with politics. To Micah Jerusalem was the home of the exploiting absentee landlords who had no love of the soil and cared not for the strength and character of Israel's yeoman class. It would seem as if this greedy exploiting group, composed largely of *nouveaux riches,* was eager to branch out and make an appearance with a country-seat. And the Shephēlā, that rich fertile district that lay between the Judean hills and Philistia, was the very place for a country home. But those country seats could be acquired only as the farmers were cleared out, and that process was in full swing when Micah prophesied. From the impassioned way in which he speaks we might well imagine him to have been a victim of this selfish ruthlessness. Like Oliver Goldsmith Micah knew the tragedy of "the deserted village" and the wasted countryside. He knew that in the extinction of that sturdy yeoman class the nation must surely bleed to death.

> Ill fares the land, to hastening ills a prey,
> Where wealth accumulates and men decay.

To Micah it did not seem of surpassing importance that Jerusalem should be spared the horrors of war: it may be he would even have preferred to see it suffer in order that some of those unthinking grandees might know something of privation and distress. It may even be—and here he differs from Isaiah—that he would have preferred to see Jerusalem fall that he might witness the rise of lowly Bethlehem (Mic. 5:2). There may be more in this than is commonly thought, much more, and we shall consider it later. For Micah knew that it was the farmer in the outlying villages and hamlets that felt war's sorest impact. And the farmer had nothing but his farming skill. If only those in the capital could learn to think with sympathy of those who were to be involved and ruined by their rash schemes! But evil is wrought from want of thought.

Thus Micah is pre-eminently the prophet of democracy, the spokesman of the poor. He represents "the forgotten man," and speaks for the inarticulate masses. His accent is the accent of the countryside; he is as plain, blunt, and direct as Amos. But Amos was only a spectator of the events he describes and the abuses he denounced; Micah felt these things in his own body. Micah speaks strongly because he feels strongly, and his style is marked by simplicity, sincerity, and sympathy. His style reflects the man.

THE TEACHING OF MICAH

From all this it is not difficult to imagine what Micah will say. Like "a plain blunt man he will speak straight onward." Concerning his right to speak the prophet does not leave us in any doubt. Like the Atlantic Charter he will claim the first of the "Four Freedoms"—the right of free speech—and in so doing he gives us a full expression of the prophet's function:

> "I am full of power by the spirit of Jehovah, and of judgment and might,
> To declare unto Jacob his transgression, and to Israel his sin." (3:8)

Micah does not appear to have been a member of the professional guild of prophets. These professionals he denounces as men false to the faith, who trim their sails to the favoring breeze of popular opinion.

> Concerning the prophets who make my people err,
> Who, when their mouths are filled, preach peace:
> But as for him who feeds them not—
> Against him they declare war.
> Therefore it shall be night for you without vision
> And darkness for you that ye shall not divine. (3:5, 6)

The term "false prophets" is not found in the Old Testament Hebrew, but it meets us in the Greek version (LXX). Here we see how the professional prophets acted and we learn something of their method. They had made the Word a mercenary thing. We learn, too, how Micah spoke, and we discern the difference. But it was not easy for their audience to distinguish between the genuine and the false; to the listening people there did not seem any difference between Hananiah and Jeremiah (Jer. 28), but one was false and the other was true.

George Adam Smith remarks that every civilisation, ancient or modern, inevitably has to deal with two questions—the land question and the liquor question.[3] The latter meets us more prominently in Amos, Hosea, and Isaiah, for it assumes greater prominence in cities than in the country. Micah has one scathing reference to the liquor question (2:11), but Micah was a countryman living on the land, dwelling beside those who had nothing but their land, and it is the Land Question that presses most heavily here.

For the land is not only the source and origin of wealth: here above all men enter into communion with Nature, and Nature is a main sphere of divine revelation. The task of the peasant may strain his body but it also enriches his soul, for all his work teaches him justice, patience, sympathy and hope. To use the words of Micah's great contemporary, who was not oblivious of the larger issues involved, and who, on one particular occasion, turned his eyes from politics and international concerns to the work of the humble farmer:

> "His God doth instruct him aright and doth teach him." (Is. 28:26)

That the peasant was deeply attached to the soil is obvious from such a story as that of Naboth's vineyard (1 Kings 21). It was not just a piece of real estate that might easily be alienated or exchanged for another. It was bound up most intimately with his very life, so that to lose one's land was like a mutilation of one's bodily members. It tore the heart asunder and destroyed life at the roots. For that reason G. A. Smith may well say:

> "Micah is no longer a book or an oration, but flesh and blood upon a home and a countryside of his own."[4]

This book was not written with ink but with the lifeblood of the prophet.

It is not difficult to understand how this question assumed

[3] Smith, G. A., *Book of the Twelve Prophets,* new edition, 1928, Vol. I, p. 408.

[4] *Ibid.,* p. 408.

serious dimensions at this period of Hebrew history. Isaiah is conscious of this problem, for its repercussions were felt in the capital, and Isaiah speaks strongly and vigorously on the matter (Is. 5:8 ff.). The prolonged wars with the Syrians and Assyrians had impoverished the farmers, and the marching of armies up and down the great roads between Egypt and Syria had filled the land with spoliation and exploitation. The farmer might plant and be able to reap, or the invading army would reap and carry off his crop. To carry on through the lean period until the soil might recoup him for his losses the farmer had to borrow money and, in the process, pledge his farm as security for the loan. Even the services of himself and his family might be mortgaged. Recurring invasion might render it impossible to pay off the loan in due time, and he and his family might be expelled from their land and home. It is this that stirs the wrath of Micah.

> Woe to them that devise iniquity upon their beds;
> In the morning they execute it, for it is in their power.
> Yea, they covet fields and seize them, and houses, and carry them away.
> So they crush a yeoman and his house, a man and his heritage. (Mic. 2:1, 2)

Doubtless this was done with due legal process, but the prophet knew that in the process something precious was dying in the national heart.

For all this there was a lack of compassion and a total failure of sympathy, and things were being exalted above persons. Human beings were being treated as chattels that could be bought and sold to make others rich. Men were being treated as means and not as ends for the selfish interest of a group of profiteers.

> They eat the flesh of my people, and strip their skin from off them;
> They make bare their bones and break them up
> Like meat in a pot, and flesh in a caldron. (Mic. 3:3)

To the prophet this was not an economic problem but a moral and religious question that had to do with human life. The hot mood of Micah is paralleled by that of the English poet, Thomas Hood, who in his poem, "Song of the Shirt," championed the cause of the underprivileged and sweated workers in England:

> It's not linen you're wearing out
> But human creatures' lives.

Micah saw all this, and saw right to the center of things. For here was a repudiation of all the ancient faith stood for.

> Ye have become my people's foe; ye rise up against them that are at peace.
> Ye strip off from those passing by in confidence booty of war.
> The women of my people ye drive away from their pleasant homes;
> From their babes ye take away my glory for ever. (2:8, 9)

In these words Micah denounces the rich, greedy exploiters in Jerusalem, and concludes:

> "Arise and go! For this is not your resting-place.
> Because of uncleanness ye shall be destroyed with destruction irremediable." (2:10)

"The earth is the Lord's," said the Psalmist, but in Micah's time the landlords had appropriated it and foreclosed upon it. God had set man in the beginning to till the ground, and the ground is the source and origin of man's sustenance. Those greedy exploiters were destroying the nation's real wealth, and the glory of the nation, its sturdy yeoman class, was being reduced to a state of serfhood. The men who did so, says Micah, were robbing God and his people of their true glory.

Fundamental here was the failure on the part of those denounced to recognise the true character of Israel's God and the demands he made upon his people. That relation which in the beginning had been moral and personal was now distorted into something juristic and mechanical. A crude commercialism, bolstered and supported by a time-serving ecclesiastical institution (2:11), had enthroned material values and lost sight of things that really matter, and "where there is no vision the people perish."

Hear this now, ye heads of the house of Jacob, and rulers of the house of Israel:
Who abhor justice, and pervert all that is right;
Who build Zion with blood, and Jerusalem with iniquity.
Her chiefs judge for a bribe, and her priests give oracles for money:
Yet upon Jehovah they lean, saying,
Is not Jehovah in our midst? No evil can befall us.
Therefore on account of you
Zion will be ploughed as a field,
And Jerusalem will be made ruins,
And the mountain of the House a wooded height. (3:9–12)

Obviously those men could not discern the signs of the times. They were sitting high and felt secure and thought things might go on so for ever. But the prophet saw to the roots of things, and reality is never what we see, but what God sees.

Isaiah could not conceive a social order without the capital and its aristocrats, but Micah has the deeper insight here. No human citadel, however lofty and towering, was essential to the upbuilding of the Kingdom of God. For God does not dwell in houses made with hands but in the surrendered lives and humble hearts of men and women. The relation of man to God is personal and not mechanical; it is inward and not outward. God will destroy Zion and take away its glory: he will sweep away the imposing external apparatus of worship to bring about an internationalisation of religion. The view of God as a charm or talisman will give place to something more intimate and personal, and the ethic of the thing done will give place to the ethic of the clean heart.

TRUE RELIGION DEFINED

Here Micah gives us an Old Testament definition of true religion just as James gives us one in the New Testament (Jam. 1:27). Here we have an insight of remarkable power wherein the prophet focuses the various rays of prophecy to one burning point of light. Samuel had emphasised obedience as better than sacrifice (1 Sam. 15:22), while the eighth-century prophets had vitalised the conception, Amos identifying it with justice, Hosea with mercy, Isaiah with holiness. It remained for Micah to blend these separate notes in a way yet richer and fuller, and thus to show forth the essence of religion.

It has been shown thee, O man, what is good.
Yea, what does Jehovah seek from thee
But to do justly, and to love mercy,
And to walk humbly with thy God. (6:8)

Justice—that means the recognition of every man's rights and the discharge of every duty in such a way as brings health and well-being to the community; mercy—the rich Hebrew word beloved of Hosea and the Psalmists, signifying loyalty to God on the part of man, and of man to his fellow-man, and of God to man—mercy that is an essential part of justice and fills justice with joy and gladness to make all our service a delight to God and man; the humble walk—the renunciation of all human arrogance (the Greek *hybris*) and one's own selfish will, and the waiting in quietness and confidence to hear and do what God the Lord will direct. This is to set life in tune with the Infinite, and this is what Micah means by religion. Nowhere in the Old Testament do we find a wider vision or profounder insight.

MICAH'S THOUGHT OF THE MESSIAH

No less plainly does Micah speak of the Messiah. His thought here is in keeping with the man. Micah is indeed very bold. And if it be not Micah who speaks, as some scholars maintain, then it is certainly a true disciple of the prophet and one who has inherited his spirit. But we believe we have here the authentic voice of Micah, and he speaks with other tones than Isaiah.

Isaiah's Messiah is of kingly stock, a scion of the house of David who reigns from Jerusalem (Is. 9, 11). But Micah pins his faith to the common stock of men, and prophesies that from such, and from the humblest sphere of service, shall arise the instrument and agent of God's purpose. Micah is democratic through and through.

> And thou, Beth-Ephratah, least among the clans of Judah,
> From thee one shall come forth for me
> Who will be ruler over Israel,
> Whose origins are of old, from ancient days,
> And he will stand and shepherd in the power of Jehovah,
> In the majesty of the name of Jehovah his God:
> For he will be great to the ends of the earth. (5:2-4)

Micah knew, as few others knew, the wealth of piety and weight of character that resides in the humble homes of the common people. With Robert Burns he shared his passion, and with the Scottish poet he could have said:

> Princes and lords are but the breath of kings:
> An honest man's the noblest work of God.[5]

From such a humble sphere God's Man will come in God's own time, as came Moses and Gideon and David in days gone by, and that Man shall, by God's grace, set his people free. A true shepherd, and no hireling like the present rulers, he shall be, and the disinherited and underprivileged shall find hope in him.

THE FINAL OUTCOME

There is no real reason to deny to Micah the vision of the better day. All prophecy is contingent and conditional,

[5] Robert Burns, *The Cottar's Saturday Night.*

and from what we read in Jeremiah and the Hebrew historical books we learn that Micah's utterance of doom upon Jerusalem led to Hezekiah's reform. The preaching of Jonah had a result other than Jonah hoped or intended, and grace triumphed. We need not judge the matter otherwise here. The better day that will dawn will be a day of universal peace, and He shall reign whose right it is to reign. Here Micah and Isaiah are one in their expression (Mic. 4:1–3; Is. 2:2–4). It may well be that both are quoting an earlier oracle.

> No strife shall rage, nor hostile feuds
> disturb those peaceful years;
> To ploughshares men shall beat their swords
> to pruning-hooks their spears.
> No longer hosts encount'ring hosts
> shall crowds of slain deplore;
> They hang the trumpet in the hall,
> and study war no more.

The song is prompted in some measure by war-weariness but it is animated by a living faith in Almighty God. And because Micah believes, like the other prophets, in the divine control of history, the ideal finds place and expression in terms of time and sense. But Micah adds a verse not found in Isaiah, and here we see the strong social interest of the prophet.

"Every man shall sit under his vine and fig-tree,
And none shall make them afraid." (Mic. 4:4)

Thus religion is brought into closest contact with life, and the vision connects hope with reality. The principles represented in the Atlantic Charter need not remain an idle dream.

6

ZEPHANIAH: PROPHET OF PURITANISM

THERE is fairly general agreement as to the position of Zephaniah in the prophetic canon, and the problems that meet us here do not arise from any literary complexity or from theological variety. The problem here is that of a mind with one idea where the point is stated with sheer and startling simplicity. It is the simplicity of Zephaniah that constitutes our problem, and the problem is not unlike that which attends any study of the Puritan character.

THE MAN ZEPHANIAH

In this instance we have a pedigree of more than usual proportions, and his descent is traced back four generations to Hezekiah. Though the text does not say Hezekiah, king of Judah, it has been assumed by most commentators that Zephaniah is descended from the good king who reigned in Jerusalem in the period of Isaiah. The assumption of royal lineage has been made in the case of Isaiah also, but there seems little ground in either case for the assumption. In any case it is certain the Hebrew prophets did not depend on such adventitious aids to establish their claim to fame, and their greatness does not depend on the presence or absence of royal pedigrees. It is physically possible that Zephaniah could have stood in this relation to King Hezekiah, but it does not seem probable. Sellin is more likely to be correct in his exposition of the verse that gives this lengthy genealogy,

> "the word of Jehovah which came to Zephaniah, son of Kushi, son of Gedaliah, son of Amariah, son of Hezekiah" (Zeph. 1:1).

Kushi means Ethiopian, and an Egyptian or Ethiopian could not be admitted to the Jewish community unless he could show a pure Jewish pedigree for at least three generations (Deut. 23:8). Why his father had given him the name Kushi is not obvious, but it may well have been that in the dark days of Manasseh some people pinned their faith to Egypt and belonged to the pro-Egyptian party in Judah, and by giving such a name to their child they revealed their political sympathies. A like procedure was observed in the war period when many parents named their children Franklin or Winston. It may have been so, for folly is not limited to one generation. The name Zephaniah means "Jah hides," and that may be a reference to the times of Manasseh of whom we read that "he shed innocent blood very much." The name may even represent the prayer of pious parents and express the wish that Jehovah may protect and cover this life, or it may have been given as a kind of charm to protect from danger in general. More than that we may not say, and only his book remains to tell us what the prophet thought and said.

THE BOOK AND ITS DATE

The book may be accepted as, in the main, coming from the hand of Zephaniah himself. Certain slight intrusions may be present, but they do not affect the general picture. Sellin and Horst accept the book with the exception of the two final verses; Schmidt would reject the last six verses (3:14–20) and Eissfeldt does likewise. With this exception we may accept the book as that of Zephaniah.

As to the date of his ministry there is general agreement among scholars that it was written about 625 B.C., just before the reformation instituted by Josiah (621 B.C.) and at the period of the Scythian invasion of Egypt and the coastlands of Palestine. This Scythian invasion is described by Herodotus,[1] but Herodotus without confirmatory evidence is not regarded too highly as an authority. His statements on this question have been vigorously contested by modern scholars, particularly by Wilke,[2] but while strong arguments are adduced they cannot be regarded as decisive. The story as given by Herodotus seems to supply a historical background for the prophecies of Zephaniah and Jeremiah.

The prophet, too, writes before the discovery of Deuteronomy, the document which formed the basis of Josiah's reformation. Zephaniah describes the situation as it was in Judah before 621 B.C.

I will stretch out my hand against Judah
  and against the inhabitants of Jerusalem;
I will cut off the remnant of Baal
  and the name of the idol-priests,
And those who upon the house-tops
  worship the host of heaven,
Those who worship Jehovah
  and swear by Milcom.

. . . . .

And I will punish the princes
  and the king's sons,
And those who clothe themselves
  with foreign apparel.
I will punish those who leap
  over the threshold,
Who fill the house of their lord
  with violence and fraud. (Zeph. 1:4–9)

[1] *Histories,* Book I, pp. 105–106.

[2] Wilke, Fritz, "Das Skythenproblem im Jeremiabuch," in *Beiträge zur Wissenschaft vom Alten Testament,* Heft 13, 1913, pp. 222–254.

These are the practices and usages of unreformed Judah. Zephaniah will thus have preceded Jeremiah by a few years, and his writing and preaching may have been partly responsible for the reform inaugurated in 621 B.C.

The book divides easily into sections: 1:2–6, 8–13 announces a general world-judgment with special reference to Judah (1:4 ff.); 1:7, 14–18 announces the coming of the *Day of Jehovah,* followed in 2:1–3 by a general call to repent. In 2:4–15 is described the judgment of Philistia, Moab, Ammon, Egypt, and Assyria. In 3:1–13 the prophet concentrates again on Jerusalem and denounces its social ills and oppressions and concludes with the thought of a scant remnant of humble people; 3:14–20 is generally admitted to be a later addition and sets forth the jubilant and happy future of the renewed community. Zephaniah's stern Puritan gospel has been softened and toned down by a later hand.

THE MESSAGE OF ZEPHANIAH

Zephaniah is a man with one idea, and that idea appears to overwhelm and overpower the prophet. That idea is judgment. He is a man after Calvin's own heart, one born ahead of Calvin's time, but with the same thoroughgoing idea of the divine sovereignty. Puritanism finds a main support in him. The mythological imagery that abounds here is employed only to set forth the omnipotence of Israel's God who controls both nature and history and directs all things to the achievement of his sovereign will.

Be silent before the Lord Jehovah
  for near is the Day of Jehovah;
For Jehovah has prepared a sacrifice,
  has sanctified his invited ones.
Near is Jehovah's great day,
  near and hastening fast:
It comes swifter than a runner,

Disaster hastes faster than a mighty man.
Day of wrath is that day,
Day of pressure and distress,
Day of stress and distress,
Day of darkness and gloom,
Day of cloud and thunder-cloud,
Day of the trumpet and the battle-roar,
Upon the fenced cities
And upon the lofty turrets.
Great fear will possess men,
And they will walk like blind ones. . . .
Their blood will be spilled like dust
And their flesh like dung.
Neither their silver nor their gold
Will avail to save them
In the day of Jehovah's indignation
And in the glow of his jealousy. . . . (1:7, 14–18)

This idea has been made memorable by the great medieval hymn of Thomas of Celano, which in its opening words has caught the main mood of the prophet. The "*Dies irae, dies illa*" has been translated by W. J. Irons and appears in most modern hymnals.

Day of wrath! O day of mourning!
See fulfilled the prophet's warning,
Heaven and earth in ashes burning.
O what fear man's bosom rendeth,
When from heaven the Judge descendeth,
On whose sentence all dependeth.

Just as Milton's poetry has had very considerable influence on Old Testament theology in general, so this hymn has had no small influence on the interpretation of Zephaniah. In both cases one might well raise a question, for, as Sellin points out, this aspect of Zephaniah has been overemphasized and our total view put out of focus. For the conception of the *Day of*

Jehovah was not introduced first by Zephaniah. Amos gave expression to the idea, and in the form of judgment as opposed to the popular idea of blessing (Amos 5:18). Zephaniah, however, develops the idea with vigor and in detailed fashion.

I will utterly sweep away everything
  from the face of the earth ('tis the oracle of Jehovah).
I will sweep away man and beast,
Will sweep away the birds of the air,
  and fish of the sea:
I will cast down the ungodly,
And root out the sinners
From off the face of the earth. (Zeph. 1:2, 3)

Everything in this book seems to be hot, fiery, and burning, cutting off and destroying. G. A. Smith says "no hotter book lies in the Old Testament." Everything here is blasted and withered and scorched; there is no dew upon the grass, no song of birds or bloom of flowers, but everywhere fire and smoke and darkness, drifting chaff, dwellings overthrown, palaces desolate, nettles and saltpits, with owls hooting on the window-sills, and ravens croaking at the door. Here surely is a picture of a God-forsaken world that has felt the full force of the divine reaction against human sin. Surely the *Day of Jehovah* is a dreadful day!

There is a width of vision here which we miss in Nahum and Habakkuk, for this judgment concerns the world. There may be a lack of clarity in the detailed working out of the vision, and somehow Zephaniah seems to leave the nations suspended in mid-air. His primary concern is with Judah, and the nations seem to be introduced more or less as a background. His vision is of a God who rules the world and controls the nations and is concerned with moral principle everywhere. This was not the popular conception of the *Day of Jehovah,* as we can gather from the words of Amos. The popular conception was of a day of victory when Jehovah would intervene as he had done in days of old to set Israel high and bring low all her foes. Its watchword was *"Israel über Alles,"* and with confidence they waited for *"der Tag."* But Amos knew the essential character of God as his contemporaries did not, and though they were encouraged in their proud conceit by a succession of chauvinistic prophets there never was lacking a succession of true spokesmen for God who could say to such a mood,

the day of Jehovah is darkness and not light.

For the purpose of Israel's election had been lost sight of by those popular orators and by those who listened to them. The nationalistic prophets faced towards the past while the dynamic classical prophets were set towards far horizons. Popular thought regarded God as bound up with Israel and standing over against a hostile world, but it is the mark of the authentic prophets that they transcended this false dualism and saw things as they really were. Unlike those other prophets they saw God highly exalted in lonely majesty and full of righteousness and truth, while over against this solitary God they saw *a whole world lying in iniquity.* Israel was part of the world, and as part of that world it was exposed to the divine judgment. All nations here are under judgment and none may escape. God has no favorites. Indeed, the judgment will be more severe in the case of Israel, for she has sinned against the clearer light and fallen from the higher height.

"You only have I known of all the families of the earth:
therefore will I punish you." (Amos 3:2)

PROPHET OF DESPAIR?

Judgment complete and final seems to be the word of Zephaniah. Amid the darkness there appears no kindly light, no thought of grace that woos and beckons and descends to hell to recover its own, as in the book of Hosea. Is there no rift in the cloud to let fall one little shaft of light on all this dismal gloom? Why, asks G. A. Smith, does the prophet never speak of the love of God? Is this another Amos or a John the Baptist? It may be, as Smith suggests, that it is characteristic of youth to run to such extremes, and to be unsparing in denunciation. Certainly the prophet reveals a strong moral sensibility and passion; he gives us the impression of an austere man.

But there was reason for this austerity. Those abuses portrayed in 1:7–13, the aping of foreign fashions in dress, the practice of heathen rites, the dishonesty that filled public life, and the dead indifference that took no account of God, the "muddy minds" that had settled on their lees, and said,

Jehovah does neither good nor ill (1:12)

might well provoke a man of God to a high degree of austerity. Isaiah had to deal with men who boasted of their "covenant with death and hell" (Is. 28:18), and these insolent rowdies seem to have been very defiant and aggressive. But Zephaniah was faced with something more deadly, the dead indifference of men who had ceased to take God into account. They thought God was dead; he had certainly ceased to function (1:12). But both Isaiah and Zephaniah knew, and spared no pains to make others know, that the ultimate issue of things is never going to be a heaven-and-hell amalgamation society. Judgment will fall, and if it will do nothing else it will at least vindicate the reality of God. It will do more. For men shall see that God is not mocked, and that finally the tares will be separated from the wheat. Zephaniah resembles Amos in the detached manner in which he speaks of all this; Isaiah is richer in sympathy.

Zephaniah, like Isaiah, had seen God in his glorious holiness, and he saw Jerusalem, which claimed to be his holy city, as a center and seat of all uncleanness. Like Isaiah he had seen things as they ought to be, and the vision of things as they were shocked him until his heart was full of holy anger and righteous indignation. But like Jeremiah he will "search Jerusalem with a lantern"; maybe he will find an honest man.

Woe to the rebellious and unclean,
the city of oppression!
She hearkened not to the summons,
did not receive instruction.
In Jehovah she put not her trust,
did not draw near to her God.
Her rulers within her are roaring lions,
her judges are night wolves
who leave nothing to the morning.
Braggarts and traitors are her prophets,
her priests defile the holy
and outrage the Law.
Jehovah is righteous in her midst
and does no wrong:
Every morning he accomplishes his judgment,
at dawn he does not fail.
I have cut off nations,
Wasted are their battlements;
Their streets I laid waste
That none passed through;
Destroyed are their cities
Without inhabitant any more.
I thought now she will reverence me
and receive discipline,
And shall not be hid from her eyes
all that I commanded her.
But only more zealously have they corrupted
all their doings. (3:1-7)

Will there not be a remnant? Will none be saved?

ZEPHANIAH AND ISAIAH

Zephaniah is influenced in considerable measure by Isaiah, and it would seem as if Zephaniah had inherited the great prophet's teaching as to the remnant. But there is a difference here. To Isaiah it is the glowing certainty of faith based on the Covenant promise of God; to Zephaniah it is at most a grudging admission. In the tensions that so often attend Old Testament theological thought, it seems at times as if the divine sovereignty left no room for human freedom. One prophet will emphasise one thought to the exclusion of another and we are left bewildered. But a closer examination will reveal that both ideas are present to the minds of the speakers. Amos may seem to emphasise judgment to the exclusion of grace, and Hosea may appear to forget judgment in his emphasis on the divine love. Isaiah joins both together in his thought of judgment and the thought of the Remnant, and judgment is viewed as part and parcel of the divine grace. Here Zephaniah is debtor to Isaiah, though he leans much on Amos in his thought of the divine righteousness and the fact of judgment. Zephaniah could appreciate the thought of Amos in regard to the remnant that would survive; it would be so small as to be scarcely worth mention.

> "As the shepherd rescueth out of the mouth of the lion two legs or a piece of an ear, so shall the children of Israel be rescued that sit in Samaria in the corner of a couch and on silken cushions of a bed." (Amos 3:12)

But the thought of the remnant is implicit in the Hebrew faith in the God of the Covenant, and Zephaniah, like Isaiah, will hold to it because he holds the faith.

But if this remnant is saved it shall be "so as by fire." "It is the same standpoint ethically as that of Christ's vision of the Judgment." [3] But whereas the aristocratic Isaiah could not visualise any social order in which aristocracy did not prevail, Zephaniah gives another turn to the thought and sees the remnant composed of "the meek and the humble" (3:12). And in the later history, as evidenced throughout the Psalter, the meek and humble were found mainly among the economically poor and oppressed. Zephaniah had seen enough of the proud arrogance of military empires (chap. 2) and had ob-

[3] Smith, G. A., *op, cit.*, p. 47.

served too often the ruthless oppression and misrule of those into whose hands the government was committed (3:1–7) to believe that there was any hope there. Thus he sets his hope on the growth of other qualities of mind and heart: Isaiah had called for *faith,* but Zephaniah calls for *meekness and humility.* That is a mood wholly other than that which says proudly,

> I am, and there is none beside me (2:15).

This is the mood of God-defying Titans who trust in their own strength and take no account of God. That is the Greek *hybris* (arrogance) which evokes the fury of high heaven. But the meek commit their way to God and wait patiently for him; they have no purpose but to do his will and do it with the whole heart. This is what Micah calls "walking humbly before God" (Mic. 6:8).

> Seek ye Jehovah, ye meek of the earth, do right;
> Seek righteousness, seek humility,
> It may be ye will be hid in the day of Jehovah's wrath. (2:3)
>
> But I will leave in thy midst a people humble and small,
> And the remnant of Israel shall trust in the name of Jehovah. (3:12)

In this matter Zephaniah is pioneering the path of individualism in the Old Testament, a path along which his immediate successor, Jeremiah, was to travel much further. Perhaps, too, we do not err in regarding him as the precursor of that movement that was to culminate in what we call Judaism, for the *poor and the humble* later come to assume almost the proportions of a definite party over against the *ungodly and the sinners.* Zephaniah may have followed his great predecessor Isaiah (8:2) and taken the first steps toward the formation of such a community who were ready to undertake the observance of certain salutary regulations. Chap. 1:4 and chap. 3:11

became part of Josiah's program in 621 B.C. Zephaniah may thus be regarded as one who prepared the way for the reception of the Law, and thus he may be considered one of the earliest founders of Judaism.

7

NAHUM: PROPHET OF VENGEANCE

WE have no information as to the person of Nahum beyond what is given in his book, and in his case legend and tradition have had free play.

The prophet is described as *the Elkoshite* but as to where Elkosh was located we are ignorant. Tradition has assigned him to Alkush, twenty-six miles north of the ancient site of Nineveh, and a tomb there is reverenced as the tomb of Nahum. If this tradition were authentic we would have to regard Nahum as belonging to the ten tribes carried into captivity in 721 B.C. But the tradition is not older than the sixteenth century A.D. and little value can be attributed to it. The evidence of the book itself is against such an origin. His home has been sought in Helkesei or Elkosh, the modern El Kauze, northeast of Ramieh and about seven miles west of Tibnin in Galilee. But Galilee does not appear to have been the home of prophets, though later it became the home of the most orthodox rabbis. The tradition is attested by Jerome but it does not seem to have historical foundation. Of Elkosh in southern Judea, beyond Beth Gabrē of the tribe of Simeon, we may know little that is certain, but this seems the most probable site of the prophet's home. For Nahum exercised his ministry in the southern kingdom: "all the evidence of his book points to the fact that he was a Judean and not a member of the north Israelite kingdom." [1] Thus we will think of his home as half-way between Jerusalem and Gaza.

[1] Sellin, *Kommentar zum Alten Testament XII, Das Zwölfprophetenbuch,* p. 23.

NAHUM

THE BOOK OF NAHUM

The book consists of three chapters, and until about the beginning of the present century it was generally regarded as a unity and assigned to Nahum. But since 1891 doubt has been expressed in increasing measure with regard to 1:1–9 (Hebrew 1:2–10), and the majority of critical opinion is against assigning these verses to Nahum. The verses referred to contain the remains of an alphabetic psalm.[2] Here, however, the alphabetic psalm extends to about only one-half of the alphabet, and though various attempts have been made to carry it through to the end of the alphabet such efforts cannot be deemed successful. They do too great violence to the text and imply a large measure of arbitrariness.

It would seem wiser to assume that this alphabetic psalm was incomplete from the beginning. Why it should be so we have no means of knowing. Perhaps a later writer quoted it from memory, and he may even have forgotten its alphabetic nature, for the letter N comes before B in the second verse and M seems to precede L in the ninth verse. Otherwise the letters follow in order as far as N. Or it may be that the writer did not wish to quote more; a minister may lop off verses of a hymn in public worship and this psalm was probably part of a worship service. Or yet again the reason may have been purely mechanical—there was not room for any more on the manuscript. Whatever the reason may have been the fact remains that Nahum's book opens with an incomplete alphabetic psalm and the form is slightly confused.

Sellin has offered an attractive solution of the problem of Nahum's book. He holds that this little book is *a prophetic liturgy,* and that it was written as a form of service or liturgy to be used as the New Year Feast in October 612 B.C. Sellin

[2] An alphabetic (or acrostic) psalm is one wherein successive verses of the psalm begin with the Hebrew letters in order. Sometimes single verses or pairs of verses are thus marked and in the 119th Psalm eight verses are given to each letter. There are 22 letters in the Hebrew alphabet and consequently the 119th Psalm has 176 verses.

further maintains that the events described in the book were written *post eventum,* that is after the fall of Nineveh in 612 B.C. Verses 1:2–9 form the opening hymn, while a divine oracle follows in 1:12, 13, 15; 2:2.[3] In 1:10, 11, 14; 2:1, 3–13 we have the first *Woe* against Nineveh, followed by a second *Woe* in 3:1–17, with a concluding couplet in 3:18, 19 indicating that all this has come to pass. This hypothesis has seemed attractive to many and in its main features it may be sound. The title *Book of the Vision of Nahum* might well suggest a liturgy. But it is not necessary, as Sellin thinks, to hold that the component parts of this liturgy were written at the same time or by the same hand. If Nahum belonged to the professional prophets associated with the temple there would be no great difficulty in thinking of a prophetic liturgy of the type suggested.

But the present writer finds it difficult to believe that the poet who wrote the superlative odes of chapters 2 and 3 also composed the artificial alphabetic psalm found in chapter 1. Such productions belong to the calm academic atmosphere of the study and they are the work of virtuosos. The 119th Psalm is the classical utterance of this scribal dilettantism and it is about the deadest thing in the Old Testament. It is worlds away from the electric atmosphere of Nahum's passionate odes. Those magnificent lyrics were surely sung, as was sung the Song of Deborah (Judg. 5) or David's Lament for Jonathan (II Sam. 1:17 ff.), with the poet's eye upon the subject. For the Hebrew "thinks with the eye." The alphabetic psalm is theological and reflective, but Nahum is no theologian. Nahum is a poet with a fine frenzy and his descriptions are concrete and vivid. The alphabetic psalm is written in 3:3 meter, while Nahum's odes employ the familiar 3:2 Kina meter, broken at times by short staccato utterances in 2:2 and a rare 3:3 meter. All canons of literary criticism would indicate that the alphabetic psalm is not by the poet of the odes.

The genuine words of Nahum thus begin in 1:10 and the

[3] The numbering in the Hebrew text is frequently higher by one.

comforting oracle to Judah contained in 1:12–15, 2:2 should be set before the first oracle against Nineveh.

While no translation can do justice to Nahum's swift and fiery utterance some understanding of his poetical merit may be gained from the following translation of the message of comfort to Judah and the first oracle against Nineveh. Most of chapter 3 will be translated in the subsequent discussion.

Surely the days of my contending are ended,
  Yea, they are past and gone.
And though I have afflicted thee
  I will afflict no more.

And now I will break his rod from upon thee,
  And thy bonds I will burst asunder.

Behold upon the mountains the feet of the messenger
  Proclaiming release:
Now celebrate, O Judah, thy festival,
  And pay the vows:
For not again will pass through thee
  Any such miscreant.

Afresh shall bloom the vine of Jacob
  As the vine of Israel,
Though spoilers spoiled him,
    Destroyed his tendrils. (1:12, 13, 15, 2:3)

First oracle against Nineveh:

Ah! thicket full of lions,
  Came there not forth from thee
A plotter of evil against Jehovah
    Who counselled rascality?

Jehovah has commanded concerning thee:
  "From the house of thy god
I will destroy both carved and molten images,
  I will lay waste thy grave."

The Hammer is come up against thee:
  Guard the rampart!
Watch the way, gird the loins,
  Strengthen might to the utmost.

Blood-red is the shield of his heroes,
  Their blades like fire;
In scarlet his mighty men are clothed
  In the day of the muster.

Through the streets rage the chariots,
  Plunging through the squares;
Their appearance is like lightning,
  Like lightning they dart.

He summons his heroes,
  His nobles gallop right onward;
They hasten to the rampart,
  And the battering-ram is set up.

The bridge-gates are opened,
  And the palace melts away;
Unveiled the Queen is brought out,
  Her maidens with her
Moaning with voice like doves,
  And beating their breasts.

As a pool of waters is Nineveh
  Fast flowing away;
Stand! stand! they cry,
  But none turns back.

Plunder silver, plunder gold!
  No end to their store!
Too heavy for all
  The weight of treasures!

Vacant and void and waste is she,
  Heart of despair and knocking of knees;
Anguish in all loins,
  Livid all faces.

Where is the lion's lair,
  And the den of young lions,
Where the lion whelps dwelt
  With none to affray them?

The lion robbed for his young,
  And strangled for his lionesses,
Filling his caves with robbery,
  And his dens with rapine.

Behold, I am against thee,
  Saith Jehovah Sabaoth;
Thy lair I will burn with fire,
  And thy cubs shall the sword devour.

Thy booty I will cut
  From off the earth;
And the voice of thy messengers
  Shall be heard no more. (1:10, 11, 14; 2:3–13)

THE DATE OF NAHUM

The date of Nahum can be fixed fairly precisely. The poet writes later than the fall of No-Ammon (Thebes) which took place in 663 B.C. and is referred to in 3:8 ff. That is the upper limit for dating and the lower limit is to be set before the fall of Nineveh in 612 B.C. In that year the city was captured and destroyed by the Medes and Babylonians. Some scholars would set the date of the oracles nearer the upper limit (663) on the ground that the memory of the fall of No-Ammon could not have remained vivid after many years. But memories of decisive battles do not fade quickly; Marathon, Waterloo, even Bannockburn and Bunker Hill, would strike a responsive chord in most memories to-day. Sodom and Gomorrah, too, seem to have left an undying impression on the Hebrew mind. These great events stand out like mountain peaks above the level plains of history, and such an event as the breaking of Egypt's power would be long remembered.

But we can come nearer to an exact date and fix those odes more definitely. The "grandeur, power, and energy" (Pusey) together with the wealth of metaphor and brilliance of description almost indicate an eyewitness of the events described. We see the besiegers draw their lines around the city, we hear the galloping of horses and the rumble of chariots. The water-gates are captured, the sluices opened, and Nineveh's folk vanish like locusts in the morning. The walls are breached, the city stormed, and the streets are filled with corpses. The mother of harlotries is wasted and the righteousness of God vindicated. All that is written in the style of Hebrew poetry at its best; the writer has his eye upon the subject. All the evidences here point to the closest proximity of the poet to the event.

We can say more. For these oracles seem clearly to be subsequent to Josiah's reformation of 621 B.C. Here is no word of Judah's sin or unrighteousness—and here Nahum stands in absolute contrast to Zephaniah—and that may be explained by the conditions prevailing after 621 B.C. Judah was now pre-eminently the people of God, and the prophetic spirit had been codified and written into the statute book of the realm. It need not be forgotten that Jeremiah saw the hollowness and futility of the reforms, but all prophets were not as Jeremiah. It may be that Deuteronomy and Pharisaism, as Davidson says,[4] came into the world on the same day but this was not obvious at the beginning even to Jeremiah. The one-sided emphasis of Nahum would seem to be due to the conditions obtaining after 621 B.C. and before the disillusionment brought about by Josiah's untimely end in 608 B.C.

[4] Hastings, James, *Dictionary of the Bible,* Vol. II, p. 577.

We may therefore assign Nahum's book to the months or year immediately preceding the fall of Nineveh and date them about 613 B.C.

THE MESSAGE OF NAHUM

It is not difficult to understand the varying estimates of Nahum's message. Few scholars would rank him high in the prophetic order, and many would regard him as a type of the narrow nationalist prophets whom Jeremiah roundly denounced. To such interpreters Nahum is no more than a jingoist, a little Englander or the hundred-per-cent American. In that respect he is akin to Jonah ben-Amittai, though his nationalism is cruder and more coarsely expressed.

But such criticisms lack both imagination and sympathy. We may pause to consider this interpretation. It is true that Nahum says nothing about Judah's sin, and that Jeremiah and Zephaniah say much thereon. It is further true that all the great prophets did lay emphasis on moral and spiritual conditions, and that they were filled with the spirit,

> "to declare to Jacob his transgression and to Israel his sin" (Mic. 3:8).

But it should not be forgotten that Nahum lived in a time of crisis when the ancient world was being shaken to its foundations. Great events were transpiring on which the fate of the world hung, and one great event occupied the prophet's mind to the exclusion of all else. That event was the siege and fall of Nineveh and the death-throes of the brutal Assyrian empire.

For the brutality of Assyria is amply attested both in literature and art. Assyria was essentially a nation of warriors whose chief delight was to plunder, ravish, and destroy. With his own hand the king would gouge out the eye of noble captives or flay them alive and pin them to the ground to perish. Impalement of prisoners was a common practice. The Assyrian sculptures show us how the king could sit down to dine with the bleeding heads of captives hung around to give zest to his appetite. Isaiah (10:14) tells us that the Assyrian plundered the wealth of nations as one would rob a bird's nest, and none dared to flutter or chirp. He tore peoples from their homes and carried them far away until all patriotism was extinguished.

The Assyrian was a combination of the Roman and the Red Indian. His lawbook has been discovered recently and the penalties imposed in these laws are the most brutal of any in antiquity. Gouging out of eyes, hacking off the hands or other members of the body, cutting off the breasts of women, slitting the nose, removal of ears, and pouring boiled tar over the head —these are the things the Assyrian did.

Nor should it be difficult for us in these days to understand what all this meant. When we think of the nations of Europe enslaved and massacred by an aggressive Herrenvolk who delight in *Schrecklichkeit*, of the tortures inflicted upon unoffending women and children, we can sense something of the prophet's jubilation in the fall of "the city of blood." When we recall Lidice, obliterated to the last man, and see "the glory that was Greece" reduced to starvation, when we hear of pogroms throughout oppressed Jewry and the diabolical destruction of beauteous Naples we begin to understand the pent-up feeling that finds expression in the book of Nahum. Here is concentrated all the pathos and passion and agony of a crucified world that awaits redemption and release. "Nahum's book," says G. A. Smith, "is one great At Last!" The day of release has dawned and Nahum gives expression to the universal feeling of relief.

That should prevent us from thinking too meanly of Nahum and his message. For plainly there is something valuable here. It may be that Nahum builded better than he knew, and expressed more than he intended. For it would appear here that we have a wide feeling of humanity, and that a universal sympathy has issued from a common suffering. Nations had become one in their common hatred and detestation of Nineveh. Nahum's voice is the voice of tortured and outraged humanity. In that sense it is Everyman's book, and it is very relevant to the situation in our war-ravaged world.

But Nahum is not merely penning a hymn of hate. His condemnation is grounded in moral considerations. Nahum has all the passion of Amos for righteousness as he denounces the ceaseless robbery of the bloody city.

The lion robbed for his young,
And strangled for his lionesses,
Filling his caves with robbery
And his den with rapine.

Behold, I am against thee,
Saith Jehovah Sabaoth;
Thy lair I will burn with fire
And thy cubs the sword shall devour.

Thy booty I will cut
From off the earth,
And the voice of thy messengers
Shall be heard no more. (2:12–14)

And again we hear the voice of the Tekoan in Nahum's denunciation of her murders and lies and robberies.

For the multitude of the harlot's harlotries,
Beauteous mistress of sorceries,
Who made peoples drunk with her harlotries
And tribes by her witchcraft,

Lo! I am against thee, saith Jehovah Sabaoth,
I will uncover thy skirts;
I will show nations thy nakedness,
And kingdoms thy shame. (3:4, 5)

Now the prophet sees "the ultimate decency of things" coming to pass and divine justice executed upon the mother of harlotries.

Ah! how do thy shepherds slumber,
  Thy nobles sleep!
Scattered are thy people on the mountains
  No more to assemble.

All they that hear the news of thee
  Clap their hands;
For on whom hath not passed
  Thy cruelty unceasing? (3:18, 19)

If we might assume genuine elements in chapter 1 we might find further reason to question the interpretation that classes Nahum with the Hananiahs (Jer. 28) and Zedekiahs (1 Kings 22:24) of the Old Testament. For there are present here elements that are characteristic of prophecy at its best. It is Jehovah who exercises vengeance on Nineveh (1:2–9), and he does so to bring salvation to Jerusalem (2:1–3). Throughout the little book Nineveh is the head and front of all offending against Jehovah. Nineveh is the seat and center of God-defying insolence (*Hybris*) and there evil has its throne (1:11). It is Jehovah who triumphs over the defiant oppressor (2:2, 14; 3:5).

I will bespatter thee with filth,
  And make thee a sight to see;
And all who behold thee
  Shall shrink away from thee.

Saying, Wasted is Nineveh:
  Who will bemoan her?
Where indeed could anyone
  Seek comforters for her? (3:6, 7)

Isaiah had seen in Assyria the instrument of the divine purpose towards Judah (Is. 10:5), but that was in 701 B.C. It may be questioned whether Isaiah would have spoken differently from Nahum in 613 B.C. A century of oppression and enslavement had altered the prophetic emphasis. The contrast between Nahum and Jeremiah need not be pressed to extremes; both were prophets in the service of a holy righteous God. Jeremiah looked within upon Judah, but Nahum looked without upon Nineveh, and both spoke the word of God to their time. God sends diverse words by diverse men and each, with his own accent and emphasis, speaks for God.

Jeremiah is the most poetical of all the prophets, and in his range of feeling he is almost modern. That is to be expected from a man of such tender nature; his heart was sympathetic toward all created things. It is in poetic ability that Nahum most closely resembles Jeremiah, for as a poet Nahum has very great merit. These odes of his stand together with the Song of Deborah or David's Lament for beauty and grandeur. Pfeiffer [5] would hardly allow the name of prophet to Nahum but he ranks him high as an outstanding poet. Certainly his poetry impresses us more than his prophetic doctrine. The reverse, however, is true of Jeremiah.

THE SIN OF NINEVEH

The weight of passion that charges the poetry of Nahum provokes reflection upon Nineveh and the Assyrian empire of which it was the center. The brutality of this empire has already been indicated and we may pass by that to survey the sheer wonder of its fall. For certain reflections are inevitable as we witness the fall of great empires, ancient or modern. There is something passing strange about the fall of Nineveh; when Xenophon and the immortal ten thousand passed that way its very site was forgotten and its memorial had vanished from the minds of men. Once there had been a great city there, but "Zeus made its inhabitants senseless and so it was taken." How are the mighty fallen and the men of war brought low!

[5] Pfeiffer, R. H., *Introduction to the Old Testament,* 1941, p. 595.

Where is the lion's lair
 and the den of young lions
Where the lion whelps dwelt
 with none to affray them?

All thy fortresses are fig trees
 With figs early ripe;
They fall, when they are shaken,
 Into the eater's mouth.

Lo! thy folk within thee turned womanish
 In face of thy foe;
The gates of thy land fly open,
 Fire has devoured thy bars. (2:11; 3:12, 13)

"Ichabod" (the glory is departed) seems to be inscribed on man's mightiest creations. How do such empires come to an end? Is there something radically unsound and impermanent in their structure?

As we look back over ancient history we see those empires rise and fall. They have their day and cease to be. We see those armies marching and counter-marching up and down the *Via Maris* (The Way of the Sea), now Egypt to Assyria and now Assyria to Egypt. Little Judah on its mountain height watches the thundering legions go by, and now and again she is sucked into the vortex of international politics. Judah never became an empire, but though empires rise and fall Jerusalem continues on its lonely mountain height, and to-day it is the Holy City to which all eyes turn. Bethlehem-Judah is sacred to all Christendom. What had Judah that Assyria and Babylon and Egypt had not? What is the secret of this people's permanence?

Perhaps it is easier to approach this matter thus, and learn the reason for Israel's permanence. No nation can persist except as its life is informed and inspired with a spiritual principle. For three things are required to constitute a nation, and these three are land, people, and an organising spiritual principle or ideal. Of these three the last is most essential. The existence of Jewry to this time would seem to indicate that a nation may survive even without a land of its own, if its history has an idealistic basis. No nation can continue to exist save as its life is grounded in a spiritual principle or ideal. This principle may be expressed formally in a constitution, as in the case of these United States, or it may remain unwritten, as in the case of Great Britain. The American democracy is not constituted by this rich continent nor by the motley assortment of peoples that go to make up its population; it is constituted by these *plus* the principle of "equality of opportunity and even-handed justice for all". If we asked a Briton concerning the constitution of his country he might speak of Magna Charta, but more likely he would tell of St. George and the Dragon or King Arthur and the Knights of the Round Table. These things are not written in any constitution in Britain, but they are expressions of spiritual ideals in the heart of the people. Written or unwritten, it is the presence of such ideals that enable a people to abide in strength. "Where there is no vision the people perish." Israel had ideals and visions; those empires had not. Those mighty empires were physical things, material entities based on force and brute power. They had nothing to satisfy but their hot greedy snatching appetites. Those empires were held together by material bonds, and when a stronger material force struck them they were broken and scattered like Nineveh when the sluices were opened.

Though thy traders be multiplied
  More than the stars of heaven;
Thy overseers as locust swarms
  And thy scribes as grasshoppers
That hive on the hedge
  In the cool of the day,
And when the sun shines forth, they flee
  No one knows whither. (3:16, 17)

The life of those empires was held together like the waters of a great dam, but when the walls of the dam were broken their life ebbed away (2:7, 8, 10). And so to-day men are digging in the dust to uncover the ruins of Nineveh and No-Ammon. A common fate awaits them all.

> Shalt thou be better than No-Ammon
> Situate on the Nile streams,
> Whose rampart was the sea,
> And waters her walls?
> Ethiopia was her strength,
> And Egyptians unending;
> Put and the Libyans
> Came to her aid.
> But she went into exile
> And came by captivity;
> Even her children were dashed
> On every street corner.
> For all her men of mark
> They cast the lot,
> And all her notables
> Were bound with chains.
> Thou, too, shalt be broken,
> And thou shalt grow faint:
> Yea, thou, too, shalt seek
> A refuge from the foe. (3:8–11)

Nineveh and Thebes of the hundred gates were broken because they were physical and material things. Israel endured and still endures because it was spiritual and its life filled with moral reality. Its life cohered like the fibrous matter around the roots of trees that are sustained and fed from unseen sources above and beneath. There was nothing permanent in those empires, for there was in them no righteousness, no truth, no compassion, in short, no moral reality. Israel's life was shot through with purpose that gave meaning to its history and significance to the life of the individual. And if we ask what was that purpose, both prophet and historian will tell us it was the purpose of God to bless Israel, that in her all the nations of the earth might be blessed. That was the spiritual principle which informed the national life and gave permanence to the nation.

Nineveh was both a physical and moral monstrosity. Its situation geographically was off the main trade routes and the commerce of the world had to be deviated and diverted from its natural paths to be brought to Nineveh. National selfishness here regarded the world as a great grab-bag and sought to exploit all lands and peoples for its own military and commercial aggrandisement. The world was not a sphere for service but a thing to be exploited; men were treated not as ends in themselves but as means to ends. Those ends were the satisfaction of the cruel whims and caprices of military colossi. But the end of this is sure; as God lives it will not endure.

> Woe to the city of blood,
>   Utterly false,
> Full of plunder,
>   Robbery unending! (3:1)

REFLECTIONS

"The history of the world," says Schiller, "is the judgment of the world."[6] Nahum stirs large and wide reflection. For there is nothing in these days more comforting than the reading of history, and nothing more solemnising. When we think of the march of empire, does it not appear as if through all the ages it had for its watchword "Westward Ho!" Away back in the distant past we see a lofty civilisation of China falling before the hordes of Mongols and Tartars. These in turn fall and empire moves westward through the Babylonians, Assyrians and Persians. They rise and they fall. Alexander the Great

[6] *"Die Weltgeschichte ist das Weltgericht."*

imposes his empire on the known world, but it sinks in ruin before the rising might of Rome. The Huns and the Goths make an end of the Roman Empire, and on its ruins comes the Holy Roman Empire, followed by the imperial expansion of Spain and the emergence of the Napoleonic Empire. Napoleon and his empire pass at Waterloo, and the British Empire expands to the ends of the earth. Has not history been always moving to the west? Can it be that even now the hegemony of the world is passing still westward and coming to these shores of America? Are we not being called to achieve a greater destiny that we ever dreamed? And as we look at all those empires that went down to the dust because they forgot God does it not behoove us to take heed to ourselves and so handle this great responsibility that the vision which inspired the founders of this Republic may abide undimmed, and that our service to humanity may suffer no diminishing? Men and nations are saved to serve, and they can persist only so long as an idealistic basis of history is present. As God lives Nineveh and all its successors must be destroyed.

If we would not see history complete the full cycle and return to where it began we shall read those vigorous odes again and pray,

> Judge of the nations, spare us yet,
> Lest we forget, lest we forget!

8

HABAKKUK: FATHER OF SPECULATION IN ISRAEL

THE name Habakkuk seems to be derived from the Assyrian and signifies a vegetable. In this respect it resembles Susanna (Lily), another Bible name from the natural world. Luther called him *Herzer* (the embracer) as if the name were derived from the Hebrew *habaq* (to embrace). The word should be more correctly spelled Habbakuk. Concerning his ancestry and place of abode we have no information of a reliable kind.

The word *Nabi'* is attached to his name in the superscription of his book in a rather unusual fashion. None of the other great prophets are so styled in the superscriptions of their books, though the same form occurs in the case of both Haggai and Zechariah. It seems probable that Habakkuk belonged to the professional guild of prophets who were attached to the temple, and this fact might account for the noble ode that closes his little book. For it is worthy of note that in the later period of the Chronicler (I Chron. 25:1) the word *Nabi'* was applied to the professional guilds of singers who were responsible for the service of praise in the second temple. In the earlier period those prophets associated with the temple were accustomed to give oracles, and striking examples of this may be found in the Psalter (Ps. 20:6–9; 85:8–13) and throughout the Old Testament (II Chron. 20:14 ff.). Nahum may have been a prophet of this type, and over against this group who were affiliated with the ecclesiastical institution stood those greater prophets such as Amos, Micah, Jeremiah, Isaiah, who looked askance on those professionals. But though they were bound to the institution they were not necessarily *false prophets.* It should be borne in mind that the Old Testament in its Hebrew form does not use the term *false prophet;* that term occurs in the Greek version, and it occurs by way of addition and interpretation. Hananiah and Jeremiah were both prophets and the people had no means of distinguishing them (Jer. 28). The method of the time servers and the devoted spirits were outwardly alike. Any man can wear a clerical collar but not all who wear a clerical collar speak God's truth; it was so then, and it is so still. But people cannot be fooled all the time, and the prophetic literature as we now have it is proof of that. There is no book of Hananiah or Zedekiah. We may thus think of Nahum and Habakkuk as belonging to the professional group, and while their message may not be on the lofty plane of an Amos or a Jeremiah nonetheless their message is permanently valid and has meaning for all time.

Where so little is known of the personality of the prophet legend has been busy. In the story of Bel and the Dragon (verse 33) Habakkuk is represented as the rescuer of Daniel, cast for a second time to the den of lions. In the Codex Chisianus of the Greek version the preface to that story reads "from the prophecy of Habakkuk the son of Jesus Joshua of the tribe of Levi." Other traditions assign him to the tribe of Simeon though the location of his home in this tradition appears to have been Beth-Sakariyeh, ten miles southwest of Jerusalem. This would set his habitation not far from that of Amos. His tomb has been shown in many places, and the only fact of which we can be certain is that he prophesied in the southern kingdom.

As to the date of Habakkuk we will not be wide of the mark if we set him about 600 B.C. The date will depend in some measure on our interpretation of the book, and the book has been dated all the way from the eighth century B.C. to the Maccabean period. But the majority opinion favors a date about 600 B.C., in the closing quarter of the seventh century.

Tradition has it that he died in 537 B.C., and this tradition is not inconsistent with the date suggested.

THE BOOK OF HABAKKUK

Though the book is small it has given rise to critical problems out of all proportion to its size. It is not necessary for us here to discuss all these problems but some of the main issues can be briefly indicated.

A main question here is whether the violence complained of in the opening verses (1:1–4) is due to internal or external causes. Are the righteous in these verses the same as the righteous mentioned in 1:13? The general assumption is that these are the same group in both cases, though the present writer holds they are not and will give reasons for that view later. Involved with this question is the other question whether the Chaldeans (1:5–11) are summoned to correct the domestic abuses of Judah, or whether they are summoned to correct an evil situation that has arisen by oppression from another nation (Assyria). Is the complaint in 1:12–17 against the ruthlessness of the Chaldeans or the oppression of Assyria, and against whom are the woes of 2:6–18 directed?

The discussion of these problems has led to readjustments of the order of the text and to various excisions. Some scholars would cut out the word *Chaldeans* (1:6) entirely—and this has certain support from the Greek version—while others, following Duhm, would substitute for Chaldeans the word *Kittim* (Cypriots, Greeks) and refer the whole work to the age of Alexander the Great. The date would then be about 333 B.C. There are many attractive elements in this solution but they are gained at the expense of too great violence done to the text. This solution must be set aside. Another solution of the difficulty inherent in the present position of 1:5–11 was first proposed by Budde, who suggested that this section should be read after 2:4. The Chaldeans, he holds, were called to correct an evil situation produced by Assyria, and the oracle in

1:5–11 is the answer to Habakkuk on his watchtower (2:1 ff.). How it came to occupy its present position is explained thus by Budde: when the Jews later had come to a full experience of the cruelty and oppression of the Chaldeans in the Exile they identified them with the original oppressor (Assyria) and removed the section to its present position. After their bitter experience they could not think of the Chaldeans as saviors. This is certainly ingenious and many scholars, including G. A. Smith, have followed Budde's lead and read the book in the order 1:1–4, 12–17; 2:1–4; 1:5–22; 2:5 ff. But this solution seems just too ingenious, and a further difficulty about it is that Assyria is not mentioned in the text, though Budde, by clever emendation, finds it in 1:11.

It may suffice to indicate the solution that has commended itself to such sound and cautious scholars as Davidson, Driver, and Kirkpatrick. There may be difficulties in their interpretation but they are less than those involved in other solutions. The righteous and the ungodly, on this interpretation, are to be referred in 1:1–4 to groups or parties within Judah, and the first complaint is concerned with domestic violence. In answer to the prophet's prayer the Chaldeans are promised as the rod of correction (1:5–11). But the Chaldeans proved cruel and oppressive, and their coming raised the problem on a wider scale. 1:12–17 are to be understood as *written some considerable time* after 1:5–11, and the book of Habakkuk, as Kirkpatrick[1] observes,

> "is the fruit of religious reflection and exhibits the communing and questioning of the prophet's soul with God."

That implies not a matter of days but of some years. In 1:5–11 the Chaldeans were a prospect of hope, but in 1:12–17 they constitute a moral problem vexing faith. Hope might be high with the fall of Nineveh in 612 B.C. but after Carchemish (605 B.C.) and Jehoiakim on the throne of Judah conditions became intolerable. Judah found she had but exchanged one oppressor for another. On this interpretation there is no diffi-

[1] Kirkpatrick, A. F., *The Doctrine of the Prophets,* 1912, p. 268.

culty in referring the righteous and ungodly in the opening verses (1:1–4) to parties within Judah, while in 1:12–17 the same terms refer to Judah and the Chaldeans. The remainder of the book presents no difficulty, and though many scholars deny chapter 3 to Habakkuk there is no cogent reason for doing so. The balance of probability in the case of the closing psalm points to its being from Habakkuk. Apart from certain insignificant additions the book may be regarded as authentic.

Sellin regards the work as a prophetic liturgy and in his third edition (1930), as opposed to earlier editions, he repudiates the view of Duhm. Both Sellin and Duhm, on different grounds and with different dates, hold chapter 3 to be integral to the book.

THE SIGNIFICANCE OF HABAKKUK

Habakkuk is significant mainly for his thought, but he is significant also for the indications he gives of the prophetic consciousness and the *prophetic technique*. Here we see something of the prophetic method and procedure. It is to be observed that the prophet undergoes a certain obvious physical and emotional stress (3:16). Both visions and auditions are part of his experience (2:2; 3:2). The mechanical side of prophecy is not as conspicuous in the case of the great prophets, though it is not absent there, and we are very conscious of it in the case of Zechariah. The prophets had to prepare themselves and put themselves in a receptive attitude to receive the divine word, and this preparation may often take outward visible form (2:1). This mechanical side of prophecy may not appeal to us but we should not overlook its presence in the prophets.

There is a limited view in this prophet which may seem to some readers unduly narrow. The wider vision of Isaiah or Jeremiah is not Habakkuk's and there is no effort to interpret world events in the light of a world purpose. Habakkuk impresses rather as "a homekeeping wit" who sees the noblest ideals in regular work and peaceful enjoyment of the rewards of labor and a commerce founded on good faith and righteousness, ideals that may sound to us commonplace and even bourgeois (2:6 ff.). But his strong moral sense is quickly roused at the sight of oppression and his faith in a mighty God of moral character is clear (1:13; 3:3). Nor is his compassion limited. In a sense his heart seems bigger than his head, and like Nahum his sympathy with a world enslaved lifts him above the nationalism so often associated with the professional prophets. Here, indeed, he reveals something of the spirit of Deutero-Isaiah and the book of Jonah, for he sees in his God the protector of all mankind and of beasts and trees.

For the violence done to Lebanon shall overwhelm thee,
  And the havoc of cattle affray thee;
Yea, the shedding of men's blood, and forced toil
  Laid on the land and city and folk therein. (2:17)

Luther's etymology may have been faulty when he translated Habakkuk by *Herzer* but his exegetical insight was sound. Habakkuk is the prophet of the big heart, and as Paul says,

> "Knowledge puffs up, love builds up." (1 Cor. 8:1; Moffatt version)

THE BEGINNING OF SPECULATION IN ISRAEL

Habakkuk is significant mainly in another aspect. For he is the father of speculation in Israel. With him religion goes prominently into the interrogative mood. "My God, why?" is Habakkuk's particular cry. Nor could this development be avoided in Hebrew thought. It was a development that led to Israel's noblest literature, and in one sense the book of Job is a footnote to the book of Habakkuk.

The question that exercises Habakkuk is one that could not arise elsewhere. It could arise only among a people who believed in an omnipotent righteous God whose righteous will was expressed through Nature and in the events of history.

Moreover, as the Hebrew had no outlook beyond the world of time and sense, save on rare occasions, it was obvious and inevitable that the familiar dogma of recompense should find a main place in Hebrew religious thought. To use the familiar words of Bacon, "Prosperity is the blessing of the Old Testament." A righteous God will reward the righteous and prosperity will accompany and follow piety. Abraham and Job are both blessed with herds and flocks innumerable. And the same God who rewards the righteous for his righteousness will not fail to punish the sinner who offends against his righteous will. Suffering thus becomes the infallible index of sin, and this main corollary to the main proposition Job's friends do not fail to state emphatically. All this, of course, might lead to a situation, as in the case of Job, where the character of a righteous man could be slain by a logical syllogism. But the time was not yet come when men could see things thus clearly, though the difficulty was becoming apparent to Habakkuk. The Hebrew could not think otherwise, for it was not possible to think of moral anomalies in a world ruled by a righteous God. Only where such belief in a righteous God is present could Habakkuk's problem arise, and men could answer the question only by denying the divine righteousness, as in Job, or by admitting and confessing sin, as in the fifty-first psalm. We need not concern ourselves here with the later developments which finally destroyed the dogma of divine recompense in its traditional form. Theology must do justice to all the facts of religious experience—and innocent suffering is one of the facts which the old dogma did not recognise—and the book of Job is part of the process of development, as is also the experience of the Suffering Servant (Is. 53). But we confine ourselves here to Habakkuk and his revelation of divine truth in reference to this perennial problem.

Seldom do we find an answer to all our hot and dusty questionings but our religious vitality is not to be measured by the answers we get but by the questions we ask. When we cease to become interrogative we cease to live and we become static men in a dynamic age. This is the real burden of Habakkuk.

> How long, O Jehovah, must I cry for help
> And thou hearest not?
> I cry out to thee 'Murder!'
> But thou savest not.
> Why makest thou me to see evil
> And to gaze upon trouble?
> Spoiling and violence are before me
> And strife and contention,
> Therefore "Torah" is benumbed
> And judgment wholly chilled,
> For the wicked circumvent the righteous
> And right is perverted. (1:1–4)

Conditions like these posed a problem to the prophet, for they raised questions as to the righteous character of God. Nor is the problem solved by the coming of the Chaldeans (1:5–11). These might be the instruments of the divine purpose to Jeremiah as the Assyrians were to Isaiah, but they only accentuated the prophet's problem, which is the character of God himself. For "that bitter and hasty nation" whose "horses are fleeter than panthers and swifter than evening wolves . . . that haste like eagles to the prey" appeared only as a new oppressor to Habakkuk. There was something passing strange in their demonic might, their military methods, and siege techniques.

> They laugh at every fortress,
> Throw up earthworks and capture it;
> Then away on! on! they storm like the wind,
> And make a god of their might. (1:10, 11)

Kings they scorn and princes they laugh at—but where is Israel's God? "How long, O Lord, how long?" These are the things that confronted Habakkuk and sent him to his watch-tower; that is the reason for his speculation.

For the problem is still with the prophet. The cure has

been worse than the disease. The Chaldeans who were to be the rod of correction have served by their insolence (*Hybris*) to sharpen the problem to a point of agony. But the prophet will not despair. If he knows there is a problem he also knows there is an answer to the problem. His faith in a righteous God abides.

Art not thou from everlasting,
 Jehovah, my holy God undying?
O Jehovah, didst thou appoint him for judgment,
 Didst thou, O Rock, call him to correct?
O thou whose pure eyes cannot look on evil
 And can'st not gaze on wickedness,
Why dost thou regard robbers and keep silence
 When the godless devours the good?
Thou makest men as fish of the sea,
 As worms that have no ruler!
He lifts them all with his trident,
 And sweeps them into his net;
He gathers up men with his drag-net,
 And rejoices exultingly therein.
And so he offers sacrifice to his net,
 And burns incense to his drag-net,
For by them is his portion fat
 And his meat plentiful.
Must he for ever be emptying his net
 And murder folk endlessly? (1:12–17)

Such is the prophet's question and he awaits an answer. He puts himself in the proper attitude to receive the revelation.

On my watchtower I will stand,
 Set myself on the outlook,
And strain to see what he will speak with me
 And how he will answer my plea.
And Jehovah made answer and said:
 Write the vision,

And engrave it upon tablets
  That he may run who reads it.
For the vision is still for the appointed time;
  It ripens to fruition and does not lie.
If it delay, wait patiently,
  For certainly it comes and will not fail.
Behold, swollen, not right, is his soul within him;
  But the just shall live by his fidelity. (2:1–4a)

This may not seem a great message and some scholars have even doubted whether it merited a revelation. To some it has seemed a case of "much cry, little wool." But it should be borne in mind that the divine revelation is "line upon line, precept upon precept, here a little, there a little," and God speaks one word at a time. The fact that Paul centered on this word of Habakkuk (Rom. 1:17) and that Luther exalted it to be the watchword of the Protestant Reformation might well suggest that there is more here than meets the eye, and that here we have a word of permanent significance. The words used by Habakkuk may not have in them all that Paul is taking out of them but they are weighty words holding a mighty seminal thought. *The prophet has discerned the fundamental truth that character alone abides.* The wild excesses of the tyrant have in them the seed of death; as G. A. Smith says, "Tyranny is suicide." That may be clear enough to us but Habakkuk was the first to think this matter through. All history emphasises its truth, and the course of the present-day conflict makes it clear again. It is being written to-day in letters of fire across the skies that all flesh may see it together. The fidelity, that is integrity, honesty, trustworthiness, of the righteous man has in it the principle of life, for he has in himself something of God's own nature. For when the Hebrew used the word *live* he used it in a full sense, meaning life under the eyes of, and by the blessing of, God.

Habakkuk here expresses his belief in the "ultimate decency of things." That may not become evident in one day but *in the long run* it does prevail. With Jehovah "a thousand years are but as yesterday" (Ps. 90:4). Nero may sit in his chariot as it clatters up the Capitol hill at Rome with a train of captives behind, and Paul may languish in a Roman jail, but a day does come when men are willing to call their children Paul and their dogs Nero. The history of the world is the judgment of the world, and as God lives and reigns in righteousness that day comes and will always come.

"Anger is one of the sinews of the soul," says Thomas Fuller; "he who lacks it hath a maimed mind." Habakkuk is not maimed in this respect, and the woes of 2:6 ff. convey the reaction of a mind that is inspired with the thought of righteousness.

Woe to him that amasses what is not his,
  Who loads himself with debts!
Shall not they suddenly rise that shall bite thee
  And they awake who shall oppress thee?

. . . .

  And thou shalt be their prey.
As thou didst spoil many peoples
  So shall the rest of the nations spoil thee.
Woe to him that getteth false gain
  And layeth up wrong for his house
To set his nest on the height,
  To escape from the hand of evil!
Thou hast devised shame for thy house
  And forfeited thy life through sin:
For the stone in the wall will shriek,
  And the beam from the rafter shall answer it.

. . . .

Woe to him who makes his neighbor drunk
  From the cup of his anger until he be drunken,
That he may look on the nakedness of men,
  And see them sated with shame!

Drink thyself from thy goblet,
 And reel about and show thy foreskin!
For the beaker from Jehovah's hand will come to thee,
 And filth shall come over thy fame. (2:6b–11, 15, 16)

Some of the allusions in these taunt-songs may escape us but they are clear in their vigorous assertion of the divine righteousness.

But while Habakkuk is the father of speculation in Israel he is no less the prophet of faith.

He fought his doubts and gather'd strength,
He would not make his judgment blind,
He faced the spectres of the mind
And laid them: thus he came at length

To find a stronger faith his own;
And Power was with him in the night,
Which makes the darkness and the light,
And dwells not in the light alone,

But in the darkness and the cloud,
As over Sinai's peaks of old,
While Israel made their gods of gold,
Altho' the trumpet blew so loud.[2]

The divine trumpet sounds in chapter 3 and in this final ode we have the triumphant expression of the prophet's faith. The vision of the divine glory sweeps away all lingering doubt and faith abides.

What though no flow'rs the fig-tree clothe,
 Though vines their fruit deny,
The labor of the olive fail,
 And fields no meat supply?

[2] Alfred Lord Tennyson, "In Memoriam", XCVI.

Though from the fold, with sad surprise,
My flock cut off I see;
Though famine pine in empty stalls,
Where herds were wont to be?

Yet in the Lord will I be glad,
And glory in His love;
In Him I'll joy, who will the God
Of my salvation prove.
He to my tardy feet shall lend
The swiftness of the roe:
Till, rais'd on high, I safely dwell
Beyond the reach of woe.

God is the treasure of my soul,
The source of lasting joy;
A joy which want shall not impair,
Nor death itself destroy.
(3:17, 18; Scots Paraphrase)

9

JEREMIAH: PROPHET OF PERSONAL RELIGION

JEREMIAH is the most intriguing of all the great prophets, and also the most revealing. Here the nature of the prophetic genius is seen in fuller light than anywhere else in the Old Testament, and the intimate revelations of Jeremiah put a key in our hands that opens many doors. The prophetic consciousness is not easily analysed, but Jeremiah helps us more than any other prophet in this matter. Here we have spiritual autobiography of a unique kind which might be called the *Confessions of Jeremiah.* In these Confessions Jeremiah is as revealing as Augustine. Other prophets impress us with their aloofness but the "Impassioned man of Anathoth" makes us feel his nearness and the warmth of his humanity. He is, indeed, the most human of all the prophets, and at the same time the most Christ-like. The story of his chequered career has gripped men through all the ages, for it is the story of divine strength perfected in human weakness. It is the tale of one who "learned obedience by the things he suffered" and shows us how he learned. "My Hosanna," says Dostoievsky, " has passed through great whirlwinds of doubt," and Jeremiah might well say the same, for the radiant certainties that sustained his life to the weary end were purchased with surprising expense of spirit. Like the Apostle Paul who fought with wild beasts and with wilder men, Jeremiah had to fight not only with his contemporaries but with himself continually, and not infrequently with God.

> Thou has deceived me, O Jehovah, and I let myself be deceived;
> Thou has been too mighty for me, and thou hast prevailed.
> I have become a laughing stock all day long,
> Everyone mocketh me . . .
> Then I said, I will think no more thereon,
> Nor speak any more in his name.
> But his word was in my heart like a burning fire,
> Shut up in my bones;
> I was weary with forbearing,
> And I could not abide it. (20:7–9)

"A man of contention and strife" was his appointed portion; loneliness and social ostracism were meted out to him, for he could not cry "peace, peace" where there was no peace. That is the cross of Jeremiah, for a nature so rich and tender craved the companionship of his fellows. But it was the will of God that he should be shut out from all the sweet and innocent joys of life (16:1).

> "The book of Jeremiah," says A. B. Davidson, "does not so much teach religious truth as present a religious personality. Prophecy had already taught its truths: its last effort was to reveal itself in a life."[1]

Here we can truly say "the word was made flesh," and a new dynamic personality appeared on the stage of Hebrew history. The man in this case is more than his book, though we may not forget Milton's word that

> "a good book is the precious lifeblood of a master-spirit, embalmed and treasured up on purpose to a life beyond life.[2]

Here is a book written with the lifeblood of a man, for in the case of Jeremiah, as in that of Hosea, the stream of revelation cut its channels deep into the experience of a suffering heart.

[1] Hastings, James, *Dictionary of the Bible,* Vol. II, p. 576.
[2] Milton, John, "Areopagitica."

> "In Jeremiah we have the purest and highest consummation of the prophecy of the Old Testament. After him One only could come who was greater than he." [3]

These are the words of one of the most sympathetic and understanding commentators on the prophet; they are large words but not too large.

THE PROPHET'S HERITAGE

Jeremiah was born at Anathoth, a little village six miles northeast of Jerusalem, and, as he claims to be "but a lad" when he was called in 626 B.C., we may assume that he was born about twenty years before that date. His family traced their origin right back to Moses, and few could boast a family tree so noble and lofty. They had, indeed, fallen on evil times, for they belonged to that priestly family that had been unfrocked and "rusticated" by Solomon on the occasion of Adonijah's rebellion (1 Kings 2:26–27). Their ancestor Abiathar had carried the ephod before Israel's greatest king, and had acted as his father-in-God (1 Sam. 30:7), had shared David's persecutions with unfaltering loyalty, and later acted as chief priest in the sanctuary at Jerusalem. But Abiathar supported the wrong side in the matter of the succession to the throne, and for that he was retired to his ancestral estates at Anathoth. Thus Jeremiah was heir to a rich material and spiritual heritage. He was steeped in the finest Hebrew piety and nourished on its sacred traditions. He owed much to heredity, but more to grace. The account of his call stirs us by its quiet intensity, its profound naturalness and its simplicity. The word of Jehovah came to me:

> Before I formed thee in the womb I knew thee,
> And before thou camest forth I set thee apart;
> A prophet to the nations I ordained thee.

[3] Cornill, C. H., *The Prophets of Israel,* pp. 98–99.

And I said,
Ah, Jehovah God!
Behold I cannot speak
For I am but a lad.
And Jehovah said to me:
Say not thou art but a lad;
For to whomsoever I send thee thou shalt go,
And whatsoever I command thee thou shalt speak.
Fear not before them, for I am with thee to help thee,
'Tis the oracle of Jehovah.
Then Jehovah stretched forth his hand, laid it on my mouth and said,
Lo, I put my words in thy mouth:
See, I put thee in charge this day
Over nations and over kingdoms
To pluck up and pull down, to build and plant.[4]

Jeremiah was a predestined man, a "man of destiny" if we may use that term which is more frequently applied to great military colossi and the masters of *Realpolitik*. The Hebrew is so used to the thought of divine sovereignty that he seems to leave practically no room for human freedom, and here again recurs one of those frequent tensions of theology. Doubtless the long line of ancestral piety had much to do with the shaping of his life and career. As Cornill remarks,

> "Such mighty and genuine piety could only have been sucked in with his mother's milk." [5]

Nature and nurture combined with the grace of God to produce this unique personality. "It is," says John Skinner,

> "the consummation of a genuine religious experience, rooted probably in the pieties of home and early life, of a growing self-knowledge and knowledge of God, which now ripens into the consciousness of a special mission." [6]

[4] Jer. 1:4-10.
[5] Cornill, C. H., *Das Buch Jeremia,* 1905, p. 21.
[6] Skinner, John, *Prophecy and Religion,* 1922, p. 27.

When Dr. A. J. Gossip was called to his first charge in the town of Forfar, Dr. Alexander Whyte, to whom he had been assistant, came to preach the induction sermon. In that sermon he informed the congregation that the act of induction that day was a matter that had been fixed in the counsels of God from all eternity, and that they, in the act of installing their new minister, were simply carrying out a decision that had been made by the Almighty before the world was founded. Such a thought might well solemnise the minds of minister and congregation, and whatever we may think of the doctrine of Predestination it will certainly save a man from making false starts, and once he is started it will keep him firm in the appointed path. Such a doctrine, of course, will not command ready assent to-day. We would seek a more natural interpretation and hold that in the prophetic experience we are presented with an elevated idea, suffused with intense emotion, entering into consciousness in dramatic form created by the imagination, and uttering itself in poetical language. It may be that these two lines of interpretation are not so far apart, but many will prefer Whyte's interpretation and Jeremiah's simple intense narrative. Be that as it may, the prophet knew himself on that day called of God with a summons he could not evade. The memory of that solemn hour was to abide as his inspiration through his long storm-troubled life.

> My heart was full: I made no vows, but vows
> Were then made for me; bond, unknown to me,
> Was given that I should be, else sinning greatly,
> A dedicated spirit.[7]

"There is no discharge in that war," and through those years of agony and tears, fightings without and conflicts within, forced to renounce the companionship of wife and children (16:1), the prophet goes bewildered on his way, and the divine strength is perfected in weakness. Thus he becomes *the father of true*

[7] Wordsworth, William, "Prelude."

prayer, wherein the needy soul at once expresses its own poverty and its impregnable confidence in God. Like a child turning to its father he is continually returning to God for illumination of his darkness and renewal of his strength. Much of the book consists of such dialogue between the prophet and God, in which the perplexed soul lays its difficulties before God and receives an answer and direction.

> Thou art in the right, O Jehovah,
> If I take issue with thee;
> Yet concerning matters of right
> I would speak with thee.
> Why is the way of the wicked smooth,
> And why are treacherous men at ease? (12:1)

To which the answer comes:

> Thou hast run with footmen and art weary,
> Then how wilt thou contend with horses?
> In a land of peace thou art ill at ease,
> Then how wilt thou do in Jordan's jungle?
> (12:5)

In this matter of constant vital communion, living and moving and having his being in God, he most closely resembles the Savior himself.

SPIRITUAL TENSIONS

In our prophet is found continually an opposition between conscience and feeling, between the voice of God and the impulse of the heart. Herein lies the essence of all high tragedy. This is something new in prophecy, and while its presence here may seem to reduce the prophetic stature of Jeremiah it elevates and heightens him as a human personality. "In him," says Volz, "the prophet and the man oppose each other: the man in him sets himself against the prophet." [8] Thus the tragic

[8] Volz, Paul, *Der Prophet Jeremia,* 1928, p. 24.

schism is set right within the soul of the prophet, and this again, is the cross of Jeremiah. Human affection constantly inhibits the divine commission. The other prophets of the Old Testament seem to stand at the side of God and hurl their words of doom down upon the people, but Jeremiah seems to stand between the people and God and gather to his own bosom all the shafts of the divine indignation.

For the hurt of the daughter of my people I am hurt,
I am black: astonishment hath taken hold of me. (8:21)

All the affection of his vast heart lies in the words "my people" and "my God"; all his thought revolves round these two poles, and all his passion is to unite them in indissoluble union.

> Let my eyes run down with tears,
> Let them not cease day or night
> For the Virgin daughter of my people is broken
> with a great breach,
> With a very grievous blow. (14:17)

Or more poignantly still:

> O that my head were waters,
> And my eyes a fountain of tears,
> That day and night I might weep
> For the slain of the daughter of my people. (9:1)

Such wealth of pathos and passion is not found again until we hear it in the words of the Savior lamenting over Jerusalem. There is something akin to the Savior's agony in Gethsemane in those quivering words that break from the prophet's lips.

> Broken is my heart within me,
> All my bones quiver:
> I am like a drunken man,
> Like one overcome with wine,
> Before Jehovah and his glorious majesty. (23:9)

Right into the presence of God with passionate remonstrance will he press his case, for here Jeremiah is akin to Job.

> Why is my pain perpetual, my wound incurable,
> Refusing to be healed
> Wilt thou be to me as a deceiver,
> And as waters that fail? (15:18)

Like a priest—and this comes from his ancestry—he bears his people on his heart to the throne of grace, while, like a prophet, he speaks the word God gives him to speak, though his heart is crushed with the burden of the word. "Man of sorrow and acquainted with grief" he was in measure above all other messengers of God. It is little wonder that many have sought to identify him with the Suffering Servant in Isaiah 53. Nor is it less wonderful that in the days of our Lord men saw in Jesus that which reminded them of Jeremiah (Matt. 16:14).

RELIGION IN THE INTERROGATIVE MOOD

In no prophet do we find religion so frequently passing into the interrogative mood. Jeremiah does not always receive answers to his hot dusty questions. Amos is seldom interrogative, for Amos is clear, forcible, and detached. Amos' head never had to struggle with his heart, and the shepherd of Tekoa was of stern fiber. Jeremiah is not detached but is involved with a deep involvement of love and sympathy in all the fortunes of his people. The nation's evil case becomes his heart's agony and the burden of his spirit. So much so that it shakes him like a physical storm.

> My bowels! my bowels! O my pain!
> O walls of my heart!
> My soul is in tumult within:
> I cannot keep quiet
> For I hear the trumpet's sound,
> The alarm of war. (4:19)

There is in such passages, and in the experiences which they reflect, a weight of passion and an expense of spirit which Amos could never fathom, though Hosea knew it well. But, while Hosea's pain seems finally turned to peace and he attains a place that is luminous with God, Jeremiah is a warring man until his life's end, and never seems to pass beyond the sense of bewilderment. His last days are hidden from us but it may well be that his last words, like those of the Savior, were, "My God, my God, why?"

HIS MINISTRY

So far we have been speaking of the man, and the man in this case is of unusual interest. But the man may not be separated from his message and ministry. He had been called

"To destroy and pull down, to build and plant" (1:10)

and his task was both destructive and constructive. On the words "Jehovah touched my lips," Matthew Henry comments in his quaint fashion, "Grace always specialises." Those lips that were to utter thoughts that breathe and words that burn were empowered with "an holy unction from on high." Grace triumphs, and this frail shrinking nature was transformed into a hero of the highest type. The fear of God expelled every other fear, and he became "an iron pillar and wall of brass" (1:18).

The growth and development of Jeremiah's thought may be measured by a consideration of his attitude to certain significant events that took place during the period of his ministry (626–588 B.C.). In the beginning his appearances are infrequent but after 608 B.C. Jeremiah attains a greater prominence. In 588 B.C. all the other prophets—perhaps we should say false prophets—are silent and seem to have vanished. Jeremiah is left as the sole spokesman for God. His recognition seems to have been somewhat belated, and we may understand the reason for this if we mark various stages in his activity and an increasing insight into the purpose of God and the nature of true religion.

JEREMIAH AND DEUTERONOMY

Jeremiah's entry into public life coincides with the discovery of the *Book of the Law* which was found in the temple in 621 B.C. Most scholars agree that this book, in the main, is identical with Deuteronomy. On its discovery Josiah immediately set about a radical reformation of religious life, and on the basis of this document all worship was centralised in Jerusalem. Jeremiah was not called in at this point, nor does he seem to have had any part in the steps taken at this time. A prophetess, Huldah, was the spiritual director of the movement. Now it would be difficult to overestimate the importance of this movement, for it meant a decided step forward in the realm of moral and religious practice. The abuses that found place at the rural shrines were all swept away by the stroke of the pen and the act of reformation. No longer would men "go up on every high hill and under every green tree" to commit fornication or continue heathen practices which the prophets had continually denounced. That was all swept away at one swoop; it was a root-and-branch policy, and doubtless much was gained by the measure, though something also was lost. For religion was no longer localised, and a shrine in Jerusalem could hardly arouse the interest that adheres to a local church. It is precisely as if the citizens of New Jersey could not worship save in Trenton or if the people in New York State had all to go to Albany for their religious services. Such an act would certainly make it possible to control the ritual and rid it of abuses. But it was bound to arouse opposition and cause a sore feeling in many quarters.

But, on the whole, Deuteronomy and the reformation based on it mark a step forward. It represented an effort to codify the prophetic spirit, to write into the statute book of the realm the ideals of Israel's great religious leaders. It is, of course, open to question whether a spirit can be codified, and whether in particular the prophetic spirit is not too elusive to be caught and fixed within the covers of a lawbook. Such an attempt must always be attended with danger and difficulty, and that very quickly became clear to the reformers themselves. Time alone could show the full significance of the movement. There is the danger that the living spirit of prophecy may be asphyxiated in the process, and that inspiration and spontaneity may give place to statute and ordinance. The vitality of the prophetic word may be replaced by the humdrum of the sage, or, worse still, by the arid legalism of the scribe. That which was once dynamic may become static and lifeless. Time made all this very clear. There is a sense in which the word of A. B. Davidson is profoundly true: "Deuteronomy and Pharisaism came into the world on the same day." [9] The religion of the book is on its way to supplant the religion of the spirit. The thing that began so well ends so ill. But we need not stay here to analyse Deuteronomy or concern ourselves further with that book. The question that concerns us here is, what did Jeremiah think of the reformation instituted by Josiah on the basis of that book?

It seems most reasonable here to think that the attitude of the prophet varied. Many scholars, however, hold that the prophet was opposed to the movement and that his attitude throughout was one of radical opposition. This seems to attribute a degree of insight to Jeremiah which is not in accord with what we read in the record. Skinner [10] makes the remark that sometimes a man has to become engaged to a woman before he discovers that it is inadvisable to be married to her. Something like this seems to have transpired in the mind of Jeremiah, and his attitude to Deuteronomy changed. At first he acted on the principle that half a loaf is better than no bread, and he welcomed the movement for what it meant in the way of removing glaring abuses. He may have gone on a preaching mission in connection with the reform (11:1–14), and such a mission on his part may well have aroused the fury of his kinsmen at Anathoth. But Jeremiah soon saw how

[9] Hastings, *op. cit.,* Vol. II, p. 577.
[10] *Op. cit.,* p. 106.

things were working out, and latent dangers became quite patent. He learned that no real improvement was taking place in the lives of the people, and that it is impossible to make people righteous by act of Congress. It was at this point his attitude seems to have changed to one of real opposition, and he was forced to think his way to a more satisfying solution. This solution is found later in his doctrine of the New Covenant. Such a reading of the situation seems most consistent with the record, although it should be said that the text presents difficulties and is open to various interpretations, as is obvious from the strongly divergent views of scholars.

Jeremiah came to see that men could not be made what God intended them to be by any external means. What was required was not reformation or reorganisation but total regeneration. Drastic surgery was required, more drastic than the reformers could apply, and, to use the prophet's expression, it was not the flesh but the heart that must be circumcised (4:4). Inward cleansing could not be effected by legal sanctions, and the best efforts of the reformers, because they were external and dealing with externals, could never reach the seat of the malady imbedded deep in the national soul. Heathen altars might be thrown down but the heathen heart still remained, and after Josiah's death in 608 B.C. that heathen heart re-asserted itself with increased vigor. The prophet had seen to the center of things, and here his power as a moral analyst is not less than that of his predecessor and mentor, Hosea. The further development of this thought is made clear by his attitude to the ecclesiastical institution as revealed in his speeches concerning the temple (chaps. 7 and 26).

JEREMIAH AND THE TEMPLE

Here we see the first approach from the negative side to his later positive doctrine of the New Covenant (31:31 ff.). The temple had become little more than a fetich to the Jews, and that which had been a vital act of faith in Isaiah's day had sunk to the level of a dead dogma—the inviolability of Zion. "That," says W. Robertson Smith,

> "has always been the law of the history of religion. What in one generation is a living truth becomes in a later generation a mere dead formula, part of the religion learned by rote, with which a living faith has to do battle upon new issues." [11]

That which in Isaiah's time had been a living experience of saving faith had turned to a dead shibboleth on the lips of men in the days of Jeremiah. Like the brazen serpent Nehushtan it had to be shattered and broken to bits.

> "Trust not in these misleading words, 'the temple of Jehovah, the temple of Jehovah, the temple of Jehovah is all this.' What? Steal, murder and commit adultery! and swear falsely and sacrifice to Baal! and then come and stand before Me in this house, and say, 'we are delivered':—in order to perpetrate all these abominations! Is it a robbers' den you take my house for? Verily as such do I also regard it, saith Jehovah. But go now to my sanctuary which was in Shiloh, where I placed my name at the first, and see what I did to it because of the wickedness of my people Israel. And now because you do all these deeds, I will do to this house in which you put your trust as I did to Shiloh; I will cast you out from my presence as I cast out your brethren, the whole seed of Ephraim." (7:8–15)

Words like these may not be spoken with impunity and the prophet narrowly escaped with his life. But the die was cast, and there could be no going back. Henceforth Jeremiah is "a man of strife and contention," and more than once his life was in jeopardy. His own familiar friends lifted up their heel against him (11:21 ff.), and kinsmen plotted his death. Cheap politicians masquerading as statesmen, and military "brass hats," clothed with a little brief authority, sought to impede and thwart him in his ministry (18:18 ff.; 20:1 ff.). "It is a

[11] Smith, *The Prophets of Israel,* p. 370.

law of spiritual history that the preachers of new religious systems have their hardest battles with the contemporary religious leaders."[12] Jeremiah is no exception and the son of the priest found his most bitter opposition in the ranks of the priests and temple prophets. Ritual to Jeremiah was nothing, but morality was everything, and election signified responsibility. The priests were there with all the influence of the institution behind them, and the Chauvinistic prophets were highly popular. Jeremiah stood alone—alone with God. Bonds and imprisonment were his portion, and strutting Pashurs (chap. 20) and blustering Hananiahs (chap. 28) seemed to have the best of things. Were it not for the kindness of a colored slave Jeremiah would surely have died at the bottom of a miry well (38:7 ff.). The swaggering ruthlessness of a Jehoiakim, who thought the penknife was mightier than the pen (chap. 36), and the shilly-shally policy of a Zedekiah, who had a wishbone where a backbone should have been, only served to show the strength and tenderness of Jeremiah's martyr life. At times it is more than he can bear, and his long patience is broken by fits of ferocity and wild recriminations towards men and God. Wild whirling words break from those sanctified lips, and in most unChrist-like fashion he invokes vengeance on his foes.

> Thou knowest, O Jehovah!
> Remember me, and visit me:
> Avenge me on my persecutors. (15:15)

> Pull them out like sheep for the shambles.
> And prepare them for the day of slaughter. (12:3)

Sometimes, as if in a perfect delirium of rage, the prophet lets himself go with complete abandon.

> Deliver up their children to famine,
> Give them over to the power of the sword:

[12] Volz, *op. cit.*, p. 31.

Let their wives become childless and widows,
And their men be slain by pestilence,
And their young men be slain by the sword in battle.
(18:21)

Duhm, one of the most incisive commentators, would regard this last passage as not from Jeremiah, but even so there is enough in the foregoing to leave us wondering. So like Christ, and so unlike!

"If thou take forth the precious from the vile
Thou shalt be as my mouth." (15:19)

Grace is to be won by selective action in the realm of speech. But the precious will appear from out the vile, and as the prophet feels the

"Desperate tides of the whole great world's anguish
Forced through the channels of a single heart"

he becomes the priestly intercessor at the throne of Grace. His cup of sorrow must surely have overflowed when Jehovah rejected all further intercession for the sinful people.

Then said Jehovah to Me: though Moses and Samuel stood before me yet my mind could not be toward this people; cast them out of my sight and let them go forth. (15:1)

It is precisely this laying bare of the prophetic heart that intrigues us and draws us to the prophet. He is so human, and yet few of the sons of men have enjoyed such intimate communion with the Father of all spirits. The secret of the Lord is with him: he is "far ben" [13] with God.

THE ESSENCE OF RELIGION

Out of this communion there came to Jeremiah finally an insight into the essence of religion. He is the first to root it

[13] Scotticé, meaning exceedingly intimate and friendly. The *ben* is the sphere of domestic family life, while the *but* is for formal austere occasions.

in the heart of man, and think of it in universal terms. He is the first to discover the individual and the real nature of piety. The ecclesiastical institution he will set aside or relegate to the background, for the pith and marrow of religion are not found there. The institution is external and impersonal, while religion consists essentially of a personal relation to the living God. Only as the springs of life are renewed can hope dawn for men. Grace must reign, for law has failed, and its failure is clearly seen. The religion of statute must give place to religion of the spirit, and the mechanical cult must give place to free and spontaneous worship. Jeremiah did not reach that thought in a day, but he did reach it finally, and all that goes before it leads up to this.

> "Lo, the time is coming, saith Jehovah, when I will make with the house of Israel (and with the house of Judah) a new covenant, not like the covenant which I made with their fathers when I took them by the hand to bring them out of the land of Egypt: seeing they have broken my covenant, and I have rejected them, saith Jehovah. But this is the covenant which I will make with the house of Israel after these days, saith Jehovah; I will put my law in their inward parts, and write it in their heart: and I will be to them a God, and they shall be my people. And they shall no more need to teach one another, every man his neighbor, to know Jehovah; but all shall know me from the least to the greatest, saith Jehovah: for I will pardon their guilt, and remember their sins no more." (31:31 ff.)

This is a great seminal thought. Here religion bursts the bounds of nationality and takes on a universal aspect. Religion is made independent of time and place, and a new era is opened in the spiritual history of men. Nothing like this emerges in history until we come to the New Testament, and mark at Antioch the narrow walls of Jewish exclusiveness falling before the potent spirit of early Christianity. Religion is here conceived as personal communion with a personal God. It is independent of time and place; God is equally accessible in Babylon or Jerusalem (chap. 29), for his dwelling-place is not a "house made with hands," but the humble and contrite heart.

THE LETTER TO THE EXILES

It may be well to pause here for a moment and consider how the prophet was led into such a profound insight. A multitude of causes may have operated here, but the immediate cause is clear. It lies in the history of the people. The prophet never loses contact with life. In 597 B.C. had occurred the first captivity under Jehoiachin, and the flower of Judah's chivalry was carried away to Babylon. In Babylon they had ample leisure to ponder the meaning of events, and the results of this reflection are obvious in the post-exilic literature and in the final editing of our Old Testament.

But the first reaction to events was not by way of reflection. The immediate reaction was one of despair and bewilderment. For Deuteronomy had made it impossible for a good Jew to live at peace in a foreign land, for the foreign land was unclean. The practice of the religious cult was impossible in the unclean land, and without the cult that had guided all their actions life could not be carried on. Men could not marry nor beget children nor plant gardens nor do anything that normal folk might want to do, for all these things implied and involved a cult action, and the cult could not be observed outside Jerusalem. And so the first thoughts of the exiles were thoughts of rebellion, and only drastic action on the part of the Babylon government kept that rebellion from flaring up and causing all the Jews to die in a pogrom. But Babylon had a short way with such troublesome people, and the leaders of the rebellion were "roasted in the fire" (29:22). The light and easy optimism that was found in Jerusalem, against which Jeremiah contended in the person of Hananiah (chap. 28), had perhaps communicated itself to the exiles in Babylon, and it is the business of the true prophet to open the eyes of these misguided people to the real facts of the situation, and, in doing so, to reveal the nature of true religion.

Thus we owe to a living situation the great letter to the exiles which is found in chapter 29. This is one of the most significant documents in the Old Testament, and it is most revealing in the study of Jeremiah's religious development. The letter may have been enlarged by later hands, but what may have been its original form is here given in the translation of John Skinner.

> Build houses and dwell therein:
> Plant orchards and eat their fruit:
> Take ye wives and beget children
> That ye may wax and not diminish.
> And seek the good of the land
> To which I have led you captive;
> And pray for it to Jehovah
> For with its welfare is yours bound up.
> For well I know the thoughts
> That I think concerning you—
> Thoughts of weal, and not of ill—
> To give you a future and a hope.
> When you pray to me I will hear;
> When you seek me you shall find:
> When you seek with all your heart,
> I shall be found of you, saith Jehovah.[14]

Here are thoughts that must have sounded revolutionary to those who first heard them. All those cult activities which they believed themselves incapable of performing in Babylon Jeremiah bids them practice. God, says the prophet, and this in opposition to Deuteronomy, is not limited to one land; the seeking heart may find him anywhere and at any time. The letter reveals Jeremiah as *the founder of Foreign Missions,* for the foreign land becomes the sphere of revelation, and there

[14] Skinner, *op. cit.,* p. 286.

God may be worshipped. Moreover Jeremiah pioneers here in another remarkable way, for he is *the first to enjoin prayer for one's enemies.* The reason annexed may seem to savor of prudential wisdom, "for with its welfare is yours bound up," but it would be unfair to emphasise the reason annexed without emphasising the injunction itself.

These are great and wonderful thoughts whose full content the prophet himself may not have fully grasped. Later generations entered into the heritage. And One was to come who would show clearly that

> "neither in this mount nor in Jerusalem shall ye worship . . . but the hour cometh when the true worshippers shall worship in spirit and in truth . . . God is spirit." (John 4:21 ff.)

The measure of such thoughts could hardly be taken in the prophet's time, but men sensed the truth inherent in his words. Others may have judged the matter on levels of expediency, but, whether on grounds of expediency or principle, the advice was taken with such thoroughness that when the day came for the exiles to return many, perhaps the majority, had no difficulty in staying on in Babylon. That may have been due less to the teaching of Jeremiah than to the fact that business opportunities were not lacking in Babylon, and bright young Daniels could find a fuller scope there than at Jerusalem. For even then men were not beyond mistaking the means of life for life itself. The records of a business house like that of Murashu & Sons, discovered by the archaeologist, show that the Jew was not slow to develop those capacities which have made him prominent in the world of business.

This large word of the prophet was to fructify and bear fruit in later days. The thought that God is not tied to particular shrines (chap. 29) nor bound to particular forms of social organisation (chap. 35) were new and revolutionary ideas. The great God whose sovereign purpose was revealed in the control of history and the lordship of Nature gives place to a deeper and even more spiritual conception, the thought of a God who finds his dwelling-place in the heart of the solitary believer. Here the prophet has both universalised religion and made it personal; he has discovered the individual. The writer of Psalm 73 and the author of Isaiah 53 are his true disciples and successors. They build on his foundation. And across the centuries Christ himself stretches his hand to grasp the thought of this herald of the dawn, when on that night in which he was betrayed, he said, "this is the new Covenant in my blood."

THE PROPHET AND POLITICS

It is natural to expect that the prophet would play in politics a less significant role than others. He was little interested in external forms and mainly concerned with the internalising of religion. Perhaps he was too high-strung and too emotional to take part in affairs of state. Isaiah dominates the politics of his time, and by his statesmanship of faith influences mightily the political life of Judah. But Isaiah is exceptional in this respect, and it may have been easy for Isaiah, who was on familiar terms with kings and princes. Jeremiah lived in a different time when kings were less inclined to listen to prophetic voices. But when Jeremiah is called upon to speak he will not keep back the word, though the word be a word of doom. Jeremiah will see the Chaldeans as part and parcel of the divine purpose that rules the world, and will say that to fight against them is to fight against God (chap. 38). That is not pleasing doctrine to chauvinists, but Jeremiah knew the real enemy of Judah was not the Chaldean but Judah's sin. Judgment must fall and independence be lost, if so be the soul of the nation is to be saved alive. The cleansing discipline of defeat and exile is imperative if religion is to become real and Israel achieve its God-appointed destiny. The cheap politicians of that day set their eyes on the main chance, but Jeremiah set his eyes on God and held to his vision. He stood alone amid the malice and jeers of lesser men—alone with God.

THE WORD WAS MADE FLESH

Strange it is how Jeremiah combined such intense love of his own land with the thought of the universality of religion. Ephraim will return (33:7 ff.), and the exiles will come again to Jerusalem, which will be the center of the divine kingdom. The national element persists here, as in Isaiah, and alongside stands this hope of a super-national religion. These two aspects create no tension in the mind of the prophet though it may be otherwise with us. For the Hebrew genius will connect the ideal with the real, and link its most distant hopes with the realities of the present life.

What a blow it must have been to Jeremiah when after the fall of the city and the ensuing confusion he was swept away to Egypt to die in a strange land. It seemed after the disaster of 586 B.C. as if state, nation, religion were all torn from their roots, but in reality the prophecy of personal religion, independent of time and place, was first fulfilled, unconsciously, in his own person. Jeremiah had not only spoken the big emancipating word; he proved it in his own experience, and demonstrated it in his own person. In characteristic Hebrew style the ideal was realised, and *the word became flesh.*

10

EZEKIEL: THE PROPHET AS PRIEST

EZEKIEL is the strangest figure in the goodly fellowship of the prophets but he is of profound significance for the history of Old Testament religion. To many he has seemed wholly unattractive, both by his own character and the nature of his teaching. Probably no book of the Old Testament is as little read as his, and it may well be the least popular, as it is the least known of the Old Testament. It abounds in allegories and apocalyptic imagery, and it operates with grotesque forms and bizzare ideas. Its complicated figures and its "wheels within wheels" (1:16) have offered ample scope for the ingenuity of Jewish and Christian commentators and for others less qualified who find delight in regarding the Bible as a book of conundrums or a volume of riddles. Whether we think of him as subject to catalepsy or as the victim of psychopathic experiences—and interpreters have thought thus of him—the fact remains that both he and his book seem to belong to another world than ours. It may be that our prejudices are based on lack of real knowledge, and that if we knew him and his book better we might judge otherwise. Doubtless he has been misjudged. Some would even go so far as to say that the result of his ministry was disastrous, and that he is to be charged with changing the vital prophetic insights into dead theological dogmas. He is held responsible for the destruction of spiritual freedom and is regarded as having laid the foundation for all the narrow pedantries of the Scribes and Pharisees. Our study of the prophet will reveal what degree of truth, if any, is in these charges, and this will become clear as we seek to ascertain his place in the growth and development of religious ideas and estimate his contribution to the general store of revelation.

THE BOOK OF EZEKIEL

Criticism of the book of Ezekiel has been particularly vigorous in recent times. Indeed the question of Ezekiel and his book forms one of the crucial points in Old Testament criticism at the present moment. Until the beginning of the present century there was almost unanimous agreement concerning the prophet and his book, and as recently as 1932 the late J. E. McFadyen—beloved teacher of the present writer—could write:

> "We have in Ezekiel the rare satisfaction of studying a carefully elaborated prophecy whose authenticity, until recently, has been practically undisputed . . . The order and precision of the priestly mind are reflected in the unusually systematic arrangement of the book.[1]

But those words would be strongly questioned to-day. The latest work on the subject, bearing the significant title *The Problem of Ezekiel*,[2] would recognize only about twenty-five per cent of the material in chapters 1–39 as genuine, while the remainder, including chapters 40–48, is attributed to other sources. Such a radical criticism is not likely to command wide assent. We need not enter here into the many other solutions of the problem suggested by various scholars; their works are recorded in the bibliography. Suffice it here to state that the writer feels himself in sympathy with such scholars as Eissfeldt,[3] Lods,[4] G. A. Cooke,[5] and Julius Bewer,[6] who regard

[1] McFadyen, John Edgar, *Introduction to the Old Testament*, 1932, p. 187.

[2] Irwin, W. A., *The Problem of Ezekiel*, Chicago 1943.

[3] Eissfeldt, Otto, *Einleitung in das Alte Testament*, 1934, pp. 411 ff.

[4] Lods, A., *The Prophets and the Rise of Judaism*, 1937, pp. 211 ff.

[5] Cooke, G. A., *The Book of Ezekiel*, 1937, 2 vols. (*International Critical Commentary*.)

[6] Bewer, Julius A., *Literature of the Old Testament*, New York 1944; revised edition, pp. 169 ff.

the whole work as, in the main, from Ezekiel, although they make varying allowance for editorial expansion and additional material, particularly in chapters 40–48. This seems the most reasonable position, for while some of the theories advanced resolve some difficulties they fail as a whole to compel conviction. Herntrich [7] is the most persuasive of such advocates, but the persuasive element in his theory does not concern the main authenticity of the book (except chapters 40–48) but rather the location of the prophet when he uttered the words contained in the book. The book is bound up with the man, and we must ask whether Ezekiel preached first at Jerusalem and later removed to Babylon.

According to the record as we now have it in the book of Ezekiel the writer was the son of Buzi and was a member of the Zadokite priesthood. He was carried away to Babylon in the first captivity under Jehoiachin in the year 597 B.C. There he seems to have lived with the exiles and mingled freely with them. It is not likely that he functioned here as a priest, for the practice of the cult in a foreign land was impossible. In the year 593 B.C. he received his inaugural vision which is described at considerable length in chaps. 1:1–3:14. Thereafter he began to address his words to the group of exiles living in the various settlements. These words are filled with hot indignation and are words of judgment and condemnation. But the words seem to be addressed to Jerusalem and its wicked inhabitants. That is precisely the point that Herntrich lays hold upon, and he maintains that those words (mainly chaps. 1–24) were delivered in Jerusalem, and that their present form is due to a later editor. This theory has commanded considerable assent and there is much to be said in its favor. But there is also much to be said in favor of the traditional view which locates Ezekiel in Babylonia from 597 B.C. A brief glance at the historical background [of the period]—and this background has in recent years been very considerably illuminated by archaelogical discovery—will make this clear.

[7] Herntrich, V., *Ezechielprobleme,* 1932.

THE HISTORICAL BACKGROUND

Josiah's reformation in 621 B.C. had written the book of Deuteronomy into the statute book of the realm, and physical sanctions had been invoked for the furtherance of spiritual religion. But in so doing the reformers had made it impossible for a Jew to be a good Jew or a religious Jew outside of Palestine. Jehovah could be worshiped only at Jerusalem. Babylon was an unclean land where the religious cult could not be operated. Thus those who were carried away were cut off from all religious consolation; they were outside the sphere where they could rightly worship their God. They could only despair, and out of that despair were born such passionate laments as that of Psalm 137.

By Babel's streams we sat and wept,
  when Zion we thought on.
In midst thereof we hang'd our harps
  the willow-trees upon.

For there a song requirèd they,
  who did us captive bring:
Our spoilers call'd for mirth, and said,
  a song of Zion sing.

O how the Lord's song shall we sing
  within a foreign land?
If thee, Jerusalem, I forget,
  skill part from my right hand.

My tongue to my mouth's roof let cleave
  if I do thee forget,
Jerusalem, and thee above
  my chief joy do not set.

(1–6: Scots metrical version)

Their desperate case led to desperate deeds motivated by false hopes kindled by false prophets. But Babylon was an orderly kingdom and it could maintain law and order among the rebellious exiles. The false prophets were summarily put to death, and their fearsome end (Jer. 29:22) was intended to be an example to any hotheads who might feel inclined to follow in their footsteps. Jeremiah in Jerusalem had to contend with the same light-hearted optimists (Jer. 28) and he took pains to deal also with the dangerous situation in Babylon (Jer. 29). It is therefore easy to understand why Ezekiel should stress the iniquity of Jerusalem and announce its certain downfall. The minds of the exiles had to be sternly disabused of all such false hopes and brought to a point where they were facing reality. After the fall of the city, when the divine judgment had become clear and the prophet's word vindicated, Ezekiel could, and did, sound another note. The fact that the message of doom ends with the fall of the city and that the prophecy of restoration follows would seem to indicate that Ezekiel was a real live preacher speaking to the varied needs of his time and the necessities of his hearers.

The exile contributed much to the historical development of Judaism, and at its beginning stands Ezekiel. To the exiles at first there was present only the thought of loss and desolation. But the exile was not all loss. Babylon was a great city and Nippur was of high antiquity, and here there was a cultural tradition longer than any Israel had ever known. The Jews could not live there without, in some measure, sharing that tradition. A syncretistic process could not be avoided here any more than it could be avoided in Canaan when Israel first entered the land. Even Ezekiel's prophecies borrow largely from Babylonian cosmology and mythology, and his imagery reflects the ideas of Judah's conquerors. The environment in which he lives obtrudes itself in all his writing and he could not escape it. All that may be only on the periphery of the Jewish faith—though with too many it seems to have reached the center—but its presence is not to be denied. Many of the exiles succumbed to this environment, and characters such as that of Daniel were rare enough to merit special mention.

But, on the other hand, the exile gave the Jews time to think and ample opportunity for reflection. Their living conditions at Tel Abib and the other settlements appear to have been fairly comfortable. They were settled in groups where the old familiar forms of social organisation were maintained. The policy of Babylon, in this respect, seems to have been humane and generous. The lessons of their national history could now be learned by the Jews, and true prophets were still present to interpret the past and give guidance for the future. Here monotheism came to its full development, and here the deeper problems of life were subjected to fuller examination in the light of revelation. Here, too, the Jewish church was organised and its faith defined. This is the constructive period of Hebrew history when the Scriptures were written down, the sacred traditions assembled, the history recorded in regular form, and steps taken to legislate for the future. Out of the exile returned a people of God, and the future of the world lay in their hands. This is, indeed, for Israel, "a period fruitful and creative beyond all others." [8] That it was so is largely due to the work of Ezekiel.

EZEKIEL AND THE EXILES

Ezekiel makes his first appearance among the exiles by the river Chebar in the fifth year of the captivity of Jehoiachin (July 593 B.C.). At that time "the heavens were opened and I saw visions of God" (1:1), and "the hand of Jehovah was upon him" (1:3). From that date until April 571 B.C (29;17 ff.) we have dated oracles from the prophet.

The appearance of the prophet is significant not only to the exiles but to himself. For it showed clearly that the word of God could be revealed in Babylon as well as in Jerusalem. But the message which Ezekiel proceeds to deliver must have sounded strange and harsh to his hearers. It is a message in

[8] Causse, Antonin, *Les Prophètes d'Israël,* 1913, p. 198.

the manner and tone of Amos, and it is delivered in peremptory tones.

> "Whether they will hear or whether they will forbear (for they are a rebellious house) yet shall they know that there hath been a prophet among them." (2:5)

Signs and symbolic actions abound in Ezekiel to a greater extent than in any other prophet, and a great many of his oracles seem to have been mimed prophecies, a kind of "dumb show" appealing to the eye. Thus he will sit for seven days, then rise to make a sketch upon a tile representing Jerusalem besieged and surrounded, with an iron plate set between himself and his drawing; all this was fearfully eloquent though no words were spoken (4:1 ff.). Again he will cut his hair with a sharp sword and scatter a part to the wind, burn a part, and smite a part with the sword, and reserve a small remainder—all this to illustrate the various fates awaiting the people of Judah (5:1 ff.). Again they see him digging through the wall of his house and carrying out his goods and chattels to symbolise the coming exile (12:1 ff.). His book abounds in such episodes and they are difficult for us to understand. But the prophet knew how to come in by the eye-gate as well as by the ear-gate. The purport of all these prophecies, mimed or spoken, is that Jerusalem must fall and its wicked inhabitants be destroyed. In that "holy city" unholy practices increased as the political situation worsened, and the state moved on uncomprehending to its doom. Jeremiah within the city and Ezekiel by the Grand Canal are one in the proclamation of judgment. The whole burden of chapters 1–24 is that Jerusalem must fall.

> "I sought for a man among them that should build up the wall, and stand in the gap before me for the land, that I should not destroy it; but I found none.
>
> Therefore have I poured out mine indignation upon them: I have consumed them with the fire of my wrath: their own way have I brought upon their heads, saith the Lord Jehovah." (22:30, 31)

JEHOVAH AND HIS PEOPLE

Ezekiel has a somewhat unique viewpoint in regard to the relations of Jehovah and his people. He differs from the other prophets who viewed the wilderness period as the halcyon days of Israel (Jer. 2:1 ff.). In his somewhat brutal allegory of the two sisters Ohola and Oholiba (chap. 23) he pictures the nation as given to idolatry and fornication from its earliest beginnings. The prophet here impresses us with his strangely detached manner, and again we are reminded of the brusque shepherd of Tekoa. This is the more wonderful in that Ezekiel was himself a member of the nation he condemned while Amos was an outsider. Ezekiel is "an hard man," and he knows nothing of the passion of Hosea or Jeremiah. It is difficult to escape the impression that Ezekiel is more concerned with sin than with the sinner. No tears will be shed when his wife, "the delight of his eyes," is reft away from him by death (24:15 ff.), nor will he weep for the fall of Jerusalem. The divine righteousness has been vindicated, Jerusalem has fallen, and the exiles can only lament.

> Our bones are dried up,
> Our hope is lost:
> We are clean cut off. (37:11)

RIGHTEOUSNESS AND RETRIBUTION

All this may be sound doctrine but it was not easy for the exiles to accept. For it ran counter to all their inherited belief. They had inherited a theology and a way of regarding things that conflicted with what was now happening. They felt they had a just grievance against life and against the God whom they believed to be in control of life. Most of those exiles had lived through the reformation of Josiah and had seen that thoroughgoing attempt to purify the national life and make Israel a veritable people of God. That such strenuous efforts to obey the divine law should be rewarded with such a measure of suffering as the captivity entailed seemed grossly unfair and inequitable. Piety should be rewarded with prosperity, and, conversely, sin should be followed by suffering: it should be so in a world ruled by a righteous God. So the Hebrew thought. This was his problem, and the problem recurs all through the Old Testament. Here, as in the book of Job, the divine righteousness was being called in question; the character of Israel's God was at stake. They complained against God and said bluntly,

"The way of the Lord is not equitable." (18:25)

The problem could not be evaded, for it sprang from the vital experience of the suffering nation.

Ezekiel did not evade the problem. Like Amos and Isaiah, Ezekiel regards Jehovah as in control of world history. He is just and righteous altogether. Side by side with this thought narrow nationalistic elements obtrude themselves, and the prophet never reaches the full compass of his great thought. Israel is the people of God and Jerusalem is his seat, but all nations are under his control, from farthest north to extreme south (25:1–32:32). Egypt and Tyre he delivers to Nebuchadrezzar, and the whole earth shall know that Jehovah is Lord.

Those lofty prophetic insights that seem to us almost commonplace were not shared by the people. Minds that could not compass such a philosophy of history were overwhelmed by their present distress and could only express their harassing doubts. Ezekiel is faced with a people who feel that God has not dealt fairly with them. They feel that they are suffering for sins not their own, and because they were plain people unable to frame a profound philosophy they express their grievance in the words of a popular proverb:

"The fathers have eaten sour grapes
And the children's teeth are set on edge" (18:2).

This sets forth their problem and their haunting doubt of the divine justice. Ezekiel will not question the divine justice and so he is forced to an interpretation of the age-long problem.

Ezckiel's treatment here runs counter to the accepted ideas of his time. For both Deuteronomy and Jeremiah held the inherited and current ideas of the solidarity of the nation. When Jeremiah heard people use the proverb just cited he could only say that in the final restoration it would no longer be true, but in saying this he admitted that at the time it was spoken there was reason for the complaint (Jer. 31:29, 30). Deuteronomy 24:16 expressly states that

> "The fathers shall not be put to death for the children, neither shall the children be put to death for the fathers: every man should be put to death for his own sin."

The historian in II Kings 14:44 ff. is careful to point out that on this principle Amaziah dealt with the murderers of his father and did not put their children to death. From these instances it may be inferred that there was a growing feeling against the idea that the innocent should suffer with, and for, the guilty.

Ezekiel's treatment of this question may seem unsatisfactory, and it is open to objection on various grounds. It is wholly atomistic and savors almost of casuistry. It is an attempt to extend to the individual the *principle of absolutely just retribution,* precisely as the prophets had applied that principle to the nation.

> "What mean ye that ye use this proverb concerning the land of Israel, saying, the fathers have eaten sour grapes and the children's teeth are set on edge? . . .
> Behold all souls are mine: as the soul of the father, so also the soul of the son is mine: the soul that sinneth it shall die.
> "Yet ye say, wherefore doth not the son bear the iniquity of the father? When the son hath done that which is lawful and right and hath kept my statutes and hath done them, he shall surely live. The soul that sinneth it shall die: the son shall not bear the iniquity of the father, neither shall the father bear the iniquity of the son; the righteousness of the righteous shall be upon him, and

the wickedness of the wicked shall be upon him. But if the wicked turn from all his sins that he hath committed, and keep all my statutes, and do that which is lawful and right, he shall surely live and shall not die."

(18:2, 4, 19–21)

Here a new emphasis is laid upon the individual, but that emphasis is stated in extreme form. For Ezekiel fails to reckon with the indubitable influence of environment and heredity and the social spread of the individual action. Ezekiel seems to tear the individual apart from the social organism and hardly leaves room for the development of what we know as character. But innocent suffering is a fact woven into the fabric of life itself, and it cannot be denied. Nor can the individual be isolated from the group: none of us liveth to himself. There is a rigidity about Ezekiel's doctrine of individualism which removes it from the sphere of life as we know it. Ezekiel himself felt the difficulty of his theory, and the survival of many evil-doers in the fall of Jerusalem left him with a problem on his hands. It is here we feel the casuistic element in the prophet, for he explains the survival by saying that they were allowed to survive that from their wickedness the exiles might understand how justified Jehovah was in overthrowing the city (14:21–23)!

The theory of the individual soul and its God should logically have led Ezekiel straight to universalism, but it did not. It led straight to Pharisaism and the righteousness of works which finds its strongest condemnation in the New Testament. For Ezekiel could not shake off the elements of nationalism, and his thought finally limited itself to the Jewish soul and its Jewish God.

Nevertheless Ezekiel himself is more than any of his theories, and certainly more than the developments which followed from them. This thought of the individual became regnant in later Judaism, for it contained valuable elements. It lent a particular urgency to the prophetic message, and it bestowed a deep significance upon individual life and conduct.

Life for the individual became real and earnest, for it presented him with the opportunity of working out his own salvation or condemnation. It assured him, too, of the help of a God who did not desire the death of any but that all should turn to him and live (18:23). Further, it lent a profound significance to the prophetic office, for the prophet was set as a watchman to warn and exhort to repentance: his was a pastoral office in which he dare not fail, else innocent blood would lie upon his soul. The prophet was held responsible for every evil-doer who died in his evil-doing without due warning from the prophet (3:16–21; 33:1–9). This is a new and solemn conception of the prophetic office; here prophet, priest and pastor are made one.

EZEKIEL'S THOUGHT OF RESTORATION

If the prophet could not speak another word than judgment there would have been no further development of Jewish religion. History and the event had vindicated the prophet, and now the time had come for another word. For under the impact of hostile circumstances men may lose heart and become desperate or wholly debilitated. Hitherto Ezekiel had been mastered by the thought of judgment (chaps. 1–24), but after the fall of the city he is mastered by the thought of restoration. Like Deutero-Isaiah the prophet recognises that men require to be comforted, and that word 'comforted' is to be interpreted in the sense of its Latin original which means "made strong, fortified." This is perhaps the most difficult type of preaching the preacher is called upon to do, and it is too often neglected with the result that men lose heart and become spiritually depressed.

Here Ezekiel displays some of his richest imagery. No more eloquent expression of Israel's hope could be found than that in chapter 37, the vision of the Valley of Dead Bones.

"And he said to me, Son of man, can these bones live? and I answered, O Jehovah, thou knowest. Again he said to me, Prophesy over these bones and say unto them, O ye dry bones, hear the word of Jehovah. Thus saith the Lord Jehovah unto these bones: Behold I will cause breath to enter into you, and ye shall live. And I will bring up flesh upon you and cover you with skin, and put breath in you, and ye shall live; and ye shall know that I am Jehovah." (37:3–6)

Or like Hosea Ezekiel will vary metaphor and simile and speak of the good shepherd.

"As a shepherd seeketh out his flock in the day that he is among his sheep that are scattered abroad, so will I seek out my sheep; and I will deliver them out of all places whither they have been scattered in the cloudy and dark day. And I will bring them out from the peoples, and gather them from the countries, and will bring them into their own land; and I will feed them upon the mountains of Israel, by the watercourses and in all the inhabited places of the country. . . . I myself will be the shepherds of my sheep and I will cause them to lie down, saith the Lord Jehovah. I will seek that which was lost, and will bring back that which was driven away, and will bind up that which was broken, and will strengthen that which was sick." (34:12, 13, 15, 16)

Nor is the hope limited to the members of the southern kingdom: the banished brethren of the north also shall be brought back (chap. 36). Mythological features enter here, and we are reminded of such thoughts as appear in Isaiah 11:1 ff., and here, too, we hear echoes of Jeremiah.

A new heart also will I give you,
And a new spirit will I put within you:
And I will take away the stony heart
out of your flesh,
And I will give you a heart of flesh. (36:26)

All this is in line with the thought of earlier prophets but Ezekiel introduces novel ideas of a theological nature and gives us a more dogmatic idea of God. Like Isaiah he feels the sublimity of God, and his recurring phrase, "Son of man," which is equivalent to "earth-born creature," emphasises the great gulf between the creature and the Creator. Like Isaiah, too, he is overwhelmed by the vision of the divine glory which is the outward revelation of the inward holiness of God. The simple restrained manner of Isaiah gives place here to strange and bizarre details (chaps. 1, 9) derived from his Babylonian environment. In Isaiah we have a spiritual emphasis but in Ezekiel we are more impressed with the physical. These strange creatures that crowd the vision of Ezekiel are the precursors of the later Jewish angels, and here we have the initial stages of what later became a full-blown angelology. The old thought of the *near God* who walks and talks with men in the early traditions of Genesis is passing away and giving place to the new thought of the *far God* who can communicate with his worshipers only through intermediaries. The theologian has superseded the storyteller.

THE REDEEMED COMMUNITY

Ezekiel's thought of individualism must not be set in total isolation from his thought of the redeemed community. The first twenty-four chapters are mainly concerned with judgment and what follows thereafter including the oracles against the various nations, concerns the future salvation. It may be that Ezekiel himself is divided in his own personality and that this division is reflected in his book. In the earlier part of his career the prophetic impulse prevails over the priestly, but in the later stages of his career it would seem that the priestly element overrides the prophetic impulse: this is particularly so in the last nine chapters, which are frequently denied to Ezekiel by critics. But the strange variety of the book may be due to the strangely composite personality of Ezekiel as prophet and priest.

In the thought of salvation Ezekiel differs from the earlier prophets, for the motivating force in Ezekiel is not the divine love and mercy but *the thought of the divine honor.* This may seem a less lofty conception than that held by his predecessors but it accords logically with Ezekiel's thought of the divine sublimity and exaltedness. There is nothing in Israel itself worthy of redemption, so feeble, creaturely, and frail it is. The motive, therefore, is found in Jehovah himself. This thought may seem to suggest something egotistical and selfish when compared to the thought of love divine. But it is consistent with Ezekiel's lofty thought of God. Jehovah will restore his people to vindicate his own honor, that his great name be no more profaned and that the nations may not continue to taunt his broken and scattered people, saying, "Where is thy God?"

Such a thought is clearly related to the doctrine of monotheism and issues directly from the thought of the divine majesty symbolised in the inaugural vision. It may be expressed in gross mythological form and accompanied with all the fantastic imagery of Apocalypse, but the thought itself is not gross. Most scholars reject the gruesome description of Gog of Magog in chapters 38, 39, and while nationalistic elements cross and mar the wider thought of universalism it is difficult to imagine the prophet reduced to such a form of particularism as would leave him finally with the thought of Israel alone in a lonely world with a lonely Jewish God. We find it difficult to think that those two chapters with their unlovely features came from the hand of the prophet who wrote:

"I have no pleasure in the death of the wicked but that the wicked man turn from his way and live." (33:11)

Chapters 40–48 give in detail Ezekiel's description of the new Jerusalem. In accord with the Hebrew genius the ideal is made real, and here we have the priestly blue-print of Utopia. It would seem, if we assume Ezekiel's authorship, that here most prominently the original priestly heritage of Ezekiel is finding expression. Prophecy is passing over into ecclesiasticism. The prophet who earlier took such lofty imaginative flights and soared on wings of strange fantasy here comes down to earth and becomes very practical and prosaic. Precise measurements and delimitations take the place of dreams, visions, and grotesque fancies. That is Ezekiel, and that must be borne in mind as we judge him. For that reason we may well believe that there is an authentic nucleus of genuine Ezekelian matter in these chapters.

Notable here is the fact that the Messianic king gives place to the new figure of a prince (*nasi'*) who is completely subordinated to the hierarchy. This form of the "two swords," the ecclesiastical and political, recurs in Zechariah where the arrangement proves less fortunate for the political representative. Ezekiel is presenting us with a veritable priests' Paradise, and it might be legitimately inferred that the prophet had lost faith in kings as a result of the events culminating in the disaster of 586 B.C. The ideal of Ezekiel is a religious community fenced and guarded by physical and spiritual sanctions.

Inasmuch as we may not draw too much from these chapters, in view of uncertainty of authorship, we need not follow all the details of the elaborate scheme. The principle of theocracy introduced by Deuteronomy is carried to new heights, and the religion of the book is firmly established. Judaism is emerging; ritualism and sacerdotalism are in the ascendant. The hierarchy has ousted the monarchy, and the people who were once a nation have now become a church. A holy God, a holy people, a holy land—these are the pillars on which the whole structure rests. No thought of missionary expansion is here but only a hard rigid exclusivism.

> "Thus saith the Lord Jehovah, no foreigner, uncircumcised in heart and uncircumcised in flesh, shall enter into my sanctuary, of any foreigners that are among the children of Israel." (44:9)

A wall of partition had been erected which later was strengthened and consolidated by Ezra and Nehemiah (Ezra 10:10 ff.; Nehemiah 9:2 ff.), and it was not thrown down until Paul went to Antioch and liberated the full Christian Gospel (Acts 15).

ESTIMATE OF EZEKIEL

It was suggested at the outset that the ministry of Ezekiel was of doubtful value and that he is to be held responsible for much religious innovation that later became subject to condemnation.

There can be no mistaking the zeal of Ezekiel. Like Elijah he is very zealous for the Lord Jehovah. "Back of all the crude, prosaic, uncouth actions that frequently offend our aesthetic feeling we feel the glow of a holy consuming fire." [9] Amid all the grotesque imagery this zeal for Jehovah shines forth. In the period in which he was called to minister no quality was more required, for he was called to reanimate a community who had lost hope and become dispirited. In this matter he is akin to the early Nabis who inspired Israel in the fight against the Philistines. His zeal infected the people to whom he spoke and kindled new hope. That, in itself, is no mean service.

This zeal for Jehovah is mainly responsible for the harsh note in his message as it is responsible also for his one-sided emphasis on the divine honor. Luther, Calvin, and John Knox did not speak soft words, and were frequently as brusque as Amos himself. There are times when the spirit of man must be stabbed awake and Ezekiel and the Reformers lived in such times. The time had not come yet for the gentler tones of Deutero-Isaiah. Men had first to be made aware of the real nature of sin and brought into contact with a reality that transcended their current thought. This also Ezekiel did for his people, and this also is no mean service.

It is easy to see how he failed in his thought of individualism. The thought of the individual and God should have led straight to the thought of universalism but Ezekiel could not

[9] Sellin, Ernst, *Der altestamentliche Prophetismus*, 1912, p. 79.

disengage this thought from the thought of Israel as the people of God. And thus he presents us with the thought of a universal God without a universal religion. Israel after the flesh did not give way to an Israel after the spirit, but Ezekiel here with his fractional insight was preparing the path which the apostle Paul was to tread. The thought, too, of a God of love who does not desire the death of any, but that all should turn to him for life was a seminal thought that ripened in the Gospel. And the thought of the prophet as one who watches for men's souls added the conception of pastor to that of preacher.

His emphasis on physical holiness, separation in space and time, may appear a throw-back to ideas of a much earlier time. It led to an emphasis upon cult and ritual, and involved the danger that the ethical may be thrust to the background. That this was a real danger is obvious from the history of Judaism, and we see it taking shape in succeeding centuries.

Every movement that is really vital has elements of danger and possibilities of misdirection. The Roman Catholic Church and the Protestant Church, in all its varieties and schisms, alike stem from the Apostolic Church, but one need not charge the Apostles with responsibility for the crudities of the Doukhobors or the ecstatic on-goings of the Holy Rollers. Nor may we attribute Scribism and Pharisaism to Ezekiel, though the possibility of such developments was present. Other developments were also possible. Ezekiel was attempting to realise the prophetic ideals, and sought to bring them into the region of daily life. The ritual may be the expression of the ethical, and for most people the ethereal atmosphere of pure spirituality is simply not possible. Ezekiel is practical though his practicalness led to grave abuses. But the abuses are not due to Ezekiel but to the hardness of men's hearts.

Moreover, it had to be so. For if Judaism was to survive and preserve its precious heritage it could only be in this way. The hard shell of Judaism had to form around the kernel of divine truth that it might be safeguarded and kept against "the fullness of the times." The law was our tutor to lead us to Christ. The "father of Judaism" is a term frequently applied to Ezekiel but it need not be taken as a term of abuse. For Judaism paved the way for the Gospel and prepared "a highway for our God."

11

OBADIAH: A HYMN OF HATE

CONCERNING Obadiah personally we know nothing at all. He is introduced in the most abrupt fashion with the simple title, "Vision of Obadiah," but as to where or when he received his vision we are not informed. Nor are we told how he came to be a prophet. The name Obadiah means servant of Jah (Jehovah), and the name occurs frequently in the Old Testament. Where so much room is left for conjecture we need not be surprised to learn that he has been identified with several characters who bore that name. The most frequent identification is with Obadiah, the good house-steward who in the days of Ahab cared for 100 prophets of Jehovah and "hid them by 50 in a cave and fed them with bread and water" (1 Kings 18:3 ff.). But there is no ground for such identification. We may well believe that this spokesman for God was too much concerned with his prophetic task to think of his own personal identity or his later literary fame.

The heading that stands in verse 1 is not likely to have proceeded from the prophet's hand but from a later editor.

We may thus class Obadiah with the Great Unknown who gave us the second part of Isaiah's book, and with those other unknowns whose names are "written in Jehovah's book of remembrance" (Mal. 3:16). Of Obadiah personally we can say no more.

THE BOOK OF OBADIAH

This book is the smallest in the Hebrew Bible, and consists of only twenty-one verses. But not all these verses are from

Obadiah. Around this little book has raged a discussion out of all proportion to its size, and the controversy cannot be regarded as settled. The little book has been subjected to searching analysis and dissected into several separate oracles. T. H. Robinson would divide it into seven separate oracles dating from before the sixth century B.C. to the middle of the fourth century B.C. But the available material here seems too scant to afford ground for such treatment, though its very scantiness seems to allow larger scope for critical ingenuity. We need not go into detail here save to say that in the critical analysis we follow Eissfeldt, who divides the book into two main sections, 1–14, 15b and 15a, 16–21. The first part may be assigned to Obadiah, but the second part, which falls into two sections, 16–18 in poetical, 19–21 in prose form, would appear to be a later addition; 16–18 might possibly be a later oracle of Obadiah, but 19–21 is certainly from a later period.

In this connection it should be constantly borne in mind that there was no such thing as literary copyright in ancient times. These writings were written down by hand and copied by very human copyists, who construed their task with what we would regard as a surprising degree of freedom. For those copyists did not hesitate to make remarks, and such remarks might be set on the margin or any place where space could be found. Those remarks were likely to be copied by a later copyist who failed to understand their precise value and meaning. If the whole skin—for the writing was upon skin—was not used, the possessor of the copy would feel at liberty to fill it with writing of his own, and this together with the original would be transcribed by the next copyist. The last clause of verse 7, "there is no wisdom in him," is superfluous according to the metrical scheme; obviously it is the marginal remark of a copyist who was ready and eager to deny the vaunted wisdom of Edom. Verse 20, according to some scholars, contains a grammatical note that the word *shebut* is written with defective form, and according to these scholars the original reading was simply "the captivity of the sons of Israel." Such notes, like printers' notations in versions of the English Bible, appear to have been incorporated not infrequently in the body of the text. The strange clause at the end of Jeremiah 31:22, "a woman shall encompass a man," would seem to be a grammatical note indicating that the masculine has been changed to the feminine in the case of the preceding nouns. Such is the judgment of Dr. Julius A. Bewer.[1] Likewise in Jeremiah 31:26 there is a verse which reads, "Upon this I awaked, and beheld, and my sleep was sweet unto me"; the verse is wholly irrelevant to what precedes or follows. It would seem that here we have the note of a copyist who records the fact that he was "overcome with heaviness" in the course of his transcribing and took time out for sleep.

Lest one should think this is fanciful, let the reader note that quite a few similar errors have crept into our printed editions of the English Bible. One issue of the Authorised Version, published in 1611, printed twice some twenty words from Exodus 14:10, and a like slip is found in the Hebrew Bible in II Samuel 6:3 ff. where the repetition is not found in the Greek version nor in the parallel passage I Chronicles 13:7 ff. In one English version (Oxford, 1716) the word *vinegar* was printed for vineyard in the heading of Luke 20, but something worse happened in an edition published in 1631 when the negative was omitted from the seventh commandment! This Bible was popularly known as the *Profligates' Bible*. Another edition, published in London in 1653, omitted the negative in I Corinthians 6:9 so that it read, "the unrighteous shall inherit the kingdom of God." Or yet again, in an edition published at Cambridge in 1805 a printer's marginal mark *to stand* (*stet*) was embodied in the text to read, "born after the Spirit to stand even so it is now" (Gal. 4:29).[2]

Thus we see how subject to human infirmity and error

[1] Bewer, J. A., *Literature of the Old Testament,* revised edition, 1944, p. 147 (footnote).

[2] For some of these details we are indebted to Cook, S. A., *The Old Testament: a Re-interpretation*, New York, 1936, pp. 8–9.

was the transmission of the sacred text. The copyists were human and they did some very human things.

OBADIAH AND JEREMIAH

It is to be noted that part of this little book is paralleled by a passage almost identical in Jeremiah. Obadiah 1–4 is very similar to Jeremiah 49:14–16, while Obadiah 5 seems almost identical with Jeremiah 49:9. The question has been raised as to whether one writer is here borrowing from the other, or whether both are borrowing from an older author. Such oracles against the nations seem to have had a wide vogue, and it may be doubted whether such oracles occurring in any particular book are to be regarded as the authentic work of the prophet in whose book they appear. Such doubt seems to be justified in the case of Jeremiah 46–51, all of which Duhm would deny to the man of Anathoth. It may be that here Duhm goes too far and that there is a real Jeremianic kernel in these chapters. Sellin would accept the passage in Jeremiah as authentic and holds that Jeremiah is borrowing from Obadiah, who, he holds, wrote about the middle of the ninth century B.C. We prefer, however, to regard Obadiah as written after the fall of Jerusalem (586 B.C.) and we regard the passage in Jeremiah as inserted there from Obadiah by a later editor. Obadiah's book, or at least the main part of it (1–14, 15b), will have been written shortly after the fall of Jerusalem. Its date will be near to that of Lamentations, and it appears to be written by one who was in touch with the events of that distressful time. Sometime, probably within a generation, after the disaster, while wounds were still bleeding and memories burning, Obadiah spoke his word.

THE HISTORICAL BACKGROUND

This, and all such oracles against Edom, goes back to a family quarrel. And few feuds are more bitter than those between brothers. Here was a vendetta that seemed to rage from the beginning of Israel's history. According to Genesis 25 this strife began in the prenatal times of Jacob and Esau. There may be in the Genesis story a reading back of later history but the fact remains that these two peoples, who by ancestry were brothers, lived in a state of continual feud. When Moses led the children of Irael through the desert to the promised land the easiest route lay through the territory of Edom. Permission to pass through was asked and denied, and Moses with his followers passed around Edom by a long weary road. Such unbrotherly conduct could not fail to rankle and leave a lasting grudge.

That in itself might not be enough to account for this continuing vendetta; other reasons entered. The main reason may be geographical rather than historical, for geography is often "latent history." Edom contained within its borders the port of Elath at the head of the Gulf of Akaba, and Elath was the terminal for important trade routes. From it merchantmen sailed to India and returned with rich argosies of freight, and from it, too, the trade routes spread across Palestine and north to Damascus. Recent archaeological discoveries have revealed great copper mines here and smelting furnaces.[3] All this meant commercial wealth and expansion. A fierce trade rivalry developed, and trade rivalries lead to wars. Thus we find Judah continually trying to hold Edom in subjection and Edom struggling against the yoke (II Kings 8:20–22). Amos 1:11 would seem to indicate that these fratricidal conflicts were conducted with brutal ferocity. In 734 B.C. Edom threw off the yoke and won independence, and for about 130 years she was a sore thorn in the side of Judah. When the Chaldean came against Jerusalem Edom was her ally. The Babylonian had learned, like the Roman and the modern Nazi, to "divide and conquer." The ancient feud was capitalised by the oppressor, and in the day of the attack Edom lined up with the invader against her inveterate foe. Obadiah 10–14 tells of the mean

[3] Glueck, Nelson, *The Other Side of Jordan*, 1940, pp. 50 ff.

part they played in the sack of the city, and the sevenfold repetition of the phrase "in the day of adversity" contains a weight of passion like that in Psalm 137:7:

> Remember, O Jehovah, against the children of Edom
> The day of Jerusalem:
> Who said, Down with it, down with it,
> Even to the foundations thereof.

Archaeological discoveries have revealed that after the fall of the city the Edomites pressed into southern Judea and occupied much of her territory. The returning exiles who came back after 538 B.C. could find a footing in the land only with great difficulty, and the hate that had grown through centuries mounted to a white heat of helpless rage. Later the region became known as Idumea, and this district gave the Jews the Herods to rule over them. The measure of hatred for the Herods revealed in the New Testament is easily understood from the historical background of these two nations. Later Edom became a symbol for Rome, and later still it symbolised the Christians. Historically Edom represented all that was detestable.

THE MESSAGE OF OBADIAH

From such a background of history and geography we have Obadiah's little book. We may not hesitate to designate it a *Hymn of Hate,* for a burning, scorching, blasting book it is. Here we have the reflection of Israel's national consciousness, which in Malachi's book will be expressed in plain blunt words:

"Jacob have I loved but Esau have I hated." (Mal. 1:2)

There is nothing here concerning justice or righteousness; here we have only a flaming fiery cry of hatred that shouts, "Edom must be destroyed." A book such as this raises serious questions and makes us conscious of the gulf between the Old Testament and the New.

Nonetheless it will reward us to think of what the prophet says. In the Old Testament there are many denunciations of foreign nations, but there are none that equal the denunciations hurled upon Edom. For brother Esau and Edom, Israel reserved her fiercest words. No feud in all her history was so bitter. If it be true that "hell has no fury like a woman scorned," it is no less true that hatred has no rage like that of a brother betrayed.

> In the day when thou stoodest on the other side,
> In the day when strangers carried off his substance,
> When strangers came in through his gates
> And cast lots upon Jerusalem,
> *Thou, even thou,* wast as one of them! (verse 11)

Never did the cry *"Et tu, Brute,"* sound with deeper passion. It was not "mine own familiar friend" who lifted up his heel against him, but a uterine brother who stood in the day of his brother's agony and laughed with loud guffaws (verse 12) at his pain.

> Because of violence done to thy brother Jacob
> Shame shall cover thee, and cut off shalt thou be for ever.
> (verse 10)

Brutus' act to Antony was treachery to friendship but this was denial of the covenant of brotherhood. Moreover it was aggravated by a stab in the back and shooting in the dark, for if the Chaldean had the nobility of the lion, Edom could only be likened to the jackal who did things the lion would not demean himself to do. Deep double-dyed treachery was theirs. All that lies behind the weight of passion that crowds the opening oracle.

> Behold I will make thee small among peoples,
> Despised among men.
> The pride of thy heart has deceived thee,
> O thou that inhabitest the clefts of the rock,
> Who settest thy dwelling-place aloft,
> Saying in thy heart,
> Who shall bring me down to the ground?

Though thou shouldst build high as the eagle,
And even set thy nest among the stars,
From thence will I bring thee down—'tis the oracle of Jehovah.
How art thou brought low!
If thieves came upon thee and should rob by night
Would they not steal only their sufficiency?
If vintagers came upon thee
Would they not leave gleaning grapes?
How is Esau searched out! rifled his treasures!
To the border they expel thee, the men of thy covenant,
Thy friends have betrayed thee, prevailed against thee;
They lay snares in thy way (there is no wisdom in him).
Will it not be in that day—'tis the oracle of Jehovah—
That I will destroy wisdom from Edom
And understanding from the Mount of Esau.
Dismayed will be thy heroes, O Teman,
That all may be cut off from Mount Esau by slaughter.
Because of violence done to thy brother Jacob
Shame shall cover thee, and cut off shalt thou be for ever. (2–10)

The memory of Edom's treachery could never be effaced: the writer describes it as if it were still before his eyes.

Gloat not over thy brother like a barbarian,
Rejoice not against the sons of Judah in the day of their ruin:
Make not thy mouth large in his day of distress,
Come not thou into the gates of my people in the day of their sorrow.
Gloat not thou on his disaster in his day of sorrow,
And lay not hands on his substance in his day of sorrow.
Stand not in the breach to cut off his fugitives,
Deliver not up his survivors in the day of distress.
As thou hast done it shall be done to thee:
Thy recompense will return on thine own head.
(12–14, 15b)

One thing we can say after reading Obadiah; he tells us plainly *how it feels*. It is difficult for us to understand the sorrow of Lidice or the agony of Poland or the stress which the blitz imposed on Britain. The rape of Nanking seems far away and the story of Japanese atrocities may not be true: thus we speak and think. If our pity is stirred, it is stirred as an emotion but not as a motive. It may be we have seen *Mrs. Miniver* in the movies, or seen pictures of holocausts in the deserts of North Africa, but we are far from knowing how it feels. It is easy to indulge in cheap sentiment when far removed from the scene, but Obadiah felt it all, and it was something that burned and scorched the soul. If we cannot share his sentiments we can at least try to understand his experience.

Reference has been made to trade rivalries, and there was certainly much there that fanned the flames of hatred. But the real cause of the feud lay deeper in the respective national temperaments. That fundamental difference the Old Testament runs right back to the very origin of the two nations; the original feud is between Jacob and Esau. Esau was the founder and father of Edom as Jacob was founder and father of Israel. From the two brothers the two nations and their differences derived.

"A PROFANE PERSON"

The character of Esau is aptly described in the New Testament (Heb. 12:16) as that of "a fornicator or profane person." *Profane* is a picture word, being derived from the Latin *fanum,* a fane or temple, and *pro,* meaning "in front of." The part in front of the temple was the forecourt where beasts were bought and sold and the moneychangers operated (John 2:13 ff.). Edom was interested solely in buying and selling things: beasts and livestock were its main concern. It was a commercial civilisation and prided itself on its business acumen and commercial astuteness. It is a remarkable fact that nowhere in the Old Testament is any mention made of the gods of Edom. Mention is made of the gods of Moab, Philistia, Phoenicia, and Syria, but never is mention made of the gods of Edom. Their religious life was wholly inconspicuous, and from the Old Testament we might well infer that they were a godless people. It is true that archaeology has supplied the lack of information on this point and that Edom had gods, but they played no significant part in the national life. Their story can be told in the Old Testament without such reference, but it is impossible to conceive the story of Israel without reference to Israel's God. Edom was known for its wisdom, and this seems to have been of a worldly kind. We might speak of them as a nation of "go-getters"; *their interest was in things*. The cultural foundations and the idealistic basis of life received scant attention from the Edomites. The scribal addition to verse 7, "there is no wisdom in him," is profoundly true.

Edom represents the proud, haughty spirit that trusts itself, and, as such, it was radically opposed to the religious mood and temper of Israel. At the center of Israel's life was a shrine and the vital thought of a sovereign God; at the center of Edom's life was a market place and beasts; the *fane* belonged to Israel but Edom was profane. Poets and prophets, visionaries and idealists were native to Israel but they were not found in Edom. In the deepest things of the spirit Israel and Edom were poles apart, and their mutual attitudes could not be other than hostile and repellent. They stood for different philosophies of life, and "what fellowship hath light with darkness?" Through the centuries the contrast deepened and hostility increased until Edom came to symbolise the incarnation of evil, as Babylon symbolised it to the writer of Revelation. It seemed so deep-seated and radical that the Old Testament writers could fix it in the eternal counsels of God (Mal. 1:2). Such a conflict, in its final analysis, is the conflict of the church against the world, of light against darkness, of God against Satan. And to the Hebrew it seemed there could be no end save by the complete destruction of Edom.

The book begins and ends with hate, and it sings of hate all through.

> And they shall go up as saviors to Mount Zion
> To punish Mount Esau,
> And the kingdom will be to Jehovah. (verse 21)

Some scholars would prefer to omit the words 'to punish Mount Esau,' but there is no adequate reason for so doing. This is a hymn of hate, and men had yet to learn the larger way of love. We can take the last words and interpret them in the larger light of the Christian dispensation, and we can believe that finally He will reign whose right it is to reign. And in that day there will be "neither Jew nor Gentile, bond or free, male or female" (Gal. 3:28), and we may add, neither black nor white, nor brown, nor yellow, for all shall be one in Him.

12

DEUTERO-ISAIAH: PROPHET OF WORLD SERVICE[1]

THE latest date mentioned in Ezekiel is 571 B.C. (Ezek. 29:17), and in 562 B.C. Nebuchadrezzar died after a reign of forty-two years. Under his rule the empire had flourished and the exiles appear to have met with humane treatment. After some preliminary restlessness the Jews had become adjusted to the new environment. But with the death of Nebuchadrezzar things took a turn for the worse and a series of less competent rulers finally ended in the fall of the empire within a generation.

The passing of Nebuchadrezzar did not make an immediate difference in the lot of the Jews, for Amel-Marduk (Evil-Merodach of the Bible), his successor, proceeded to show distinct favor to the Jews and released their former king Jehoiachin who had long languished in prison (II Kings 25:27–30). But Amel-Marduk reigned only two years, and was succeeded by his murderer, Neriglissar (562–556 B.C.), who in turn gave place to his son, Labashi-Marduk. This last-named monarch was incompetent and after a few months a revolution set Nabunaid (Nabonidus) in his place. But Nabunaid (556–539 B.C.) was more interested in archaeology than in govern-

[1] The term "Deutero-Isaiah" (or Second Isaiah) is used to designate the author (or authors) of Isaiah 40-66. Most scholars are agreed that these prophecies are not from Isaiah of Jerusalem who prophesied between 740 and 701 B.C. Here we have a great anonymous prophet from the period of the Exile; the historical background is 150 years later than the period of Isaiah of Jerusalem.

ment, and by tactless procedures he contrived to alienate the influential ecclesiastical authorities in Babylon. This continued friction between the hierarchy and the monarchy resulted in the king spending most of his time at Teima (Biblical, Teman) in Arabia and the actual work of government was left in the hands of his son, Belshazzar. In such circumstances it would seem that the lot of the Jewish captives deteriorated and the march of events fanned to flame a smoldering discontent.

For at this time the tempo of history was strangely quickened. Cyrus appeared on the political horizon and things began to happen. Cyrus was a romantic figure and his rise to power was rapid. As king of the little land of Anshan he was subject to Astyages, king of Media, but by 550 B.C. the unpopularity of Astyages and the military genius of Cyrus combined to establish the latter on the throne of Media, while a year later he became king of Persia and the most considerable figure of the East. His advance to fame was swift and surprising and in 546 B.C. he defeated Croesus of Lydia and was in control of most of Asia Minor. Babylon fell in 539 B.C. and the Jews found themselves vassals of the Persian empire.

These stirring events could not fail to move the minds of men everywhere and the Jewish exiles could not remain uninfluenced by them. A great many of these exiles, perhaps the majority, had given heed to Jeremiah's word to settle down in Babylon (Jer. 29); they had settled and had given so many hostages to time that when the voice of the Eternal sounded they could not, or would not, hear. Jerusalem was far away and Babylon was near, and after all "a bird in hand is worth two in the bush." Idealism had given place to sordid realism.

But there were others—it may have been a minority—who had kept the faith and still believed in an idealistic interpretation of history. They were waiting "for the consolation of Israel" and lived in hope of the Day of Jehovah. Some may have construed this narrowly in the old concept of national exaltation and looked for judgment upon Babylon; such thoughts are found in small anonymous oracles that have lodged themselves in the book of Isaiah (Is. 13; 21:1–10). Others may have been ready to share a larger view, and thus when a prophet arose to interpret events in the light of a comprehensive divine purpose he had a responsive audience (Is. 41:2–4).

THE PROPHET: PLACE AND DATE

We have no knowledge of the personal life of this prophet; he is wholly anonymous. He is but a voice, an unseen, though not unheard, herald of the dawn, the harbinger of the new day. Where he lived and spoke we are not told: Babylon, Phoenicia, Palestine, Egypt have all been suggested as his habitation, but as the speaker seems to have events before his eyes we may well believe he lived in Babylon. The evidence of his presence there seems even stronger than in the case of Ezekiel.

Wherever he lived he was a prophet of profoundest insight. To speak of him as a religious genius does less than justice to his greatness. Nowhere in the Old Testament are we more impressed with "the lively oracles of God"; there is a unique flair about this prophet which has caused his words to grip and hold the imagination of all the centuries.

> "No other prophet shows such a combination of smoothness and passion. Amos is fiercer and colder; Hosea and Isaiah are more allusive and cryptic, especially the former; Jeremiah is plainer, and has an entirely different method. The whole of these chapters forms one magnificent outburst of joy." [2]

Perhaps he mingles the character of religious philosopher with that of prophet, but nowhere in the Old Testament do we meet with a nobler vindication of the character of God or a more incisive interpretation of the real meaning of redemption. The prophetic inspiration here reaches its apex, and the thoughts here expressed, whatever may have been their origi-

[2] Robinson, T. H., *Prophecy and the Prophets,* 1925, p. 163.

nal reference, have found their completest and most obvious fulfilment in the words and works of our Lord.

The date of the prophecy can be fixed with a fair degree of accuracy. Cyrus had already entered upon his victorious career when the prophet began his work. Terror was already upon the peoples, and his rise had forced the powers to make a coalition against him. Croesus had sought support from Babylon, Sparta, and Egypt, but such alliances did not avail against the conquerer. Babylon had not yet fallen nor was Cyrus' edict yet published; thus we may date the prophecy between 549 and 539 B.C. Within the prophecy we perceive development, for in chapters 40–48 the prophet uses argument to enforce the meaning of events, while in chapters 49–55 the situation seems to have become clear for all to see. These latter chapters must have been spoken on the very eve of Babylon's fall.

Within these chapters are found the *Servant Songs* (42:1–4; 49:1–6; 50:4–9; 52:13–53:12) and in these songs we have some of the loftiest insights of the Old Testament. Are these from Deutero-Isaiah or from another writer? If from another writer, is that other writer earlier or later than the prophet? The songs are so closely interwoven with the context that many scholars think they cannot have been incorporated by another hand; the fact that scholars differ as to the precise extent of these songs shows how closely they are woven into the main structure. The present writer, however, inclines to the opinion that the prophet here is utilising material from an earlier writer of remarkable insight. The prophet was not alone in his larger views of God and the divine purpose, and in these songs he may be using the words of another to correct certain narrow conceptions that are found in the oracles outside these songs. But whatever the prophet borrowed he made his own and stamped it with his own seal. Thus, despite apparent differences in the understanding of the Servant's character, we may assume that in chapters 40–55 we have the work of the prophet. Chapters 56–66 seem to reflect conditions of the post-exilic period and most scholars would regard these chapters as from about the same period as Malachi.

THE MESSAGE OF DEUTERO-ISAIAH

The message of Deutero-Isaiah is a message of comfort and consolation. His book is frequently called "The Exiles' Book of Consolation." The keynote is sounded in the opening words, made memorable by Handel in his great oratorio:

> Comfort ye, comfort ye, my people,
>   Saith your God,
> Speak ye comfortably to Jerusalem,
>   And proclaim to her
> That her warfare is accomplished,
>   That her iniquity is pardoned,
> That she hath received at Jehovah's hand
>   Double for all her sins. (40:1, 2)

In our study of Ezekiel we have seen that the exiles were in grave danger of spiritual depression. A torpor had crept over the spirit of Judah and faith was at its lowest ebb.

> "Why sayest thou, O Jacob, and speakest, O Israel: My fate is hidden from Jehovah and my right ignored by my God?" (40:27)

The sight of Babylon's imperial splendor and the pressure of circumstances had wrought into their hearts a haunting fear that Jehovah had forsaken his people or was unable to stand up against the pagan deities.

> "But Zion said: Jehovah has forsaken me, and my Lord forgotten me." (49:14)

Israel was in danger of succumbing to the insidious influences of heathen polytheism. Had it not been for Ezekiel and Deutero-Isaiah the exiles might finally have lost their identity and become lost like the northern ten tribes of Israel. In this sense the ministry of Deutero-Isaiah is not merely timely; it is of momentous interest for the history of religion.

In such a situation the prophet is called upon to overcome those deadening doubts and inspire the hearts of men with a mighty creative faith. It is worthy of note here that the prophet almost never uses the word "faith" but emphasises rather the courage and resolution that are the outward attitudes and expression of faith. "Fear not" and "Wait" are his favorite words, and by these terms the prophet signifies the militant aspect of faith, the capacity to stand up to things and the ability to hold on to the very end. For the prophet is bringing glad tidings of great joy. He comes at a time when Israel was ground down to the dust, and he comes with an evangel, and that evangel is grounded in, and guaranteed by, the character of God.

Deutero-Isaiah is the most theological of all the prophets, and that of necessity. For while Cyrus makes history the prophet interprets it in the light of divine purpose and shows the real significance of those momentous happenings. Behind all the international politics of his time he sees, and shows, the unfolding of Jehovah's purpose. And this he does to comfort hearts that were trembling and souls that were fainting amid the convulsions of that time.

Thus the prophet expounds the character of God. He does not seek to prove his existence but proceeds to take his stand on history, adduce the evidences, and dwell upon the attributes of God. Here we reach the full monotheistic view which not only expresses its faith in one God but also expresses its disbelief in any other gods.

> Thus saith Jehovah, the King of Israel,
> Yea, his redeemer Jehovah Sabaoth:
> I am the first and I am the last,
> And beside me there is no god at all.
>
> Be not afraid nor be disquieted,
> Did not I of old proclaim and declare it?
> Ye are my witnesses. Is there a God
> Or a Rock beside me at all? (44:6, 8)

Israel's God is the Creator of heaven and earth; he is exalted and transcendent.

Who hath measured the waters in the hollow of his hand,
And determined the heavens with a span
And comprehended the dust of the earth in a measure,
And weighed the mountains in scales,
And the hills with a balance?

. . . .

Lift up your eyes on high,
And see, who hath created these?
He who brings out their host by number
And calleth them all by name:
So great is his strength and mighty his power
That not one is out of its place. (40:26)

His wisdom and power are unlimited, and to him nothing is impossible (40:12–16; 41:17–20). He is omnipotent and omniscient, without peer or parallel.

"To whom will ye liken me that I shall be equal to him? saith the Holy One." (40:25)

Source and origin of all, first and last, he is ever consistent, and all that comes to pass moves by his will to an end which He has ordained.

Remember the former things of old

. . . .

For I am God and there is none else,
Elohim and there is none like me;
Foretelling the end from the beginning,
From of old things not yet accomplished;
Saying, My purpose shall stand,
And all my pleasure will I accomplish:
Who have called from the East a bird of prey,
The man of my purpose from a far country—
As I have spoken I will bring it to pass;
As I have planned I will accomplish. (46:9–11)

As Creator of a world so vast he stands unique and incomparable; why should the exiles fear when such a God was theirs? The gods of Babylon, for all their apparent magnificence and costly equipment, are but wood and stone, incapable of speech or action. In the day of distress they can do nothing, for they are nonentities (*elilim*) ; made by man, they are no gods.

> Declare the things which are to come,
> That we may know that ye are gods;
> Yea, do something either good or bad,
> That we may see it and marvel.
> Behold, ye are nothing,
> And your work is nothing at all!
> An abomination is he that chooseth you. (41:23, 24)

In grim sardonic fashion Isaiah shows the futility of those man-made deities, and with savage irony he points at them dangling from a cart as they are transported out of Babylon.

> Bel boweth down, Nebo stoopeth;
> Their images are a burden to the beasts,
> Laid as a load upon weary cattle.
> They stoop, they bow down together:
> They could not deliver the load,
> But themselves are gone into captivity. (46:1, 2)

The gods who should have lifted and sustained and carried men are only so much deadweight to be loaded on a truck! They cannot interpret the great events that are afoot; they can do nothing, for they are but *nothings.* But Israel's God brought these things to pass and foretold them long ago by his prophets (41:22; 43:9; 44:7) and his prophet is now at hand to interpret these happenings with reference to the final goal.

All this development in prophetic teaching is remarkable inasmuch as a parallel development was taking place at this time in Greece. The early Greek philosophers had prepared the way for Plato and Socrates, and on that foundation these erected a remarkable edifice of thought. There emerged in Greece at this time a monistic philosophy that differed only externally from Jewish monotheism. But the Hebrew did not reach his system by metaphysics; his foundation was wholly ethical.

> "It is not the pure reason which guides them, it is the practical reason, and their basis is essentially ethical rather than metaphysical. This means that they were able to develop their doctrines from the standpoint of real personality, and thus they avoided the pantheistic snare which lies in wait for those who seek to evolve a theoretical monism from intellectual abstractions."[3]

Israel's God is incomparable, and his purpose with his people is a purpose of grace. The intention of the divine heart is redemption, and that on a world scale.

> Turn unto me and be ye saved,
> All ye ends of the earth!
> For I am God, and there is none else.
> By myself have I sworn—
> A true word has gone forth from my mouth,
> A word that will not be recalled:
> That unto me every knee shall bow,
> Every tongue swear.
> Only through Jehovah has Jacob
> Victories and strength;
> On his account shall they be shamed and confounded
> All that were incensed against him;
> But in Jehovah shall all the seed of Israel
> Triumph and make their boast. (45:22–25)

This relation of Israel to Jehovah the prophet sets forth in many a tender similitude. Jehovah is Israel's husband (54:5), her shepherd (40:11), her vindicator or redeemer, *gōēl,* signifying the nearest kinsman who undertakes to redeem

[3] *Ibid.,* p. 167.

(44:24). With more than a mother's love does he love Israel (49:14, 15); he chose Abraham as his friend (41:8, 51:2), and that friendship cannot be broken. Here the prophet will reinterpret the doctrine of election which Amos had assailed, and will rescue it and set it in its original light. Jehovah will be shown to be "a just God *and* a Savior" (45:21). All ethical and spiritual values are preserved and maintained here, as in the case of Hosea, and with an echo of the earlier prophet Deutero-Isaiah speaks twice of Jehovah as Israel's "compassionater" (49:10; 54:10). Righteousness that was inflexible and austere in Amos is linked with grace and is almost identified with the liberation of Israel and becomes practically synonymous with salvation (51:4, 6, 8; 45:8, 24; 46:13). He has proved his love to Israel by forgiving all her sin (44:22), and her name is graven upon the palms of his hands (49:16). For her sake he will sacrifice other nations (43:3, 4). To bring about her release he has raised up Cyrus (41:2), and the purpose of grace which had been frustrated by Israel's sin is about to find its fulfilment. The "covenant of peace" is established (54:10), the "everlasting covenant, the sure mercies of David" is confirmed to the nation on condition of obedience, and filled with larger hopes and promises (55:3–5).

In all this we see the real nature of prophecy. The prophet stands forth as the spokesman of God to interpret events. Cyrus might not think of himself as this prophet thought of him—his own records show he did not so think—but Cyrus did not know the inner secret and the prophet did. Cyrus may seem to others just another military colossus bestriding the earth, but to the seeing eye and understanding heart of the prophet he is more. Cyrus is Jehovah's friend (48:14), his shepherd (44:28), his Messiah (45:1). Cyrus is the instrument and agent of Jehovah's purpose as that purpose concerns the world (45:13; 46:11; 48:14). There is something unique in these words spoken concerning a foreign king. Nowhere else in the Old Testament do we find a foreigner designated as Messiah.

All this Jehovah brings to pass that his people may go forth and return safely to their homeland (49:20, 21). Here the local and national element appears, and without this national appeal the prophet would have found no response to his message. The Zionist movement is no new thing originating in our time. No one loved Zion with more affection than this prophet, and none spoke of it in more glowing terms. But he loves it because he sees it related to the universal purpose of God, and because he sees it as the center of a world religion. That which is transpiring in Babylon is a manifestation of the divine glory (40:5; 41:20), and it is of world-wide significance (44:23; 48:20). Israel is saved to serve, and all the earth is to be blessed in her (49:22; 55:4, 5). Divine truth shall go forth from Zion. Ezekiel had cut off Zion from the world with a strict exclusiveness but Deutero-Isaiah takes the world for his parish. Jerusalem and Israel appear here as they appear in other prophets but the terms have now a wider significance. *They cease to be local terms and become religious thoughts.* Israel is the Servant of Jehovah and Jehovah is God of the whole world.

THE SERVANT OF JEHOVAH

This lofty thought of missionary vocation is set forth clearly in the four *Servant Songs* (42:1–4; 49:1–6; 50:4–9; 52:13–53:12). In these songs the universality of the Servant's mission is set forth, and the spirit in which his ministry is to be exercised is described (42:1–4; 49:1–6). Unlike the earlier prophets, this ministry shall be without loud noise or tumult; but, like the earlier prophets, the Servant will meet with opposition and persecution (50:6), and will finally be done to death for the cause which he has at heart (53:3–9). His life will seem to many to have ended in utter failure, but further reflection upon the matter will lead to the conclusion that his suffering was the will of his God, and those sufferings will be seen to be the Servant's highest glory, for those sufferings of the Servant atone for the sins of others and have mighty redemptive power (53:10–12). The great cause is won at great cost.

When Philip overtook the Ethiopian eunuch on the road to Gaza he found him reading this last *Servant Song,* and in response to Philip's inquiry, "Understandest thou what thou readest?" the eunuch put the question which most of us might put to-day:

Of whom speaketh the prophet this? (Acts 8:34)

The answers to that question are numerous and varied, and we need not detail them here. They are set forth in tabulated form by Volz [4] in his commentary on the book. There are those who see here in the Servant the portrayal of an individual, and the variety of interpretation arises from the different individuals proposed. Jehoiachin, Zerubbabel, Jeremiah, Josiah, the prophet himself, and even Moses have all been proposed at different times and by different scholars. One scholar (Sellin) has made three of these identifications and now seems ready to vote for a fourth. Nor is it difficult to understand why men should think that an individual is here portrayed, for the features are so highly individualised, particularly in the fourth song, that we can scarcely think of any other interpretation than the individual. But others have seen here the nation Israel, either in its real or ideal aspects. Such is the Jewish interpretation, and Christian scholarship is one with the Jew on this question. The nation Israel is the Servant of Jehovah.

It may help us toward an understanding of the question if we think of a peculiar conception of Hebrew thought. We refer to the concept of Corporate Personality. This typical Hebrew way of thinking may seem strange to us who think in a way almost diametrically opposite, and it may be that our main difficulty in the matter of interpreting these songs is due to our failure to recognise how the Hebrew thought. Dr. H.

[4] Volz, Paul, *Kommentar zum Alten Testament,* IX, Jesaia II, p. 167.

Wheeler Robinson has set forth the profound significance of this thought not only in relation to these songs but in relation to the Old Testament in general.

> This is a conception strange to the modern mind, for our sense of social solidarity is of a different order, denoting as it does the combination of individuals on the basis of common interest or obligation. 'Corporate Personality,' on the other hand, denotes the primitive idea of a family, a clan, a tribe, or a nation as one, so that on occasion the whole group and the individual member of it may be treated as identical whether in law or religion, with fluidity of transition from the one to the many and vice versa. Thus the prophet can feel not only that he represents Israel but that he is Israel.[5]

We begin with the thought of individual rights but the Hebrew could not conceive of an individual apart from the nation; the nation was the unit of his thought, and for him our thought of the individual was not easy. Achan's sin (Josh. 7:1 ff.) is the sin of the "sons of Israel," and Achan's whole family must be rooted out, root and branch, to atone for that sin. Achan is his family, and the family is Achan. When Israel fought against her enemies they thought of the tribe or nation as the unit and they exterminated all that breathed. Parallel to this is the thought behind the law of blood revenge; the *gōēl* (avenger, vindicator), the next of kin, did not say his kinsman's blood had been shed; he said, "*Our*" blood has been shed. This also springs from, and illustrates, the Hebrew thought of Corporate Personality. It is not easy for us, who have been indoctrinated with other conceptions, to understand how the Hebrew thought, but it is worth trying to understand the Semitic way in this matter.

Thus the prophet will think at times of the whole group, and then he will think of the group narrowed to a single representative. But the whole group is in that representative, and

[5] Robinson, H. Wheeler, *The Old Testament: Its Making and Meaning,* 1937, p. 85. Used by permission of Abingdon-Cokesbury Press.

that representative is the whole group. Israel may be represented by its choice men of prophetic spirit who make an offering of their own individual and the nation's sufferings. There is a strange fluidity here, and we meet the same fluidity in the Psalter, where frequently the first person singular will exchange in the same psalm with the first person plural. It bewilders the interpreter but it was natural to the Hebrew (e.g. Ps. 129). This, too, would explain the individual features in the portrait of the Servant and why some have thought of the prophet himself as the Servant of Jehovah. Just as Elijah could think of faithful Israel narrowed to his own person so that he alone was left, or as Jeremiah seems to think the whole cause of Jehovah rests upon and is embodied in himself, so the Servant here can be regarded as the small minority group of faithful Jews, and this group may even be narrowed to his own person. This line of thought would solve the apparent contradiction that seems involved in the attitude towards the Servant in the oracles outside the four *Servant Songs:*

> "Who is blind as my Servant and deaf as my messenger?" (42:19)

But there need not be any difficulty here. Israel in exile was a people of varied spiritual insight and attainment. Nor is it otherwise in the church. The church is the Servant of Jehovah, but there is much dumbness and deafness and lethargy in the church, and the church has yet to inspire and evangelise the majority of its members. Her duty lies within, like that of the Servant of Jehovah, to her own members, and it lies without in the obligation to be a missionary people and win the heathen world to the true religion.

Deutero-Isaiah was a prophet of daring faith and splendid vision. He is unique in that he makes explicit what was implicit in the earlier prophets and reaches a complete monotheism. A wider and fuller interpretation was given to the original revelation, and Deutero-Isaiah opened prospects and vistas akin to those of the Evangel. But he paid the penalty of greatness; his lofty insights were too lofty for Israel. Judaism followed the lines laid down by Ezekiel, and narrowed itself with an iron-clad exclusiveness which only the dynamic of the Gospel could break. The book of Jonah is animated by the same wide and generous spirit but it stands alone. Deutero-Isaiah had to wait until Christ came before men could clearly envisage the prospect of a universal kingdom and understand fully the glory of vicarious suffering.

13

PROPHETS OF THE PERSIAN PERIOD

HAGGAI, ZECHARIAH, AND MALACHI

THE HISTORICAL BACKGROUND

WHEN Babylon fell on the 29th day of the tenth month of the year 539 B.C. a way was opened for the development of that period in Hebrew history which is generally referred to as post-exilic Judaism. The beginnings of this significant period lie further back in history but it is from Babylon and the returned exiles that the main influences stem which were to shape and mold the final forms of Hebrew religion and Jewish polity. In the various deportations that had taken place through the years 597, 586, 581 B.C. the best part of the nation had been carried away to Babylon. We need not think that the majority of the population were deported, for it seems probable[1] that not more than one eighth of the population was removed, but the ablest and most competent leaders, secular and ecclesiastical, were taken to Babylon. Those left behind could be described by Jeremiah as "a basket of very bad figs," while the exiles were "a basket of good figs." (Jer. 24: 1 ff.)

During those years of exile Israel had time to think and ample leisure to reflect upon the meaning of events. It may be an exaggeration to say that Israel went into exile a nation and returned as a church, but such a statement has meaning. For Israel developed in the exile along lines other than those of the pre-exilic period and returned with a new view of life

[1] Lods, *The Prophets and the Rise of Judaism*, p. 174.

and life's responsibilities. Out of the experiences that came in the exile Israel extracted experience, wisdom, maturity so that she was not likely to make the same mistake twice. It was a chastened people that came back, and in the prophets of this period we mark something new and distinct. We observe the rise and growth of Judaism.

But the religious development may not be understood apart from knowledge of the historical background, and this must be set forth first. Here, fortunately, we have outside sources to supplement the record of the Old Testament; these external sources are the Cyrus Cylinder, the Chronicle of Nabonidus, and the works of Josephus. The Old Testament record is found in Chronicles-Ezra-Nehemiah together with the prophets Haggai, Zechariah, and Malachi. Some parts of Isaiah 56–66 seem to be written against the background of this period. The value of the evidence in Chronicles-Ezra-Nehemiah is variously assessed by scholars and it must be evaluated with critical care.

THE PERSIAN EMPIRE

This empire emerges with the rise of Cyrus, who became king of Anshan under the suzerainty of the king of Media in 559 B.C. Cyrus rebelled against his overlord in 550 B.C., and by 546 B.C. he had overwhelmed Croesus, king of Lydia, and proceeded to pass from victory to victory. Isaiah 41:2, 3 hails him as the "Messiah of Jehovah" and represents Jehovah addressing "Cyrus, my friend (or shepherd)." Nabonidus, king of Babylon, was first driven from Teima (O. T., Teman) in Edom, where he had been spending his time in the study of archaeology in complete forgetfulness of his kingly duty. He had lost favor with the priestly class at Babylon through his long absence from the capital, which made it impossible to observe the religious ritual as it should be observed. When he returned it was too late. The hierarchy had formed a fifth column within the city, and it fell to Gobryas, Cyrus' commander, without a fight. In 539 B.C. the Jews passed under Persian domination.

Contrary to the hopes and expectations of the Jews, the city was not destroyed. A policy of remarkable humaneness was adopted by the new ruler towards the subject peoples. Unlike the previous empires, the Persian did not engage in ruthless deportations; instead of carrying away, there were restorations of exiled peoples to the lands from which they had been torn. Cyrus describes his procedure on his own Cylinder.

> "The gods who dwelt in them (i.e. in Asshur, Susa, Agade, Eshmunak, Zamba . . . with the territory of the land of Gutium) I brought back to their places, and caused them to dwell in a habitation for all time. All their inhabitants I collected and restored them to their dwelling-places. And the gods of Sumer and Akkad whom Nabonidus, to the anger of the lord of the gods, had brought to Babylon, by the command of Marduk, the great lord, I caused them peacefully to take up their dwelling in habitations that rejoiced the heart." [2]

There is no mention here of the Jews or their land, and as they had no images of their deity there is no mention of any gods in this connection. But according to Ezra 6:5; 5:14 ff., Cyrus is said to have given orders that the temple vessels, which had been taken from Jerusalem to Babylon by Nebuchadrezzar, should be restored and returned to the temple at Jerusalem, and that the temple there should be rebuilt. There is no reason to doubt this, though there is reason to doubt the number of these vessels—five thousand four hundred—as given in Ezra 1:11. There is no inherent improbability in the statement itself, for we learn from Papyrus No. 21 of the Elephantine Papyri [3] that in the year 419–418 B.C. Darius II issued instructions to the Jews living in Egypt as to the celebration of the Feast of Unleavened Bread.

[2] Rogers, R. W., *Cuneiform Parallels to the Old Testament*, 1912, p. 383.

[3] Cowley, A., *Aramaic Papyri of the Fifth Century B.C.*, 1923, pp. 60 ff.

THE RECORD AND THE RESTORATION

The day of release had dawned for the exiles; the night of sorrow was past and gone. It was now possible for the Jews to return to their own land. Did they go back? As to what precisely took place we cannot speak with any great degree of certainty, for the Old Testament sources are both ambiguous and scanty. According to Ezra 2:64 and Nehemiah 7:66 the number of those who returned in the beginning is given as 42,360 men with 7,337 slaves of both sexes, and 200 or 245 singing men and women. The record does not seem too reliable, for the detailed lists work out in the case of Ezra to 29,818 and in the case of Nehemiah to 31,089, while First Esdras in the Greek version gives the figure as 30,142. These variations may not signify a great deal, but the figures seem excessive in view of other facts. For those figures refer only to males (except where it is expressly stated otherwise) and the figures here given would imply a caravan of about 100,000 souls, including women and children. According to Jeremiah 52:28–30 the Babylon community in 581 B.C. amounted to about 4,600 males, and it scarcely seems possible that this community should have reached such large proportions as those mentioned in a period of little more than forty years. Both history and archaeology show that there were Jews in Babylon after the presumed restoration, and one cannot escape the feeling here that the records have "telescoped" the history and are giving us figures of a census of pure-blooded Jews resident in Judah in the time of Nehemiah.[4] These records were written probably about 300 B.C.[5] long after the events which they narrate. These later writers seem to have thought of Judah as wholly desolate of people after 586 B.C., and this opinion has been shared by many later writers. But it certainly was not so, and when the exiles returned they found there a

[4] Lods, *op. cit.*, p. 191.

[5] Oesterley and Robinson, *Introduction to the Old Testament*, p. 126.

resident population. Judah had not ceased to be occupied. The return, however, cannot have taken place in such volume as Ezra and Nehemiah indicate, though there is no reason for taking the position of Kosters, who denies that there was any return of the exiles from Babylon. The return took place but not in the way the later writers assert; it took place in piecemeal fashion as will be seen from a closer examination of the available sources.

THE EDICT OF CYRUS

From what is recorded in history concerning Cyrus it may be considered highly probable that he gave orders for the repatriation of the Jews. Though no mention is made of such an order or permission on the Cyrus Cylinder, there is reference in the book of Ezra to an edict of Cyrus. This edict is cited twice (1:2–4; 6:3–5), although there is little resemblance between the two versions. The first citation occurs in a peculiarly Jewish form that has not failed to arouse suspicion. For it does not seem at all probable or reasonable that Cyrus should call on the other peoples to contribute to the cost of a Jewish temple, nor was he likely to refer to the Jews as guests sojourning in his domains. The imperial authorities were much more realistic. But it seems unwise to discredit the version that appears in chapter 6. Here we have reference to a *roll* or writing discovered at Ecbatana, and although the Persians did not write on rolls but on clay tablets the error as to form of the document should not induce scepticism as to its substance. For the document bears the marks of authenticity. It reads as follows:

> "A record: In the first year of Cyrus the king Cyrus made a decree: Concerning the house of God at Jerusalem let the house be builded, the place where they offer sacrifices. The height thereof threescore cubits, and the breadth thereof threescore cubits; with three rows of great stones and a row of new timber; and let the ex-

> penses be given out of the king's house: and also let the gold and silver vessels of the house of God, which Nebuchadrezzar took forth out of the temple which is at Jerusalem and brought unto Babylon, be restored, and brought again to the temple which is at Jerusalem, every one to its place, and thou shalt put them in the house of God."

Despite objections which have been made to the form and contents of this edict, it seems not unreasonable that Cyrus should have stated the style and size of building. "He who pays the piper calls the tune," and if Cyrus was paying for the building he was entitled to say what kind of building it was to be. The subsidy for this purpose may have been taken out of the provincial taxes, but those taxes were not subject to any claim by the Jews. They represented a royal bounty and were recognised as such. The edict as it here appears has a genuine ring and accords with all we know of Persian practice. It would appear that there was a definite instruction in the matter, and that this instruction, or a copy of it, could be found in the royal archives twenty years later when questions were being raised as to the rebuilding.

The book of Ezra is less trustworthy when it proceeds to give an account of the events that followed 539 B.C. In chapter 3:8–13 it is stated that the returned exiles "in the second year began to set forward the work of the Lord" (537 B.C.). In that year the foundation of the temple was laid under the combined leadership of Joshua, the high priest, and Zerubbabel, the governor. But here we have contemporary evidence in Haggai and it is clear from Haggai (2:15–18) that in his day (520) nothing had been yet done towards rebuilding the temple. Haggai further makes it clear that he inspired both Joshua and Zerubbabel to begin the task.

Moreover, Ezra has another account of the matter in 5:14–16 where it states that the sacred vessels were committed to Sheshbazzar, who had been appointed governor of the province by Cyrus, to be delivered at the temple of Jerusalem.

> "Then came this same Sheshbazzar and laid the foundations of the house of God which is at Jerusalem: since that time until now hath it been in building, and yet it is not completed."

The writer is here speaking of the days of Haggai and Zechariah, and is citing the words of their contemporaries. But both Haggai and Zechariah are in direct contradiction to Ezra on this point. Not only so, but the writer in Ezra contradicts himself when he says:

> "Then ceased the work of the house of God which is at Jerusalem; and it ceased until the second year of Darius king of Persia." (4:24)

Zechariah states plainly that Zerubbabel laid the foundation, and Haggai (1:14; cp. 2:15–18) seems to imply the same. That the writer in the book of Ezra is not to be trusted as a competent historian is clear from the additional fact that he regards Xerxes (486–65) and Artaxerxes (465–24) as having reigned between Cyrus and Darius. If he made that confusion there, it is very probable that he confused the second year of Darius with the second year of Cyrus.

From all this it is clear that we may not accept without question the testimony of those later writers, and that their witness must be carefully evaluated. The writer of Ezra is reconstructing history on the basis of inadequate data, and he writes in full view of later feuds and animosities that issued finally in the Samaritan schism.[6]

THE PROBABLE SEQUENCE OF EVENTS

The real historical situation becomes clear when we turn to the contemporary witnesses who acted prominently in the events of the period described. The oracles of Haggai and Zechariah are dated most precisely, and although Dr. Welch[7] questions this exact dating there is no real reason for such

[6] Oesterley and Robinson *ibid.*, p. 127.
[7] Welch, A. C., *Post-Exilic Judaism*, 1935, p. 162.

scepticism. According to these witnesses the course of events seems to have followed some such plan as we now describe. The sacred vessels were committed to the custody of the government official for delivery to the authorities at Jerusalem. Sheshbazzar may be the same as Shenazzar mentioned in I Chronicles 3:18 and he was probably a son of Jehoiachin the king, whom Nebuchadrezzar carried away to Babylon in 597 B.C., and who was released by Amel-Marduk in 562 B.C. Many scholars (e.g. Welch, Hölscher) dissent from this identification but it is generally accepted. Moreover, it seems probable, for, as Herodotus tells us:

> "It was customary for the Persians to respect kings' sons, and to restore them their power and their crown, even though their fathers had rebelled." [8]

That any great company travelled with the royal official, who would move post-haste to his position, may be doubted. He may have been accompanied by some eager spirits who could not wait, but that he was attended by the motley throng suggested by Ezra and Nehemiah seems highly improbable.

Nor is it likely that the resident Jews in Babylon could have set their affairs in order so speedily. Many held lucrative positions and had large stakes in trade. Their holdings could not be liquidated at a moment's notice; the Jew does not usually act in this rash manner, and there is no reason to think he did so in Babylon. Farmers knew the good agricultural possibilities of Babylon and they would not readily give them up for a chance on the bare wind-swept heights of Judah. Many reasons conspired to keep them there. "Many abode in Babylon," says Josephus, "because they did not wish to leave their possessions." [9] The advice of Jeremiah (Jer. 29) had been taken to heart, and the Jews had sent down their roots by the waters of the Tigris and Euphrates, so that they could not, or would not, pull them up readily. Most of those resident in Babylon could not have known another home, and the fierce

[8] *Histories,* III: 15.
[9] *Antiquities of the Jews,* xi, i, 3.

passion for Zion that had inflamed the hearts of the first exiles must have been largely quenched. That many remained behind is clear from the business documents of the house of Murashu & Sons, a great trading corporation on the banks of the Tigris. These documents,[10] found at Nippur, belong to a century later, but in them occur many Jewish names of clients and associates. Names like Benjamin, Gedaliah, Hananiah, Pedaiah bear witness to the fact that many remained in exile. They may have subscribed to the expenses of those returning, but for themselves they preferred to stay where they were. And who will blame them?

THE RETURN FROM BABYLON

But that many did return is clear, though we may not say when they returned. Sheshbazzar disappears from view, and in the time of Haggai and Zechariah we find Zerubbabel, grandson of Jehoiachin and nephew of the first governor, in charge of the province, and Joshua as high priest. That this was the arrangement in the year 520 B.C. is clearly attested by both Haggai and Zechariah.

It is not difficult to imagine the situation as it appeared to the returning exiles, nor is it difficult to see how the later writers, Ezra and Nehemiah, imagined it to have been. These writers seem to have the idea that after 586 B.C. the land was emptied of its population, and the poetical descriptions of Isaiah, Jeremiah, and Ezekiel might well suggest this. Jeremiah speaks of the land as "desolate without man or beast" (Jer. 32:43), while Deutero-Isaiah refers to Jerusalem as uninhabited (Is. 44:26; *cp.* Ezek. 36:33–38). But this is the language of poetry and is not to be treated as sober historical record. The fact is clear from Jeremiah 41:4, 5 that shortly after the fall of Jerusalem in 586 B.C. worshipers were making their way from Schechem, Shiloh, and Samaria to offer sacrifice and

[10] *Babylonian Expedition of the University of Pennsylvania,* IX: 28, 76.

worship at Jerusalem, the central shrine. They certainly knew of the destruction of the city, for two months had passed since its fall; they came, too, with all suitable signs of sorrow, "having their beards shaven and their clothes rent and having cut themselves." Haggai certainly implies that the temple, dilapidated as it may have been, was still there (1:4) and that the sacrificial system was in operation (2:14; *cp.* Zech. 7:1–7). Dr. Welch holds that Jerusalem was the spiritual center of both kingdoms through this period, and all we know of Hebrew history confirms this. Welch goes further, however, and maintains[11] that Nehemiah 10 contains the terms of a pact by which the religious life of the combined peoples was regulated. Apart from any judgment on this question all our sources indicate that from the days of Hezekiah there had been a *rapprochement* between Israel in the north and Judah. The dream of a re-united kingdom never died. This movement was furthered by Josiah, and there is no reason to think it would be interrupted more than temporarily by the events of 586 B.C. Rather it would be increased and strengthened as the remanent Jews and their brethren in the north felt the pressure of a common sorrow.

Of all this the later writer in Chronicles-Ezra-Nehemiah knows nothing. He proceeds on the assumption that the exiles who returned came back to rebuild the temple and set the religious cult on a sound and proper basis. The fidelity of the Jews who had carried on through the hard and difficult times succeeding the fall of the city and the loyalty of like-minded brethren in the north are passed by or, worse still, it is maligned and denied. Welch's volume may be regarded as in large part a vindication of "the forgotten man" in Judah and Israel in the period 586–538 B.C. These are the men who in a mean and hard time held fast to the faith of the fathers. The temple and the altar at Jerusalem, ruined as they were, formed the rallying point of all who held the true faith of Israel. When the day of release came it was to this temple that the exiles

[11] *Op. cit.,* pp. 69 ff.

returned, and to this temple Cyrus sent back the sacred vessels.

We have set forth this historical background at length because it is one of the dark periods of Hebrew history, and the background is essential to a proper understanding of the prophets of this period. These prophets are Haggai, Zechariah, and Malachi. Joel chaps 1 and 2, together with parts of Isaiah 56–66, are assigned by many scholars to this same period. Before we proceed to the study of these individual prophets it will be necessary to set forth some general features that distinguish them from the great pre-exilic prophets.

THE PROPHETS AND JUDAISM: THE RELIGIOUS BACKGROUND

There is something in these prophets which an observant reader cannot fail to note. It is the stress on ritual and the apparatus of worship. To Amos, Isaiah, and Jeremiah this was anathema: in their day the ethic of the thing done had taken the place of the ethic of the clean heart. Rites had supplanted right, and religiosity had displaced religion. Worship and wickedness were synonyms to the great prophets. Public morality was at its lowest ebb when the temple was thronged (Amos 5:21 ff.; Is. 1:10 ff.). But to those prophets the spirit was everything and the form nothing; now that seems to be reversed and increasing value is set upon the cult and the temple. No greater contrast could be imagined than that between the words of Jeremiah (chaps. 7, 26) or Amos (5:23) and the teaching of Haggai and Zechariah as they summon men to rebuild the temple and restore the ritual.

Perhaps the difference is not as great as we imagine. The post-exilic prophets would have agreed with Samuel and Hosea that obedience is better than sacrifice (1 Sam. 15:22; Hos. 6:6) but they would have hastened to add that *obedience is evidenced by a willingness to sacrifice*. It is not that they exalt the ritual above the moral: to them the ritual was the expression of the moral. There was, however, danger here, and what was latent in this attitude soon became patent. The living spirit of the prophets when poured into legal molds was to end in the deadwood of Pharisaism. For men will always find it easier to do than to be. Almost inevitably the ritual becomes an end in itself and moral and spiritual values recede into the background. The "tithing of anise and cummin" and the cleansing of "the outside of the platter" may come, as in the Gospel story (Matt. 23:23 ff.), to constitute the main part of religion. And with this comes a subtle change in men's thought of God wherein his sovereign will is lost to view, and they come to regard him as a partner in an agreement or bargain. Religion assumes the form of a *quid pro quo,* and righteousness is of works (Hag. 2:18; Zech. 6:15; 8:16 ff.; Mal. 3:7 ff.). Haggai, Zechariah, and Malachi stand near the source of this development, and their combination of the moral and ritual elements makes them highly significant in the history of Old Testament religion.

POINTS OF DIVERGENCE AND DEVELOPMENT

The divergence from the earlier prophets is revealed in the case of one or two main ideas. These ideas concern the Messianic age and the person of the Messiah. Zechariah seems to show a peculiar development of the idea of revelation, but as this is confined to Zechariah it need not occupy us here in the general view.

The Messianic hope is common to all the prophets and is implied by the Hebrew faith in the living God. But a difference arises here between the pre-exilic and post-exilic prophets. The earlier prophets had always represented this hope in the form of judgment and restoration: only after a searching and fearful purgation of the nation—or the world—could the new era appear. Amos, Isaiah, and Jeremiah are one in this view. But the later prophets occupied another standpoint. They saw the judgment already accomplished in the iron discipline of the Exile; Israel had "received of Jehovah's hand double for all her sins" (Is. 40:2), and the new and brighter day is breaking. The kingdom of God is at hand. To the earlier prophets that kingdom seemed afar off beyond the smoke and fire of judgment. Haggai, Zechariah, and Malachi feel themselves standing on the threshold of the blessed era.

For this reason we need not be surprised at what Sellin calls the "crass materialism" of this hope in the post-exilic prophets. It must not be forgotten that the Hebrew hope of salvation had always a large material element; this could not be otherwise where a clear view of immortality was lacking. The Hebrew did not normally pass beyond the world of time and sense in his thinking. Even the Christian hope for many people has a strong material element. But—and this is the point of divergence—the earlier prophets centered on the preceding judgment, and perforce emphasised moral and religious values more than the material elements of the subsequent salvation. In the post-exilic world of those later prophets the ideal took shape in thoughts of world empire and material riches (Hag. 2:7; Zech. 2:7 11; 8:20–23; Mal. 3:10 ff.), though they were not unmindful of the need of spiritual purgation and preparation (Zech. 1:1–6; 8:14 ff.).

THE MESSIAH

For a similar reason the form of the Messiah becomes more concrete and definite. The word becomes flesh and is incorporated in the person of Zerubbabel (Hag. 2:23; Zech. 6:9 ff.). Isaiah's dreams are realised (Is. 9, 11). It was perhaps inevitable that when the vision tarried too long men should seek to hasten the purpose of God. Hope deferred makes the heart sick, and prophecies unfulfilled gave rise to visionary apocalypticists, on one hand, or to men like the Zealots, on the other, who were willing to force the hand of God and bring about spiritual ends by physical means. There is an undue sense of urgency here that can only precipitate a crisis; Zerubbabel disappears we know not where or how. The Persian authorities were taking no risks and the scheme was nipped in the bud. The miscarriage of those plans made inevitable the appearance of another religious type in Israel, and Ezra and Nehemiah are the necessary sequel to the activities of these post-exilic prophets. The prophets had failed and another way must be tried.

ATTITUDE TO THE NATIONS

As to the future of the nations these prophets shared inherited ideas. Haggai appears to suggest that the nations will be destroyed and their wealth bestowed upon the temple at Jerusalem (Hag. 2:6, 22). The lofty missionary ideas expressed in Deutero-Isaiah find no echo in Haggai. Zechariah and Malachi reveal a more tolerant attitude, though in both cases it would seem that theoretical universalism exists side by side with an intense nationalism. But that is not peculiar to the post-exilic prophets; it occurs also in Isaiah and Jeremiah. Both Zechariah and Malachi could say *Amen* to the word that appears in Isaiah 2:1 ff. and Micah 4:1 ff., where nationalism and universalism are combined. But it is doubtful if either would, or could, appreciate such a word as Amos 9:7 or Micah 3:11. A study of the individual prophets will reveal the peculiar features of each.

LINKS IN A CHAIN

So far we have considered the background of religion from the negative side. But there were developments as well as divergences, and something positive emerged. Haggai and Zechariah and Malachi are links in a chain that extends from Zephaniah through Josiah and Ezekiel to Ezra and Nehemiah, and the final issue is the hard legalism that might be called the "Hard Church," the church without a heart that meets us in the Gospels. Davidson's word on this is justified; something that began well and meant well turned out very ill. Deuteronomy stimulated Pharisaism, and the ritual supplanted the moral.

Haggai is perhaps most significant here, and from him stems the later unlovely Judaism. This seems the fairest reading of the difficult oracle in Haggai 2:14, and both Sellin and Rothstein interpret it so, though Welch dissents strongly. Here we have the first appearance of that fierce national exclusiveness that was furthered by Ezra and Nehemiah and which finally culminated in the Samaritan schism. The words of Zechariah 7:1 ff. seem to express the same attitude as that of Haggai, and the feuds and hostilities that are reflected in Ezra and Nehemiah find their origin here.

Against this background of history and religion we can now proceed to an examination of these prophets.

14

HAGGAI: THE PROPHET AS REALIST

THERE are two prophets of the Restoration whose books stand side by side in the Old Testament. They function at the same time, and that time is most precisely determined by the dates affixed to their oracles. Something might be gained by dealing with both together, for they supplement each other in remarkable fashion. Here the idealist and the realist combine in a common service: the blueprints of the idealist Zechariah are executed and carried through by the practical ability and executive skill of the realist Haggai. Such combinations have frequently been very effective in the affairs of men, and one can readily recall similar associations in the case of Paul and Barnabas, Luther and Melanchthon, Calvin and Zwingli. But inasmuch as our purpose is to set forth the distinct personality and teaching of these separate prophets we will here deal with them separately.

HAGGAI THE MAN

Nothing definite is known about Haggai personally. Some have sought to infer from 2:10 ff. that he was a priest, but that passage would rather seem to indicate precisely the opposite. Nor is there any reason to think of him as a man advanced in years as some have imagined on the ground of 2:3 ff. In view of the energy displayed in the drive to rebuild the temple, we would imagine him to be a man in the prime of life; the qualities which he reveals are not usually found in old men. Finkelstein [1] speaks of him as "a militant nationalist," and

[1] Finkelstein, Louis, *The Pharisees*, 1938, p. 501.

both the vigor of his speech and the intensity of his practical activities are not inconsistent with such a description.

The name *Haggai* is rather strange in Hebrew and its origin is not clear. But names to the Hebrew usually had a very definite meaning and were not bestowed without thought. *Nomina sunt realia.* The most probable derivation of the name is from *haj,* which means dance or festival. If Haggai's nature is signified by this name, then we may well believe him to have been a man of fervent and exuberant spirit: the name would signify *the festive one*. He seems to have possessed the capacity to enthuse and inspire, and his fervent spirit proved a stimulus to his more lethargic colleagues, particularly those in authority. He has all the marks of an apostle of the strenuous life, and from his direct emphatic injunction,

> "Go ye up to the mountain and bring wood and build the house," (1:8)

we might get the impression of what someone once called "a steam-engine in trousers." Pfeiffer's [2] reference to Haggai's *single-track mind* need not derogate from Haggai's worth, for intensity is the mark of the Hebrew genius, and intensity means narrowly channeled force directed to a single end. Oesterley and Robinson's remark that "his mind was concentrated on earthly things," and B. C. Clausen's [3] striking title, "Haggai who said it with bricks," both confirm our impression that Haggai was a man with a remarkable genius for organisation and a capacity for getting things done.

THE BOOK OF HAGGAI

The book is small and consists of only thirty-eight verses. It appears to be a report of Haggai's oracles and not a direct record by the prophet himself. In this respect the book resembles that of Jonah. The reports given here would appear to be based on the prophet's own memoirs and there is no reason to doubt their authenticity.

[2] *Introduction to the Old Testament,* p. 607.
[3] Clausen, B. C., *Pen Portraits of the Prophets,* 1926, p. 135.

The book contains four separate oracles, 1:1–11; 2:1–9; 2:10–19; 2:20–23. The last two oracles were delivered on the same day. The first oracle contains the summons to rebuild, while the second offers encouragement to those who faltered in the sacred task because they felt their building could never equal that of the first temple. The third contains a reasoned exhortation based on an instruction of the priesthood as to clean and unclean. This is the most religiously significant of Haggai's oracles, and it has much to do with the growth and development of Judaism. The fourth oracle is the summons to Zerubbabel and reveals the strong realism of Haggai; here *he identifies Zerubbabel with the expected Messiah.*

The first oracle is dated "in the second year of Darius the king, in the sixth month in the first day of the month"; as the sixth month begins at the end of August we may date this oracle about September 1, 520 B.C. The second oracle will then fall on October 21, while the last two oracles were given on December 24, 520 B.C. In November of the same year Zechariah spoke his first word (Zech. 1:1–6). Within this brief period Haggai exercised his ministry as a prophet.

THE MESSAGE OF HAGGAI

All the words of Haggai have but one aim, and that aim is to bring about the rebuilding of the temple. To achieve that purpose Haggai uses the language of rebuke (1:1–10), encouragement (2:1–9) and exhortation (2:10 f.).

It is easy to depreciate the teaching of the prophet, and many would deny the presence of any spiritual message here. Oesterley and Robinson [4] seem unduly severe in their judgment:

> "His whole mental outlook and utilitarian religious point of view (see 1:9–11) is sufficient to show that he can have no place among the prophets in the real sense of the word."

[4] *Introduction to Books of the Old Testament*, p. 409.

But this seems to be an undue despising of the day of small things, and Haggai deserves better treatment than that. It is true that Haggai sounds no stirring call to repentance, and that his book contains no denunciation of social injustices such as is found in the earlier prophets and recurs in Zechariah and Malachi. There is nothing of the strong ethical and spiritual emphasis we find in the great prophets; there is only an absorbing concern with stone and timber for the temple. But it should not be forgotten that Haggai lived in a poor and mean time, and that he spoke to the circumstances of his day and to the folk who were enduring them. They had lost heart and a lethargy had descended upon their spirit. They had to be shaken out of this lethargy, and Haggai is the man to do it. He summons them to a collective effort that will take them out of themselves and give some meaning to their lives and a purpose to their national existence.

Doubtless there were progressives in that far-off time who had learned in Babylon that the temple was not essential to the service of God, and that the whole sacrificial system could be dispensed with. Jeremiah's letter to the exiles (Jer. 29) had exercised its influence, and men had come to know that the broken heart and the contrite spirit are the dwelling-place of God, and that these alone are his effective sacrifice (Ps. 51:17). But while all that may be true to some extent, and while choice spirits may find it possible to live in such a rarefied atmosphere of spirituality, ordinary men and women require that religion should have a local habitation and a name. For most people religion must be embodied, and that embodiment will take shape in wood and lime. That is how the plain man thinks of religion.

It is the merit of Haggai that he perceived this matter aright and that he knew that the material aids to religion which are required by plain folk must not be forgotten or overlooked by those who find their satisfaction in the pursuit of a spiritual ideal. Haggai saw that the nation could not prosper without a temple: a rallying point for the social and religious life of the people was required. History has vindicated the good sense and judgment of Haggai. His temple was more than a building where men could worship and sacrifice: it was the source and origin of sacramental power on which the whole life of Judaism was based. The temple was the visible evidence of God's presence and continuing grace, and plain folk need such "sensible signs."

Thus the prophet begins with a call to thought. "Consider your ways" (1:5, 7). "An unexamined life," says Plato, "is unworthy of a man." Evil is wrought from want of thought, and the times were evil. Haggai well knew that the fault

> is not in our stars,
> But in ourselves, that we are underlings.[5]

The fault was in the people themselves. The prophet is full of sense; he is a realist and looks at things as they really are. God's dwelling-place is still unrepaired, though the people have had time and money enough to build for themselves ceiled houses. This is not as it should be, and the lean harvests and bad times which they were now experiencing are evidence of their failure to consider. They have shown a strange lack of thought. For God uses Nature to proclaim his moral judgments, and the very facts which they adduce to excuse their remissness are shown by the prophet to be the result of their failure to discharge what should have been their first and main concern. They have failed in the business of life because they have failed in their duty to God. Again, "consider your ways." God's gospel may be hid in those sufferings and their present sorrows may be the roots of their future and most lasting joys. The building of the temple is the way back to success and prosperity. "Seek ye first the kingdom of God and his righteousness and all these things shall be added unto you" (Matt. 6:33). Haggai comes dangerously near to a doctrine of merit, and both in style and spirit he is closely akin to Malachi. But though all this savors of utilitarianism such arguments found

[5] Shakespeare, *Julius Caesar*.

ready entrance into the minds of the people, and with a right ready will they set themselves to the task. They were determined to command success. The work as it took shape seemed so poor and mean compared to the glory of the former temple, and those who had seen its former glory could not but lament the small proportions of the new edifice. Here there was no more the

> high embowèd roof
> With antique pillars massy-proof,
> And storied windows richly dight,
> Casting a dim religious light.[6]

Perhaps we make too much of the dim religious light, and men like Haggai are not impressed by it. "Hats off to the past: coats off to the future," is the cry of such ardent spirits. And in this respect he stands high in the order of God's encouragers. However small it may seem, the enterprise that is now taking shape will exceed in its final glory all that has gone before.

> "Yet now be strong, O Zerubbabel, saith Jehovah; and be strong, O Joshua, son of Jehozadak, the high priest; and be strong, all ye people of the land, saith Jehovah, and work: for I am with you, saith Jehovah of hosts, according to the word that I covenanted with you when ye came out of Egypt, and my spirit abode among you; fear ye not." (2:4, 5)

The present enterprise is linked to the mighty redemptive activity of God that first made Israel a nation, and this is the foundation of greater glory yet to be.

> "For thus saith Jehovah of hosts: Yet once, it is a little while, and I will shake the heavens, and the earth, and the sea and the dry land; and I will shake all nations, and the desirable things of all nations shall come, and I will fill this house with glory, saith Jehovah of hosts. The silver is mine, and the gold is mine, saith Jehovah of hosts. The latter glory of this house shall be greater than

[6] Milton, John, "Il Penseroso".

> the former, saith Jehovah of hosts, and in this place will I give peace, saith Jehovah of hosts." (2:6–8)

"The Messianic ideal built the second temple." So says H. Wheeler Robinson,[7] but the ideal would not have sufficed without the strong realist Haggai to make it assume visible form. The form in Haggai's second oracle is not too definite but in the last oracle (2:20–23) the Messiah is clearly identified with Zerubbabel, and the word becomes flesh.

> "In that day, saith Jehovah of hosts, will I take thee, O Zerubbabel, my servant, the son of Shealtiel, saith Jehovah, and will make thee a signet: for I have chosen thee, saith Jehovah of hosts."

Perhaps we might say there was too much of the flesh here and too little of the spirit, and the movement quickly came to nought. Some airy castles are not built by divine inspiration, and even a prophet may at times identify his own wishful thinking with the divine afflatus. The prophets, too, were not above making the mistake of identifying national and monarchical interests with the high purposes of the kingdom of God. Hosea (1:4; 8:4) does not hesitate to denounce the revolutions brought about by the earlier prophet Elisha. Time proves all things, and some things it wholly disproves, and sane men will examine themselves and "try the spirits." Exuberance and energy must be controlled by intelligence and insight.

Haggai had his limitations. Perhaps Finkelstein's epithet best suits the case—a militant nationalist. But it was precisely these qualities that were best fitted to preserve in a period of transition the heritage of Israel. If it be the case, as seems probable, that he took the most decisive step towards creating an exclusive community (2:10 ff.) we need not censure him too hardly. For only under this husk of exclusive Judaism could the precious kernel of Israel's faith be preserved, and out of this emerged in the fulness of the times the Christian Church.

[7] Robinson, H. Wheeler, *The History of Israel,* 1938, p. 147.

15

ZECHARIAH: THE PROPHET AS IDEALIST

CONCERNING Zechariah we have a little more information than was available for his contemporary Haggai. He is called *the son of Berechiah the son of Iddo* (1:1), but in Ezra 5:1 and 6:14 as also in Nehemiah 12:16 he is simply called *the son of Iddo.* It was possible for the Hebrew to use the term "son" as equal to grandson, and this may be what Ezra and Nehemiah have done. But there is reason to think that the name Berechiah has been inserted here in error, and that Zechariah was the son of Iddo. Zechariah was a priest and probably came up with the returning exiles from Babylon: Haggai seems to have been a member of the resident community at Jerusalem. As Zechariah is mentioned in Nehemiah 12:16 as a functioning priest in the restored community, we may infer that "he was a prophet in his twenties" (Sellin). Though his life seems thus to have been rather lengthy, his prophetic activity is confined to the years 520–518 B.C. His first oracle can be dated in November 520 and his last prophetic word is recorded under date December 518 B.C.

Where so little is known concerning the personality of the prophet the imagination may be allowed to range. Something, too, may be gathered from the background of the oracles. While Haggai impresses us with his bustling activity, Zechariah, as becomes a priest, would appear to be a profound student of Scripture, a man likely to see visions and dream dreams. We might not err in thinking of him as like Cassius, with "a lean and hungry look," who from much study and meditation is "sicklied o'er with the pale cast of thought." Haggai will handle the hammer and nails, but Zechariah will supply the blueprints of Utopia. The spiritual insight of the idealist will be wedded to the practical drive of the realist. Strangely enough neither prophet refers to the other in his oracles, though they could not have lived in the small community without knowledge of each other. One purpose occupied both men, and that purpose was to rebuild the temple and make Jerusalem the center of a new world.

THE BOOK OF ZECHARIAH

A critical question arises here. Some scholars contend that the whole book as we now have it is from the prophet Zechariah, but the weight of critical opinion is strongly against such a view. Only the first eight chapters may be regarded as from the hand of Zechariah, and chapters 9–14 constitute a later addition. These chapters we will examine later, and for our present purpose we shall treat Zechariah's book as *consisting only of the first eight chapters.*

With the exception of a few minor details the text is generally regarded as giving us the contents of the prophet's teaching. This consists, for the greater part, of a series of eight visions (1:7–6:8). These visions are all reported in the first person and they follow a uniform pattern. First comes an introduction, follows the vision and the prophet's question as to its meaning, and lastly the interpretation of the angel. The scheme would appear monotonous but Zechariah knows something of literary art and style, and with slight variations he saves his scheme from becoming monotonous.

The text in 6:10 has undergone alteration in view of historical developments, and most scholars agree that the crown was not offered to Joshua but to Zerubbabel (v. infra). The book may be difficult to interpret but it lends itself easily to analysis, and we may set forth briefly the contents of the book. The introduction (1:1–6) is dated November 520 B.C. and certifies Zechariah's commission as a prophet and calls upon the people to repent and return to God. The visions are all on one night and the report of them is given in chapters 1:7–6:8 The date is February 519 B.C.

(1) The four horsemen among the myrtle trees who report the earth is quiet and God's plans are ready (1:7–17)

(2) The four horns and the four smiths, signifying the oppressors of Judah and the punishment of them (1:18–21)

(3) The man with the measuring line, the vision of the city without walls, whose protection and glory is Jehovah (2:1–5)

(4) The vision of Joshua, the high priest, accused by Satan but upheld by God and vindicated against all charges (3:1–10)

(5) The seven-branched lampstand flanked by olive-trees, representing Zerubbabel and Joshua (4:1–6a; 10b–14)

(6) The flying scroll that spreads the divine curse upon all thieves and perjurers (5:1–4)

(7) The ephah and the woman, signifying the lifting away of all wickedness in Judah and its transportation to Babylon (5:5–11)

(8) The four chariots that bear God's wrath to the nations (6:1–8)

6:9–15 contains a word addressed to Joshua and contains instructions in regard to the crown or crowns; this will be discussed later.

7:1–7 gives directions as to the facts, while 7:8–14 contains a résumé of earlier prophetic teaching to which their fathers failed to pay heed and suffered for their disobedience. Chapter 8 contains a series of undated oracles, ten in number but usually reduced to three. 8:1–8 deals with the unfolding prospect, 8:9–17 contrasts the future with the past, while 8:18–23 foretells a season of joy and gladness that will succeed the present distress, and the Jew will be the envy of all because of his high privilege.

MESSAGE OF ZECHARIAH

There is a notable advance here beyond the thought of Haggai, and the teaching of Zechariah is noteworthy. Like Plato he moves in the realm of ideas, and like Moses he seeks to have all things formed "according to the pattern revealed in the Mount." Zechariah is the idealist and his ideas are theocratic. His aim is to establish the rule of God.

The moral and spiritual emphasis of the earlier prophets is strongly present here, but the tumult and turmoil of war are absent. Zechariah, as Finkelstein says, is a pacifist compared with the militant nationalist Haggai. The city of God that is to be built comes

> "not by might, nor by power, but by my Spirit, saith Jehovah of hosts." (4:6)

Three main elements are here, and these the prophet sets himself to realise. In the movement towards theocracy there must be a purified church, an anointed ruler, and a worthy people. With these main matters five of the visions are concerned, while the other three (first, second and eighth) deal with Israel's relation to the world.

Haggai's Messianic hopes had been stirred by the commotions in the Persian empire that followed the accession of Darius (522–486 B.C.). Like other subject powers Haggai seems to have thought that Judah could fish best in troubled waters. But while Zechariah shares the common hope he deprecates the methods of Haggai; not so comes God's kingdom. As Zechariah looks upon the scene in the first vision all seems quiet on the Eastern front. Darius has apparently succeeded in quelling the rebellious vassal states, and the convulsions of empire, from which Haggai expected so much, have ceased.

But God is neither sleeping nor dead: God is awake and his purposes are ripening fast, though in ways undreamed of by Haggai. God's hour is about to strike, and when that hour strikes God's man will appear. Let Israel hope in Jehovah.

> "So the angel that talked with me said unto me, Cry thou, saying, Thus saith Jehovah of hosts: I am jealous for Jerusalem and for Zion with a great jealousy. And I am very sore displeased with the nations that are at ease; for I was but little displeased, and they helped forward the affliction. Therefore thus saith Jehovah: I am returned to Jerusalem with mercies; my house shall be built in it, saith Jehovah of hosts, and a line shall be stretched forth over Jerusalem. Cry yet again, saying, thus saith Jehovah of hosts: my cities through prosperity shall yet be spread abroad; and Jehovah shall comfort Zion, and shall yet choose Jerusalem." (1:14–17)

The first word Haggai addressed to the depressed community was a word of rebuke; the first words of Zechariah were "good words, comfortable words" (1:13).

The second vision sets the stage for those succeeding. This also is a word of comfort; the nations that oppressed Israel and even now stand in the way of her reaching the theocratic goal are to be destroyed. All impediments to the achievement of the divine purpose shall be removed: the work of destruction precedes the construction that is to follow.

Thus the five succeeding visions are concerned with the new community. And first is the vision of the new Jerusalem, the city without walls, spreading itself village-wise upon the mountains (2:1–5). There is something full and expansive about this thought that has provoked the lyric epilogue that follows. Those prophets often builded better than they knew, though the insights they attained were fractured and broken. But here is the prophetic dream of peace and an ideal which a war-weary world might well try. Walls are divisive and separating, and all modern history shows that high walls lead only to high explosives, and that never in this way can we come by universal peace. Walls shut out and exclude, and walls shut in and breed nationalism and racial pride. The prophet will have Jerusalem an open city, open to the world, that its religious inspirations may flow forth to the ends of the earth, and that the ends of the earth may have free access to the city of God. The Christian church began with the throwing down of the exclusive wall of Judaism, and we are not going to make progress by erecting new walls of a nationalist kind. Here Zechariah is akin to Isaiah and Micah (Is. 2; Mic. 4), and here his universal viewpoint is clear.

> "And many nations shall join themselves to Jehovah in that day, and shall be my people: and I will dwell in the midst of thee . . . and Jehovah shall inherit Judah for his portion in the holy land, and shall yet choose Jerusalem." (2:11, 12)

Zechariah emphasises the prerogative of Judah in a way Amos would not have done, and we might say with Sellin that Zechariah is universalist only in theory. But, as already stated, that point could be made against most of the Hebrew prophets. Jeremiah was a Jerusalem man out-and-out, and Isaiah was no less so, yet none will deny the presence of universalism in their teaching. It may be that it is only the intense nationalist who can be a real internationalist. For patriotism begins at the center and grows outward to the circumference till in its final issue it embraces the whole world. The tragedy of what we call nationalism is that patriotism there suffers from arrested growth. Zechariah will not say, "My country, right or wrong, my country." He would have us rather cease saying, "My country against your country," and learn to say, "My country *with* your country for the good of the whole world." Instead of high walls and vertical divisions between nations we must set horizontal lines and international co-operation.

Zechariah may seem at times to come close to the danger of identifying the church with the kingdom of God, but we need not find fault with his thought of the purified church which is essential to the spiritual growth of the community. Haggai construed this too much in terms of ritual, and Zechariah has much of the same teaching. His ideal tends towards sacramentalism. But the vision of Joshua accused by the Satan (3:1–5) contains the essentially evangelical thought that God is a forgiving God, and that plenteous mercy is found in him. Joshua, moreover, is the representative of the nation, and the forgiving grace given to him is bestowed upon the people. Here Zechariah's thought of God is rich and tender. But forgiveness is based on moral considerations: it is ethical through and through.

> "If thou wilt walk in my ways, and if thou wilt keep my charge, then thou also shalt judge my house, and shalt also keep my courts, and I will give thee a place of access among those that stand by. . . . In that day, saith Jehovah of hosts, ye shall call every man his neighbor under the vine and under the fig tree." (3:7,10)

With the purified church goes the anointed ruler, and to both Haggai and Zechariah the Messiah or "Branch" is a scion of the royal house of David. But Zechariah goes a step further than Haggai and gives to the thought a new and strange turn. In this he is debtor to Ezekiel, who had sought to combine the hierarchical and monarchical ideas in a novel combination. We have here again the dangerous doctrine of "the two swords," a secular and an ecclesiastical ruler. Here is the problem of church and state, and Zechariah offers the solution of dual heads. But all history bears witness to the difficulties involved in such a scheme, and Zechariah's plan was soon found to be impracticable. The disappearance of Zerubbabel left the way clear for the growth and development of the hierarchy, and this we find in later Judaism.

It is unfortunate that the text of 6:9 ff. has been corrupted. As already indicated, most scholars are agreed that the crown mentioned here was to be set on the head of Zerubbabel, but in view of later events the name of the high priest was substituted for that of Zerubbabel. The text may be reconstructed with the aid of the Greek version, and would seem to have read thus:

> "Behold the man whose name is the Branch . . . and he shall build the temple of Jehovah, and he shall bear the glory and rule upon his throne; and Joshua shall be priest at his right hand, and there shall be counsel of peace between them both." (6:12, 13)

This might seem an ideal arrangement and conceivably it might find place in a heavenly scheme of things, but ideals have a way of becoming shattered on the hard facts of human nature and human history. The Persians, being less than heavenly-minded men, did not like the look of all this, and Zerubbabel disappeared. We know nothing as to the "manner of his taking-off," but he vanishes from the scene. Zechariah, like Plato, had given his ideal form of government.

In sequence with the foregoing is the thought of a worthy people, a nation whose God is Jehovah. Here the prophet emphasises those moral and spiritual demands that had formed the burden of the great prophets. This emphasis is conspicuous in all the teaching of Zechariah, though it is wholly absent from Haggai. The vision of the flying scroll (5:1–4) and of Madame Wickedness (5:5–11) carried off in a barrel to Babylonia to "be set there in her own place" may seem somewhat mechanical and bizarre. It is not a very long way from these sacramental conceptions to the elaborate ritual of the Day of Atonement (Lev. 16); Zechariah may speak as a prophet but his speech betrays him for a priest. Perhaps we should not scrutinise the contents of the visions too closely, and despite their strange language and symbolism there can be no mistaking Zechariah's profound ethical interest. Such admonitions abound throughout the book. He will not suffer men to stray for lack of moral [and spiritual] instruction.

> "These are the things that ye shall do; Speak ye every man the truth with his neighbor; execute the judgment of truth and peace in your gates: and let none of you imagine evil in your heart against his brother: and love

> no false oath: for all these things I hate, saith Jehovah." (8:16, 17)

Zechariah knows his God and understands as well as Amos or Isaiah what God requires of man. He is clear, too, on the point that a great un-sinning process and purification must precede the coming of the kingdom. Only people who are worthy can inherit the kingdom of God.

But when all things are ready it comes. Thus the last vision (6:1–8) returns to Judah's relation to the world. The four winds are ready to go forth bearing the wrath of God to the nations.

> "Behold, they that go toward the north country have quieted my spirit (i.e. have assuaged my anger) in the north country." (6:8)

The anti-theocratic forces are overcome and he will reign whose right it is to reign.

The final issue will be Jerusalem the joy of all the earth—here speaks the nationalist—and all the nations, fascinated by her beauty and grace, will seek to share her high privilege. Zechariah's last word is universalism.

> "Thus saith Jehovah of hosts: In those days it shall come to pass that ten men, out of all the languages of the nations, shall take hold of the skirt of him that is a Jew, saying, We will go with you, for we have heard that God is with you." (8:23)

16

ZECHARIAH: CHAPTERS 9-14

THESE six chapters raise a literary problem of considerable complexity, and inasmuch as the spiritual message is rather scanty we may devote attention here to the question of literary criticism.

There are three separate oracles or little groups of oracles appended to Zechariah 1–8. Each of these begins with the unusual phrase, "oracle (Heb. *massa'*) of the word of Jehovah," and this expression occurs at 9:1, 12:1, and Malachi 1:1. In the last instance we have a separate little book ascribed in error to a presumed author named Malachi. Malachi is Hebrew for "my messenger" and occurs in this form (Mal. 3:1), but it was later taken in error to be a proper name. But the book of Malachi is anonymous, as are also the two preceding sections introduced by the same formula. On a first view it might seem reasonable to believe that here we have a group of loose floating oracles that were finally attached to the roll that concluded with Zechariah 1–8. In one manuscript (Kennicott 195) there appears to be a gap or blank space between Zechariah 1–8 and Zechariah 9–14, and this, with other considerations, might lead to the inference that they did not belong originally there. Zechariah 11:12, 13 is cited in Matthew 27:9 but it is cited as from Jeremiah, and this is noteworthy, for it was the observance of the fact that the quotation was attributed to Jeremiah that led to the fuller and later literary criticism of Zechariah. It is noteworthy, too, in this connection that a passage from Deutero-Isaiah is cited in II Chronicles 36:22 ff. and attributed to Jeremiah. That may be a slip on the part of the writer of II Chronicles but there is also the possibility that Isaiah 40–66 was once attached to the roll on which Jeremiah was written. In any case it was Matthew's quotation of Zechariah 11:12, 13 and its assignment to Jeremiah that first set Joseph Mede[1] (died 1638) to question the Jewish tradition:

> "Nay, indeed, there is reason to suspect that the Holy Spirit (through Matthew) desired to claim these three chapters, 9, 10, 11, for their real author. For there are a great many things in them which if one carefully consider them, seem not to suit the time of Zechariah as well as that of Jeremiah."

As to what things might suit the time of Jeremiah better than the time of Zechariah we need not be in doubt. Thus when we look at chapters 9–11, together with chapter 13:7–9, which seems to have been displaced from its original position after 11:17, we observe that there are features here which suggest a pre-exilic date. The kingdom of the ten tribes is referred to as still in existence (9:10; 11:14), Assyria and Egypt are named together (10:10, 11), and diviners are mentioned as active in the religious sphere (10:1 ff.). The nations threatened in 9:1–7 are familiar to us from Amos (Amos 1:3, 6, 9) and Gaza still seems to be ruled by a king (9:5). All these references constrained earlier critics to assign these prophecies to a period even earlier than Jeremiah, and the writer was regarded as contemporary with Isaiah of Jerusalem towards the close of the eighth century B.C.

But there are equally clear references in these oracles to a post-exilic period, and these references are so woven into the general scheme of the text that they cannot be regarded as later additions. 9:11 ff. and 10:6–9 clearly presuppose the captivity of the northern kingdom (722 B.C.), while in 9:13 the Greeks are spoken of not as a distant unknown people but as a world power and as Israel's most aggressive enemy. This

[1] Cited from the *International Critical Commentary* volume, *Haggai, Zechariah, Malachi, Jonah,* p. 232.

could not be before 333 B.C., and to this period, or later, almost all scholars now assign these oracles. The signs and evidences of pre-exilic date may be explained by the writer's use of old material, or more probably the writer is writing in the style of Daniel and Enoch and veiling his meanings. The terms *Ephraim* and *the house of Joseph* will thus be symbols denoting the component parts of the Messianic kingdom. Assyria likewise is used in a broad general sense to describe the foe from the north, whether that foe be Alexander himself or the Seleucidae who divided his empire. Herodotus informs us that "the people whom the Greeks call Syrians are called Assyrians by the barbarians" [2] and to the Greeks the Jews were barbarians.

It should be noted also how far the conditions reflected in these six chapters differ from those in Zechariah 1–8. In the latter the main concern is the rebuilding of the temple, the consolidation of the hierarchy and the institution of Zerubbabel as Messianic ruler. Everything there is dated precisely and there is a feeling of sobriety in those first eight chapters. But it is altogether different in chapters 9–14. The whole picture of the Messianic age is different and the national prospects and outlook are wholly other than in 1–8. There it was peace and security (1:17–21; 2:9–11; 3:10; 8:3–8, 12), but here all is war and tumult, rapine and plunder (14:2), and only after all those Messianic woes will salvation dawn for Israel (14:6 ff.). Of all this a cautious and sane critic such as S. R. Driver writes:

> "The author of chapters 1–8 uses a different phraseology, evinces different interests, and moves in a different circle of ideas from those which prevail in chapters 9–14." [3]

The internal evidence and the contents confirm the separation of chapters 1–8 from 9–14.

So far we have reached the conclusion that these six

[2] *Histories,* 7:63.

[3] Driver, S. R., *Introduction to the Old Testament,* 8th edition, 1909, p. 354.

chapters are not by the same writer as that of chapters 1–8, and that those chapters reflect the historical background of the Greek period or later. This is the practically unanimous verdict of modern scholarship, but the unanimity is broken when we come to consider whether these six chapters constitute a unity in themselves or whether we have within these chapters evidence of separate writers.

IS 9–14 A UNITY?

The introductory formula in 9:1 and 12:1 might well suggest that here we have separate oracles and might suggest two different authors. Thus some scholars speak of Deutero-Zechariah and Trito-Zechariah. Others, again, would divide these chapters into a group of several unconnected oracles, but this seems unnecessary. Chapters 9:1–11:17 plus 13:7–9 reveal an obvious connection of thought, and though 11:4–16 is in prose while the rest of this section is in poetical form there is no reason to deny the section to one writer. Chapter 12:1–13:6, together with chapter 14, in form mingled prose and poetry, may well be a unity, for there is a continuous development of thought here. But the thought in this section differs from the thought in the section 9–11 plus 13:7–9. The last three chapters make no mention of the northern kingdom, and the shepherds who appear so prominently in chapters 10 and 11 do not appear in chapters 12–14. The difference, however, need not be considered great enough to warrant the predication of two authors, and many scholars hold to unity of authorship. Those who claim two separate writers would date both about the same time. Stade and Sellin hold one writer is responsible for the whole work, and Eissfeldt is inclined to the same opinion, though certainty may not be claimed here.

As to the date of the oracles Stade [4] in his searching examination of the documents would date the oracles in chapters

[4] *Zeitschrift für alttestamentliche Wissenschaft,* 1882, pp. 293 ff.

9–14 somewhere in the earlier years of the Greek period and suggests a time between 306–278 B.C.[5] In this he has been followed by many such eminent scholars as Cheyne, Wildeboer, Cornill and Staerk. There are good reasons for holding to such a date, but unfortunately we know very little of the history of this period. Much more is known concerning the succeeding period, the Maccabean age, and the reference in Zechariah 11:8 to three shepherds cut off in one month finds more than one fairly satisfying interpretation in the events of that stormy period. Various identifications of the three bad shepherds and the good shepherd have been made by both Sellin and Duhm and others. But there is a certain doubt about all such identifications and it is very questionable whether we can carry the date down to 150 B.C. or even later (Duhm). Pfeiffer objects to such a dating on the ground that the prophetic canon was closed about 200 B.C. but perhaps that objection is not as strong as Pfeiffer thinks. Canonisation was not completed until about 90 A.D. and additions might be made to the end of the roll even after 200 B.C. Driver is of opinion that if the date is as late as that suggested we should have expected a different Hebrew style. But the Hebrew *literati* of the late period were quite capable of writing classical Hebrew, and many of the psalms bear witness to that fact. Pfeiffer[6] himself regards Psalm 2 as an acrostic psalm written to commemorate the marriage of Alexander Jannaeus in the year 103 B.C. and there is no fault to be found with its Hebrew.

On a review of the evidence it seems most reasonable to hold to the date suggested by Stade, although the scantiness of the historical material does not permit us to identify the figures referred to in the text.

THE MESSAGE OF ZECHARIAH 9–14

These oracles probably represent prophecy at its lowest ebb, and one need not look for any lofty message here. There

[5] *Ibid.*, pp. 461 ff.

[6] *Introduction to the Old Testament*, p. 630.

is little that is ethical and much that appears unethical; the comparative sobriety that characterised Zechariah ben-Iddo here gives place to an extravagance of feeling that is characteristic of Apocalypse; the pessimism and ruthless cruelty that figure in the latter form of writing abound here. Prof. Edward Robinson aptly remarks:

> "To pass from chapters 1–8 to chapters 9–14 is to pass suddenly from the calm of a summer's evening to the inclemency of a winter afternoon." [7]

The words of 13:7 might be taken as the keyword of Deutero-Zechariah, "Awake, O sword." The ruthless cruelty, which Charles calls a mark of Apocalyptic, is here in full measure. At times this develops to something like savagery: "And they shall drink their blood as wine" (9:15). In 13:1 we see how the ritual has triumphed over the moral, while 13:3 shows the complete discrediting of prophecy. Strange it is that prophecy, the noblest fruitage of the Hebrew genius, should perish so ignobly. Only one passage worth mentioning meets us in these chapters, and it is like meeting a fine quotation from the Bible on the pages of the yellow press. We may close with this passage.

> Rejoice greatly, O daughter of Zion
> Shout aloud, O Jerusalem:
> Behold, thy king cometh unto thee!
> Righteous and victorious shall he be,
> And humble too, riding upon an ass,
> And upon a colt, the foal of an ass.
> He will clear away from Ephraim the chariots
> And all horses from Jerusalem;
> The battle bow shall be cut off.
> He will ordain peace for the nations,
> He shall rule from sea to sea,
> From the Euphrates to the ends of the earth. (9:9, 10)

[7] *The Speaker's Bible, Minor Prophets,* 1930, p. 182.

17

MALACHI: MESSENGER OF GOD

THE prophet who stands last in the Old Testament is named Malachi, but Malachi is not a proper name. Malachi is a Hebrew word meaning "my messenger," as we have seen in the previous chapter, and it occurs in this form in chapter 3:1, "Behold, I send my messenger (malachi)." A later interpreter misunderstood the meaning here and treated the word as a proper name, and this now stands as the title of the book. George Adam Smith [1] suggests that

> "the prophet . . . writing from the midst of a poor and persecuted group of people, and attacking the authorities both of church and state, preferred to publish his charge anonymously. His name was in *the Lord's own book of remembrance*" (Mal. 3:16).

This, however, seems improbable, for the prophet was hardly likely to remain hid in such a small community, and his words would not have had any weight unless they were recognised to be those of a known prophet. Malachi was the messenger of God to the people of his own time, and as such he was known and recognised.

The absence of a definite name in this instance, as in many others, has led to various conjectures. The Jewish Targum reads in verse 1, "by the hand of my messenger (or angel) who is called Ezra the scribe," while the Greek version reads,

[1] *Book of the Twelve Prophets,* Vol. II, p. 345.

"by the hand of his messenger." Jerome ascribed the book to Ezra, while other traditions attribute it to Zerubbabel or Nehemiah. Others, again, refer to Malachi as a Levite and member of the "Great Synagogue." In the absence of definite knowledge such traditions rise and flourish, but no weight can be attributed to them.

That we have here a true prophet and an heir of the genuine prophetic inheritance will become obvious as we consider this little book. For while there is here something that might suggest Ezra there is also something here that suggests one of larger understanding and deeper insight than "the ready scribe in the Law of Moses which Jehovah the God of Israel had given" (Ezra 7:6). Malachi stands last in the canon of the prophets, but his significance is not least, and some extraordinary insights will be found here.

THE BOOK AND ITS DATE

With the exception of a few additions or glosses the book is regarded by most scholars as a unity. Chapters 2:11, 12 are regarded by many as an intrusion, while 4:5, 6 (Hebrew text 3:23, 24) is generally regarded as a late addition. Sellin holds 1:2–5 to have been accidentally severed from 3:6–11, but while such dislocations did occur in manuscripts there is no real reason to think we have one such here. With these minor exceptions we may regard the book as authentic.

Concerning the date of the book we cannot speak as definitely as in the case of Haggai and Zechariah. Dr. Welch,[2] in his recent work on post-exilic Judaism, has suggested a new reading of the history of this period, and has interpreted the documents in a somewhat revolutionary way. As a result of his examination he would date Malachi before Haggai and Zechariah. His argument is sustained with considerable weight of evidence but it is not sufficient to carry conviction. It still seems most reasonable to assign Malachi to the period subsequent

[2] *Post-Exilic Judaism*, p. 113.

to Haggai and Zechariah, for Malachi in his book appears to indicate a situation that has developed since their time. The point from which we start in our search for a date must be after 518 B.C., and as Malachi is generally recognised to have written before the time of Nehemiah the lower limit in dating will be 458 B.C. If we accept the recent reconstruction of the history which sets Nehemiah before Ezra and holds that Ezra came in the seventh year of Artaxerxes II (397 B.C.), then Nehemiah will have made his first visit in 444 B.C. and his second visit in 432 B.C. On the traditional reading of the history Ezra came to Jerusalem in 458 B.C. and thus preceded Nehemiah; this interpretation would appear to be due to the priestly editors who desired to give the precedence to the scribe. For our present purpose it does not greatly matter which interpretation of the sequence of events is taken. Malachi does not reflect the situation that confronts us in the books of Ezra and Nehemiah; he is earlier than both of these.

For it is to be noted that Malachi is quite familiar with Deuteronomy but does not reveal any knowledge of the legislation of the Priestly Code which is plainly assumed in Ezra and Nehemiah. Malachi's language is strongly reminiscent of Deuteronomy, and if in regard to tithes (3:10 ff.) he differs from Deuteronomy and suggests the later legislation, that may be explained by the fact that he is living in the period between these two bodies of legislation. The ritual was in process of development; it had not yet reached the final fixed form given to it in the Priestly Code.

Malachi, like Deuteronomy, does not draw any distinctions between priests and Levites: he regards both as possessing equal dignity (2:4; 3:3). Moreover the times in which he writes suggest a period of decline, and a spirit of scepticism pervades the land. The times have deteriorated since the days of Haggai and Zechariah, and even good folk were being assailed with harassing doubts. "There come times," says John Buchan,

"when a nation seems to move from the sun into the twi-

> light, when the free ardor of youth is crippled by hesitations, when the eyes turn inwards, and instinct gives place to questioning." [3]

Malachi lived in such a time. It was the winter of Israel's discontent, and the period seems to reflect a spiritual famine in the land. The destruction of Edom by the Nabateans, suggested by 1:4, can hardly be assigned to a date earlier than 500 B.C. Fleming James [4] would date the book (though with a mark of interrogation) about that time, but it seems wiser to descend a decade or two more and place it around 470 B.C. The circumstances of that period correspond most closely to those set forth in the book of Malachi.

STYLE OF MALACHI

An attentive reader of the book cannot fail to observe that we have here something new in the way of literary style. Here we are presented with a literary artifice that reminds us strongly of Socrates, and G. L. Robinson refers to the prophet as "the Hebrew Socrates." This is the style that became current among the Rabbis and is common to the Talmud. On this point Sellin makes the observation:

> "The last hour of the immediate spirit-inspired prophetic word has struck, and the hour of the synagogue lecturer has come." [5]

Though it has not pleased God to save the world by dialectic this now became the fashion in Judaism, and Malachi stands forth as the forerunner of scholastic Rabbinism.

The new style is simple enough and is used with striking effect. The prophet first states the truth which he desires to teach, then comes the objection which it is supposed to provoke, and finally the prophet's reply which restates and substantiates the original proposition.

[3] *Life of Montrose*, p. 15.
[4] James Fleming, *Personalities of the Old Testament,* 1939, p. 413.
[5] *Kommentar zum Alten Testament,* p. 587.

I have loved you, saith Jehovah.
But ye say, wherein hast thou loved us?
Was not Esau Jacob's brother, saith Jehovah?
Yet I loved Jacob but Esau I hated,
And made his mountains a desolation,
And gave his heritage to jackals of the wild. (1:2, 3)

The argument itself need not concern us here, but the form is typical. There are no less than seven such formal arguments in the book's fifty-five verses, and the phrase "but ye say" occurs eight times (1:2, 6, 7; 2:14, 17; 3:7, 8, 13).

THE RELIGIOUS SIGNIFICANCE OF MALACHI

Though this book is small it signifies much, for with the doubtful exception of Joel (chaps. 1–2) this is the only document[6] that illuminates the religious life of a period which is largely dark so far as historical records are concerned, that is, the period of half a century that follows Haggai and Zechariah. In our study of these prophets we observed how the Jewish nation tended more and more to become "the people of the book," and how increasing stress was laid upon ritual and the right observance of ordinances. Ecclesiastical mechanism began to displace prophetic inspiration and the static supplanted the dynamic. Of course the prophetic ideals had to be translated into life, and both priest and scribe played a worthwhile role in this matter. The difference between prophet and priest is often exaggerated,[7] and it is forgotten or overlooked that the prophet might at times exercise the priestly office (e.g. Hosea, Ezekiel, Zechariah, and perhaps Jeremiah). But there was an ever-present danger here, and later history showed how those two interests could be divorced and separated. It is the merit of those post-exilic prophets that they sought to weld the moral and the ritual in an indissoluble

[6] Parts of Isaiah 55–65 may originate in this period.
[7] Dr. A. C. Welch has dealt with this point in *Prophet and Priest in Old Israel*, 1936.

bond. Thus George Adam Smith can refer to Malachi as "Prophecy within the Law," which was a living thing totally different from prophecy under the Law, where later the prophetic spirit is completely asphyxiated by legalism and intellectualism. That stage was not yet reached but in Malachi's time it was clearly coming into view. The faint outlines of the unlovely religious life that meets us in the pages of the New Testament can be perceived: the great river that flows to the sea has its source and origin far away in tiny upland rills and streams.

Nevertheless it would be unfair to dismiss these prophets as mere formalists whose main interest is the correct performance of a church service or the proper discharge of an ecclesiastical rite. Most of all in the case of Malachi is this caution necessary. He stands in spirit too close to the warm glowing spirituality of Deuteronomy to become wholly absorbed in ritual. Sacrifices and tithes are important to Malachi but only because they are the outward index of a right inner spirit. Because there is a fundamental lack of reverence toward God (1:12), and because his people refuse the divine grace (3:7), things have gone wrong in the community and distress prevails.

Thus we need not feel surprise at some statements of the prophet, for these reveal the true prophetic spirit and are far from arid legalism. We will find in Malachi insights that exceed anything found in the prophetic literature, insights so startling that commentators have sought to set them aside as impossible in Malachi's time or compatible with Malachi's own thought. Such passages are 1:11 with its universal outlook and 2:11 ff. with its high doctrine of marriage. These we shall examine presently in our consideration of his teaching. The significance of these great words cannot be overestimated.

One last remark may be made here concerning the religious significance of Malachi. In his thought of judgment he seems to confine its scope and range to Judah; that is not the general view of Judaism, and it is worlds away from the viewpoint of Joel.

THE TEACHING OF MALACHI

The teaching of Malachi is very practical, as we might expect from one who was faced with a bewildered people asking many questions. His words are addressed to three separate groups: (a) the people as a whole, (b) the priests as spiritual leaders, (c) the doubting saints. The addresses were probably delivered at various times, but there is a close connection between the sections.

Malachi begins with a statement as to the fundamental principles of Hebrew religion (1:1–5), which we have cited earlier as an example of the prophet's literary style. God loves: he is gracious and abundant in mercy. This might be substantiated by a review of national history, or even by the story of the Restoration, wherein the divine grace had been so signally and recently revealed. But Malachi does not choose any of these instances. He sees rather the divine love revealed in the destruction of Judah's inveterate foe, Edom. This may seem to us an ugly feature in the prophet's message, but Malachi spoke the language of his time and used an argument which his contemporaries could understand. Might we not see the love of God revealed in the defeat of our enemies? What Malachi says here is that God's purpose of election still stands, and that it is being substantiated by the events of history. Israel may have lost sight of the divine purpose, but it could not be obscured for ever. Israel was called because she had something that Edom had not; there is no need to read into the passage any excess of nationalistic feeling and reduce the prophet to a jingo or equate him with the hundred-per-center.

But Malachi will emphasise more than the love of God. The divine love is holy love, and it is precisely the divine holiness and majesty that have been forgotten by the people.

"A son honors his father, and a slave his master:
If I am a father, where is my honor?
And if I am a master, where is my fear?" (1:6)

This is addressed to the priests who should have been the

spiritual leaders of men. But it was "like priest, like people," and all was on a very low level. Because they had low ideas of God and his requirements there was confusion in human relationships and defective social adjustments. One thing leads to another, and it is easy to follow the development of thought here.

We are far removed from the thought of fatherhood as the Hebrew understood that thought. We have put into this thought a great deal of slushy sentimentality which is foreign to the thought of the Old Testament. The Hebrew thought on this was vigorous and stern. The first thought about a father was

Honor thy father and thy mother,

and the fundamental mood of the Hebrew in relation to God as father was a mood of profound reverence and awe. The word *father* summons to his mind thoughts of majesty and exaltedness. A Hebrew father had power of life and death over his children, and he ruled his home with a rod of iron. All the Roman *patria potestas* is here and more, and that is how Malachi thinks. The New Testament may contain larger elements but it did not drop these older elements, and Malachi will teach us to remember that there is nothing of slushy sentiment in the Bible thought of the divine fatherhood.

A SURPRISING INSIGHT

Because men thought more of the governor and the king than of Him by whom kings reign and princes decree justice they thought to fool God and get away with it. Worship became fraudulent and insincere; the lie entered the soul and it was so because the priests did not know their proper business. Nor did they know the real character of the God whom they presumed to serve. And now, as in the days of Amos, outsiders will be called upon to behold the shocking immoralities of Israel and to utter condemnation. Those heathen in their blindness put Israel to shame and it were better far that the temple should be closed altogether than that this ghastly thing should continue.

"O that there were among you that would shut the doors, that ye might not kindle fire on mine altar in vain!
I have no pleasure in you, saith Jehovah of hosts,
Neither will I accept an offering at your hands.
For from the rising of the sun to the going-down of the same my name is glorified among the Gentiles, and in every place incense is offered to my name, and a pure offering.
For my name is glorified among the Gentiles." (1:10, 11)

This surprising insight was too much for the men of King James, who gave us the Authorised Version of the Bible (1611), and they translated the tenses as future and read "will be glorified." But the tense refers to the present. Horst rejects the verse as a late interpolation and holds Malachi was too nationalistic to harbor or express such an expansive thought. Others have taken the reference to be to the Jews living in the Dispersion. But there is no need to resort to such interpretations. The passage means just what is says and must be received as it stands. We have here a large-hearted tolerance and a universalist view such as is seldom found in the Old Testament. The closest parallel is found in John 4:21 ff. and Acts 10:35.

There need be no difficulty in accepting the verse, for seemingly illogical and inconsistent ideas often come into the human mind. Isaiah has a similar combination of nationalism and universalism, and Jeremiah is likewise. Those great insights of the Old Testament prophets were never wholly mastered by their recipients and the full content could only be expounded by their successors. We need not deny those visitations of the inspiring and illuminating spirit to the prophets, but we do need to revise our own ideas of what may be possible in the sphere of divine revelation.

This sense of true religion and worship of the great God by, e.g., the devoted worshipers of Ahura Mazda reveals a breadth of understanding sympathy that is quite unusual in the Old Testament. It is the same prophetic insight as is found later in the book of Jonah, but it was not the common possession of Judaism.

A MIRROR FOR MINISTERS

Poor and slovenly ideas of worship are bound to follow from inadequate ideas of God, and it is these poor ideas that Malachi sets himself to correct and improve. That improvement can come only when the priesthood is lifted to a higher level through a fuller conception of God and a stern new conscience in the discharge of its ministry. And to that new conscience, born of a proper understanding of God and the divine demands that the prophet call those priests in words which reveal an adequate ideal for the ministry in any or every age.

"For the priest's lips should keep knowledge,
And men should seek direction at his mouth,
For he is the messenger (angel) of Jehovah of hosts." (2:7)

An uneducated ministry can only bring about a general lack of vitality in the national religious life. Where the spirit of consecration is absent the word of God will have no effect.

This weakening of the religious life is immediately apparent, for it has serious social repercussions. Where the altar is unclean life suffers, and the result is a lowered morale. A wrong view of God and a false and fraudulent form of worship lead to confusion and turmoil in society. The prophet here centers on the question of marriage and divorce, for these were burning questions in his time. The loyalty and conscience that were lacking in the fundamental relation to God are revealed in a false and fraudulent attitude to one of the most fundamental institutions of human life—Marriage.

MALACHI'S HIGH DOCTRINE OF MARRIAGE

It is not precisely clear what was happening in the community but it was something that merited and received the heavy censure of the prophet. Whether it was only the returned exiles (thus Welch) or the general population (as generally assumed), and whether it was Jewish wives or Gentile wives that were being divorced is not quite clear. The most probable interpretation would seem to be that the people in general were putting material things before moral considerations and were ready to compromise the faith of the fathers for temporal advantage. This, moreover, they were doing in a fashion that wrought great suffering on the defenceless class, the women and children. It must have appeared a gain to the returning exiles to ally themselves with those who occupied the land and had acquired social standing through their material possessions. They may have been mongrel Samaritans who had been imported into Israel after the fall of Samaria in 722 B.C., or they may have been from the peoples round about, including Edom, who had insinuated themselves into the choicer lands after the fall of Jerusalem in 586 B.C. They may have been descendants of those inferior groups who were left behind when the best of the folk were carried to Babylon. These, according to Jeremiah, were "a basket of very bad figs, which could not be eaten, they were so bad" (Jer. 24:2). It was with those varied groups the returned exiles had to make adjustments and it was no easy matter. But to achieve their aim they were willing to abandon and divorce their legitimate wives. This step may have been demanded by those with whom they sought alliance, or it may have been spontaneous action on the part of the exiles. But it was wrong, and it wrought great harm. There is no sadder sight in the East than that of the cast-off wife.

The prophet does not argue here (2:10-16) on economic grounds but lifts the discussion to the highest level. He deals with it in the light of religious principle. Here, as already indicated, he speaks a large and noble word that has no parallel in the Old Testament. The text is obscure and verses 11, 12 seem to be a later addition. To the prophet marriage is something that must be entered into "in the fear of the Lord."

It is a divine ordinance and covenant that binds a man to his wife, and that covenant is no less sacred and indissoluble than the covenant that binds man to God. This is indeed high doctrine, and it finds its closest parallel in Paul's word in Ephesians 5:28 ff. The text may be translated thus:

> Did not One (i.e. God) make us and preserve our spirit alive?
> And what does the One require? a godly seed!
> Therefore give heed to your spirit and let none deal faithlessly with the wife of his youth.
> For I hate divorce, saith Jehovah the God of Israel.
> (2:15, 16)

How far in advance of his time Malachi really was in this view may be gathered from the rendering of verse 16 in the Jewish Targum:

> If thou hatest her, send her away.

The Targum has turned Malachi's absolute prohibition into a permission of divorce, and the Greek version stumbled in the same way. Such a doctrine was too high for common folk, and the hardness of men's hearts led to the confusing and corrupting of the text.

EDIFYING THE SAINTS

Malachi understood the business of preaching and knew well that it is the preacher's business not only to convert sinners but to edify the saints. These have to be built up in faith and spiritual stature. The times were sadly out of joint, and even good people were beginning to wonder whether religion was worthwhile. According to the general thought of the Old Testament there should be a certain correspondence between a man's inward piety and his outward prosperity. Men believed in a piety that was rewarded by God in material form. Such a belief was logical enough, for a righteous God in heaven will not permit moral anomalies on earth, and the Old Testament did not have the distant prospect of the New. The facts of life were causing people to doubt, and the saints were forced to a mood of interrogation that cried "My God, my God, why?" The problem that finds its classical expression in the book of Job is here: men are beginning to doubt God himself.

> "Ye have wearied Jehovah with your words.
> But ye say wherein have we wearied him?
> In that ye say, Every one that doeth evil is good in the sight of Jehovah, and he delighteth in them; or where is the God of justice?" (2:17)

The prophet assures these doubters that God will come, and his coming will be for judgment. The apparent anomalies will disappear, faith will be confirmed, and his judgments made visible to all.

Once again the prophet speaks to those doubters and summons them to more diligent service. Faith must find its swift expression in attention to the tether and ritual requirements. When these demands are met the blessing will surely come.

> "Bring ye the whole tithe into the storehouse that there may be food in my house, and prove me now forthwith, saith Jehovah of hosts, if I will not open the windows of heaven and pour you out a blessing that there shall not be room enough to receive it." (3:10)

Here we seem to pass from the moral to the ritual, and emphasis seems to fall upon works. But the ritual is here the expression of the moral and spiritual. The words of comfort to the faltering faithful are brightened with another beautiful promise of

> "a book of remembrance for them that feared Jehovah and that thought upon his name, and they shall be mine; and I will spare them as a man spareth his own son that serveth him." (3:17)

The sifting judgment will come, and the tares will be separated from the wheat, the sheep parted from the goats, but

> "unto you that fear my name shall the sun of righteousness arise with healing in his wings: and ye shall tread down the wicked; for they shall be like ashes under the soles of your feet in the day that I make, saith Jehovah of hosts." (4:2, 3)

It would be a pity if the last book—or any book—of the Bible ended on a note like that. But it did not end so. For whether it be Malachi or another we have a last word, and a right salutary word, enjoining us to give heed to

> "the law of Moses my servant which I commanded him in Horeb for all Israel, even statutes and ordinances." (4:4)

The last two verses (4:5, 6) would seem to be a later addition giving expression to the undying hope of Israel.

18

JOEL: PROPHECY AND APOCALYPTIC

JOEL is described simply as the son of Bethuel, for which name the Greek version reads Pethuel, and we know nothing more about him personally. His book stands second in order in the collection of the Twelve Prophets in our Bible, and this fact has led many scholars to assume that he lived in an early period of Hebrew history. No significance, however, attaches to the position of the book in the collection: Jonah stands before Micah and Nahum though it was certainly written later than either of those books. No argument can be based on the position of this book, or any book, in the canon.

THE BOOK OF JOEL

The personality of Joel recedes behind his book, which raises problems of various kinds. The main purpose of the book as it lies before us is to announce the coming of the *Day of Jehovah* and to describe what will happen on that day. The book contains three chapters in the English version which are represented by four chapters in the original, 2:28–32 of the English version constituting chapter 3 of the Hebrew.

The first two chapters of the Hebrew (A.V. 1:1–2:27) describe a plague of locusts and the awful damage done thereby (1:1–12), in consequence of which a fast is proclaimed and the priests make supplication to God (1:13–20). In chapter 2:1–11 appears a second description of the locust plague in heightened terms that have led some scholars to question whether we are here dealing with real locusts or with symbols. Here again the locust invasion is regarded as a preliminary to the coming of the *Day of Jehovah* (2:1c; 2:2a; 2:11b) and again there is an urgent call to prayer, humiliation, and supplication (2:12–17). Follows thereafter the divine answer promising rain and fruitful seasons once more (2:19–27). 2:28–32 (Heb., chap. 3) follows with a sign of the *Day of Jehovah;* there will be an outpouring of the spirit upon all flesh accompanied by supernatural signs in heaven and on earth. This day, we learn, will be a day of release for Judah but a day of judgment and condemnation for the nations (Gentiles) assembled in the vale of Jehoshaphat (3:1–8; Heb. 4:1–8). A somewhat lively description of the final judgment is given and the final issue is seen to be the salvation of Judah and Jerusalem and the complete desolation of Egypt and Edom (3:9–21; Heb. 4:9–21).

Such are the contents of this little book and they have given rise to much discussion. For we must know first whether the events referred to in 1:1–2:27 are regarded as future or whether we have here the report of something that has already taken place. We must know further whether the locusts are real locusts or an allegorical interpretation of something else. On the answer to these two questions will depend our conception of Joel's book and our judgment as to its unity. Earlier commentators were generally agreed that the first two chapters contained prophecy regarding the future, and they saw in those locusts of the first chapter apocalyptic creatures like those in Revelation 9:3–11, while the locusts of the second chapter were regarded as an allegorical representation of the peoples from the north (*cp.* Gog and Magog, Ez. 38, 39). But most modern scholars are of opinion that such an interpretation is unsound and does violence to the text. We are forced, therefore, to the conclusion that in the first two chapters we are dealing with a real invasion of real locusts. The description may seem somewhat hyperbolic but it should be remembered that hyperbole was the natural mode of expression to the Hebrew. Travellers in the East and other lands who have witnessed this natural phenomenon describe it in terms very like those of Joel. G. A. Smith [1] has assembled the evidence of not a few travellers and their statements are all closely parallel to those of Joel.

Such a phenomenon might well appear to Joel as a sign of the great *Day of Jehovah,* and there might not be great difficulty in regarding the book as a unity. But a strong body of scholarly opinion regards the references to the *Day of Jehovah* in those first two chapters as subsequent additions by a later writer who contributed the last two chapters (A.V. 2:28–3:21). This writer, it is assumed, desired to give an eschatological cast to the earlier sections dealing with the actual plague of locusts. This is the general attitude of modern critical scholars in regard to the character of the book, and while most critics would prefer here two separate writers to account for the difference between the first two chapters (in the Hebrew) and the last two the assumption of one writer for the whole work is not impossible. For Joel himself may have subsequently added the apocalyptic section and may have made those adjustments in the first two chapters. Perhaps here we will have to be content with the Scots verdict "not proven," and if we assume Joel to be the writer of the book we will not lack adequate critical support.

As to the date of the book we find it set variously from 837 to 360 B.C. But the fact that Joel seems to quote most of the earlier prophets, including Malachi, that he does not refer to the northern kingdom, or Assyria, or Babylon, that he does refer to the Greeks, and that he emphasises the ritual of the cult as early prophets did not, and that his language tends in places toward Aramaic—all these converging lines of evidence would seem to indicate a date considerably later than the Exile. Driver would date him after Haggai and Zechariah, perhaps even 100 years later. Most modern scholars would

[1] *Book of the Twelve Prophets*, Vol. II, pp. 391–395.

favor a date somewhere in the first half of the fourth century B.C. If two authors are involved, the date of the apocalyptic section will be even later.

THE MESSAGE OF JOEL

The first two chapters (A.V. 1:1–2:27) are occupied with the terrible plague of locusts and the drought that accompanied that plague. It is characteristic of the Hebrew that he judges the locust plague not as a physical or economic fact but as a religious index. Behind the locusts he sees Jehovah who is lord of Nature and expresses his holy righteous will through natural events. For the Hebrew was wholly unconscious of any secondary causes; Jehovah is the source and origin of all that comes to pass. Through this disaster, which makes impossible the offering of the regular daily sacrifice, God reveals his displeasure with his people. Their sins have separated between them and God. The cessation of sacrifice meant for them the cessation of communion with God, and means had to be taken to restore that communion. Josephus tells us that such a cessation of sacrifice came again at the time of the siege of Jerusalem by Titus, and thus the people were deprived of the presence and power of God precisely at the time when they most needed him. This was, indeed, one of the defects in Old Testament thought of God and its doctrine of divine recompense.

In such a situation the immediate necessity was to humble oneself before God, confess sin, and implore the divine forgiveness. There may seem something mechanical about this procedure, and it tended to become more and more mechanical. But Joel is not unconscious of spiritual realities. To him the temple sacrifices were means of grace *when they were attended by the right spirit.* "Rend your hearts and not your garments" (2:13) is how the Hebrew makes that emphasis, and his speech could not make it otherwise. In such an act there was bound to be rending of garments, but the rending of garments was vain unless accompanied by rending of the heart. To Joel, as to Malachi, the outward act is valid only as it is the expression of inward spirit. A time was to come, and was already on the way, when men would think it enough to wash platters and make the outside clean while inwardly they had the heart of ravening wolves. That time we see fully arrived in the Gospel story. But Joel here insists emphatically on inward piety, and he knows that the acceptable sacrifice of God is "a humble and contrite heart."

Perhaps Joel would never have been heard of were it not for the continuation of his book. And whether it be from Joel, as we assume, or from a later hand we are here concerned with the teaching of his book. In this latter section represented by 2:28–3:21 of the English version (chaps. 3 and 4 of the Hebrew) we have an apocalyptic vision of the final issue of things. As to the relation of prophecy and apocalyptic we shall speak in the following section. Meantime we may consider what Joel has to say in regard to the end of things.

It must be admitted that the vision has a nationalistic basis and that the future glory of Judah and Jerusalem involves the annihilation of all her foes.

For lo! in those days and at that time
When I change the fortunes of Judah and Jerusalem
I will assemble all the nations,
And bring them down to the Vale of Jehoshaphat,
And will hold assize for them there,
For my people and Israel my portion
Whom they scattered among the nations
When they portioned out my land,
Giving a lad for a harlot's hire,
And selling a maid for wine.

. . . . . .

Proclaim yet this among the nations:
Hallow a war, rouse the warriors;
Let the fighting men muster and go!

Beat your ploughshares into swords,
  Your pruning-hooks to spears!
Let the weakling say, I am strong
  And the coward become a hero!
Hasten and come all ye nations around,
  Yea, assemble yourselves together;
Let the nations be roused and go down
  To the Vale of Jehoshaphat,
For there will I sit in judgment
  On all the nations around.
Put in the sickle, for ripe is the vintage;
  Go, tread, for the winepress is full,
The vats are running over,
  For their wickedness is great.
Tumult upon tumult in the Vale of Decision.
  For near is Jehovah's day in the Vale of Decision.
Black are the sun and the moon,
  And the stars withhold their shining;
Jehovah roars from Zion
  And from Jerusalem he shouts
  While earth and heaven do quake.
But Jehovah is a refuge to his people,
  A fortress to the sons of Israel.
So shall ye know that I am Jehovah your God.
  Dwelling in Zion, my holy hill.
Jerusalem shall be sacred territory
  And strangers shall pass through her no more.
On that day it shall come to pass
  That the mountains shall drip with sweet wine
  And the hills be liquid with milk:
All the wadis of Judah shall flow with water,
  And a spring shall issue from Jehovah's house
  To water the Vale of Shittim.
Egypt shall be desolate,
  And Edom a bare steppe
  For the violence done to the sons of Judah. . . .

But Judah shall be inhabited for ever,
And Jerusalem from age to age. . . .
And Jehovah shall dwell in Zion.
(A.V. 3:1–3; 9–21; Heb. 4:1–3; 9–21)

This represents the prevailing mood of Judaism after the Exile though it was not the only mood. There were some magnanimous spirits who conceived Israel's function to be that of missionary to the Gentiles and who recognised that they had been saved to serve. Deutero-Isaiah and Jonah gave expression to this nobler attitude, but it did not prevail generally.

We need not condemn this attitude of Joel and the apocalyptic writers. Rather we should seek to understand it. For here was something that had been bred in the bone, and it came out in the flesh. Nor could it be otherwise in view of Hebrew history. For Israel's fundamental heritage was the heritage of the desert.[2] The Hebrews came originally from the desert and life in the desert of necessity must be wholly self-regarding. The attitude of the desert nomad must always be that of the sentinel and he must always be on guard. For while the desert is the fruitful mother of men she is a cruel nurse. The nomad must protect himself against the cruelty of Nature and against the wild life of the desert. There every sound and every movement must be interrogated swiftly if men would live and not die. Wild beasts or wilder men may be upon him ere he knows it. Like Ishmael his hand will be against everything and everybody. That is the desert life and man must walk warily there. That self-regarding element was nurtured in the desert and it got into the Hebrew blood to stay. Not all the tirades of her prophets or exhortations of her preachers could exorcise that spirit. The Jew inherited it and he kept it, and to-day that element may not be omitted in any appraisal of the Jew.

Furthermore, in the desert he learned a marvelous

[2] We are indebted for some of these ideas to G. A. Smith's Scweich Lectures (1910) on the *Early Poetry of Israel in Its Physical and Social Origins.*

patience that has remained with him through the ages. But that patience was broken at times by fits of ferocity that startle and amaze us. The impatient "How long, O Lord, how long?" sometimes gives place to a wild fury that could sate itself with nothing less than the cursing psalms. We may feel that here we move on a sub-Christian level but we need not forget what the Jew has had to suffer—and still suffers—and we need not marvel if at times he comes by a delirium of conscience that springs from a famine of justice.

This has to be said not by way of condonation but for the purpose of understanding these outbursts of nationalistic feeling. "Joel draws a magnificent picture of Jehovah's coming to judgment," says S. R. Driver,

> "but its figurative and ideal character must not be misunderstood. The Day of Jehovah can never come precisely in the form in which Joel pictured it; nevertheless, it is a day which comes constantly to nations and also to individuals, and often in ways which they do not expect. That is the sense in which Joel's picture must be practically applied. Jehovah's face is set against cruelty and oppression, but he does not extirpate it by mowing down nations wholesale: and the true antithesis is not between Israel, even though invested with ideal perfections, and the other nations of the earth, but between those who, in whatever nation, 'fear God and work righteousness' (Acts 10:35) and those who do the reverse. Joel sets forth in striking imagery some of the eternal principles of divine righteousness and human duty . . . but, as is the case with the prophets generally, these truths are set forth under the spiritual forms of the Jewish dispensation, and with the limitations thereby imposed, which even the most catholic of the prophets were rarely able to throw off." [3]

We repeat again that the Old Testament insights are fractured and broken. These far-off spokesmen for God blazed trails which only their successors could follow to the end. And

[3] *Cambridge Bible, Joel and Amos,* pp. 33–34.

so on that great day of Pentecost Peter could take up the words of Joel and use them to interpret that great experience of the Christian church.

> And it shall come to pass after such things
> I will pour out my spirit upon all flesh:
> And your sons and daughters will prophesy
> And your old men dream dreams
> And your young men see visions.
> Even upon menservants and maidservants
> I will pour out my spirit in those days.
> And I will give signs in heaven and on earth
> Blood and fire and pillars of smoke.
> The sun shall turn to darkness
> And the moon to blood
> At the coming of Jehovah's day,
> The great and terrible day.
> And it shall be that everyone who calls
> On Jehovah's name shall escape:
> For on Mount Zion shall be escaped ones
> As Jehovah hath promised,
> And in Jerusalem shall be
> Those whom Jehovah calls.
> (A.V. 2:28–32; Heb. 3:1–5)

Those seminal words received at Pentecost a fuller significance and a wider range, and Joel's *Israel after the flesh* gave place to Paul's *Israel after the spirit*. For the gift of the spirit is the abiding possession of the Christian church, and where that spirit is there is liberty and life for all.

PROPHECY AND APOCALYPTIC

What precisely is implied by these terms, and wherein do they resemble each other, or in what respects do they differ one from the other? A good deal of confused thinking seems to obtain here and it will be worthwhile to determine the precise significance of these terms. Perhaps, also, we should be clear as to the meaning of a third term—eschatology.

It may be well to begin with the last term. Eschatology is derived from the Greek word *eschatos,* meaning last or final, and *logos,* meaning word or doctrine. Eschatology is thus the doctrine or teaching concerning the last things. Such a doctrine is common to both the prophets and apocalyptic writers, for both speak of the final end of things. That it existed in Israel from early times is clear from Amos' reference to those who eagerly desired the *Day of Jehovah* (Amos 5:18 ff.). Equally clear is the fact that this popular expectation contained elements which the prophet must repudiate. But Amos himself appears to have held a doctrine regarding the final consummation, though it was expressed in terms diametrically opposed to the popular doctrine. "The *Day of Jehovah* will be darkness and not light" (Amos 5:18). How that popular expectation first arose may not be determined exactly; it may be that when men first thought about the origin of the world they also began to think about its end. Israel may have met with this hope first in Canaan and it may be of alien origin. But clearly it was an eschatology of weal and blessing, while the prophetic eschatology was *mainly* an eschatology of woe. It was not, however, exclusively of woe, though until recently critics were wont to strike out every prediction of final blessing found in the earlier prophecies, on the ground that the great prophets did not prophesy anything but doom. Such an attitude on the part of critics has been called in question, and a wider examination of parallels in ancient literatures shows that such procedure is unjustified. Thus we can say that while the earlier prophets prophesied mainly of woe (Jer. 28:8 ff.) they did not do so exclusively. Isaiah's doctrine of the Remnant will readily occur to the mind as an instance where a great prophet prophesies other than doom. The later prophets certainly prophesied more of blessing than of doom, for, with Deutero-Isaiah, they felt this was necessary. The prophet spoke comfortably to Jerusalem—literally "to her heart"—for she had received of Jehovah's hand double for all her sins (Is. 40:1). The Exile had the effect of shifting the prophetic emphasis.

Such is the general content of the prophetic eschatology, and the sphere of its revelation is this world. The final revelation of salvation is given in terms that are largely material and it comes in the sphere of history. In the Apocalyptic eschatology we find a variety of elements and these are set forth in rather confused form. The crude material element still remains but spiritual elements of a higher kind enter and there is distinct advance. Here, indeed, the foundation is laid for much that meets us in the New Testament, and without a thorough understanding of the religious developments of the last two pre-Christian centuries one cannot hope to understand Christianity itself. For it was in this period that thoughts of resurrection, immortality, and God's Messiah came to clear and full expression. The various elements, as has been said, are somewhat confused but a fairly clear doctrine emerges regarding resurrection, judgment, and the Messiah. Ample evidence of all this can be found in the canonical books of the Old Testament, particularly in the book of Daniel, and in the little Apocalypse that has found its way into Isaiah and now occupies Isaiah, chapters 24–27.

Between Prophecy and Apocalyptic there were profound differences but there were also similarities. In the later period of Hebrew history Apocalyptic definitely takes the place of Prophecy; in Haggai, Zechariah, and their successors we can observe the gradual drying-up of the prophetic stream, and we can understand the plaintive cry of the later writer:

> "Our signs we see no more: there is no prophet any more;
> There is none among us who knows how long."
>
> (Ps. 74:9)

The real roots of Apocalyptic are hidden in Prophecy although the Apocalyptic writers have affinities with the Sages and the Scribes, for the Apocalyptist, as we shall see, was one who studied and searched the Scriptures diligently. From its treasury he brought forth things old and new.

Both Prophecy and Apocalyptic claim to be revelations of God, and both claimed to speak of his purpose for men and of the laws and nature of his kingdom. They were alike, too, in the similarity of their materials and methods; dreams and visions are common to both, and eschatology is a common feature.

But the differences are striking and significant. Professor Porter, however, goes too far when he writes:

> "They represent two contrasted conceptions of the nature of revelation, two ideas of the supernatural, two estimates of the present life, two theologies, almost two religions." [4]

This is to stress the differences too much and to neglect the points of resemblance. It should be noted that while Prophecy did not exclude the idea of prediction those spokesmen for God were primarily concerned to interpret the divine purpose *to their own day and generation.* They called upon their fellow-men for faith in God and absolute obedience to his demands; they sought to make God real in the life of the nation. They emphasised the moral and spiritual basis of life. Their words were spoken because Jehovah commanded them to speak, and there is an immediacy and urgency about their message.

All this is otherwise in Apocalyptic. For *Apocalyptic was not spoken but written.* Nor was the word immediate but rather the result of prolonged study of Scripture and particularly of unfulfilled prophecies. Moreover the writer of Apocalyptic did not usually speak in his own name but assumed the name and mantle of some ancient patriarch or seer: thus we have the Book of Enoch, the Apocalypse of Abraham, the Testaments of the Patriarchs, the Assumption of Moses, and many others of the same type. For this reason the writings are generally classed as Pseudepigrapha, signifying that they are not by the writer whose name they bear. While pseudonymity is a general characteristic of this literature it is not universal.

[4] Porter, F. C., *The Messages of the Apocalyptical Writers,* 1905, p. 71.

Joel, we have seen, is an apocalypse which bears the author's own name, while Revelation (Apocalypse) in the New Testament, as also the Pauline apocalypse in II Thessalonians 2 are exceptions to the general rule. The Shepherd of Hermas outside the New Testament is not pseudonymous. But normally the literary device of pseudonymity was used. The whole purpose of this study of Scripture on the part of writers and the aim of their writing was to *unveil* (*apokalyptein*) the last things. The Apocalyptist was not interested in the present world, of which he wholly despaired, but he did look for a city whose builder and maker is God. He sought to give the details concerning that city. The prophets had interpreted the present and the future arising out of that present and they kept their feet firm on the ground of history. The Apocalyptist, on the other hand, saw no organic connection between the present and the future, and his thought is apt to employ mechanical terms. The kingdom to come lay wholly outside the present world order.

Again, while Prophecy did not limit the freedom of God it did suggest that God moves within the realm of the normal and the natural. Drought, famine, plague, foreign invasion, and all such natural disasters were regarded as expressions of the divine purpose. The Assyrian, or the Chaldean, or Cyrus the Persian were but instruments and agents which Jehovah used for the furtherance of his righteous will in the world. Prophecy was thus the interpretation of natural events in terms of God and his purpose. Apocalypse, on the other hand, takes flight from experience and dwells in a fantastic world of dreams and visions. Here Jehovah manifests his power not by using normal means but by interference with such means; in Apocalypse *the abnormal becomes normal.* All is super- or supra-natural. God enters by way of cataclysm and catastrophe. The world as men knew it ceases to be, and there are signs in heaven above and on the earth beneath, the sun being turned to darkness and the moon to blood while the stars withhold their shining (A.V. 2:31; Heb., Joel 3:4) and by the might of his own marvelous hand Jehovah achieves his purpose.

Furthermore, in Prophecy the divine activity is morally motivated. God is righteous and loves righteousness; his hand is against evil-doers everywhere, against Israel as against the inhuman brutalities of Moab, Edom, Philistia, and Damascus (Amos 1). God is no respecter of persons. But this does not seem to be so in Apocalyptic. Here the moral seems to recede into the background and is obscured by a dark cloud of crude nationalism. This is perhaps truer of the earlier rather than the later Apocalyptists where the cruder forms of the early time tend to become spiritualized. Ezekiel and Joel will readily come into the mind as examples of the early writers in the apocalyptic vein. There the Jews stand over against the Gentiles, the Jews alone with their God over against a wicked world. No thought of missionary vocation or world evangelism is there. The heathen are only for extermination, or as a Moslem once said to G. A. Smith concerning the Christians, "they were made only to fill up hell." The heathen are to be totally destroyed. At the end the Jew alone remains in a lonely world to demonstrate that there is no God but Jehovah and Israel is his people.

The prophets throughout were conscious of a divine purpose which gave meaning to the national history and significance of the individual. Apocalyptic ceased to see any purpose in history and despaired of the present world. It pinned its faith and hope on a new world that was to be born through conflagration and catastrophe. Necessarily it became deterministic in its thought, and with its literary record of pseudonymity it became easy to think in terms of an ideal evolutionary scheme of things that moved inevitably to its foreordained goal. For that reason its conception of history, as stated, was mechanical rather than organic. The secret had been imparted in the beginning to Enoch, Abraham, Noah, or some other of the ancients, and it was the business of the Apocalyptist to unveil (*apokalyptein*) that secret and make it known. Some explanation of the accumulating power of evil had to be given and the Apocalyptic writers gave it. It was all part of the divine purpose and plan from the beginning foreordained and decreed and working itself out inevitably. But the final judgment upon it was also foreordained and the *finale* was at hand. Ezekiel, Zechariah (9–14), Joel all speak of this final showdown and it takes a uniform aspect. The heathen nations will be gathered in a final assault upon the city of God but they will be broken in that process. God's people do nothing, can do nothing but wait; the issue is sure. The present rule of evil was ordained but the day of its end was set. The Apocalyptic writers write in the darkness just before the dawn of that great day.

The later forms of Apocalyptic need not concern us here. Apocalyptic is related to Prophecy but it marks a real descent. It has limitations, but we need not seek to minimise its worth or its significance for the New Testament. It expresses a deep and abiding faith in God and it well knows that "Salvation is of the Lord." The final victory is his, and his ultimate purpose is the redemption and renewal of his people. Apocalypses are usually tracts written for bad times, and they supplied hope where it was most needed. Says an old Midrash:

> "If thou seest the kingdoms in conflict with each other, watch for the feet of the Messiah." [5]

The continued influence of Apocalyptic can be observed in the words of the New Testament:

> "When these things (i.e. the Messianic woes) begin to come to pass, then look up and lift up your heads, for your redemption draweth nigh." (Luke 21:28)

[5] Cited from Israel Abrahams, *Some Permanent Elements in Judaism*, 1924, p. 34.

19

JONAH: A PLEA FOR UNIVERSALISM

THE book of Jonah differs from the other prophetic books in that it is not written by the prophet whose name it bears. Several centuries lie between the prophet whose ministry is described and the writer who gave us this book. The early prophet is used here by the later writer as a peg on which to hang his teaching. He uses the figure of Jonah to point a moral and adorn a tale. The reason for this selection will become obvious as we proceed to examine the book and observe the purpose that the writer had in view. For it assuredly had a purpose, and it is written with a didactic aim.

JONAH BEN-AMITTAI

As to the person of the chief character of the story we are not without definite knowledge. Jonah ben-Amittai was a prophet who flourished in the days of Jeroboam II (782–743 B.C.), who

> "restored the border of Israel from the entrance of Hamath unto the sea of the Arabah, according to the word of Jehovah the God of Israel, which he spake by his servant Jonah, the son of Amittai, the prophet of Gath-hepher" (II Kings 14:25).

From this reference we may conclude that Jonah was a prophet with a strong strain of nationalism, such as characterised the early prophetic guilds. "Israel *über alles*" would appear to have been the keynote of his preaching, and the writer, who knew well the danger of slogans, evidently judged Jonah to be a proper representative of a narrow bigoted Judaism which he desired to combat in his own day. Jonah is the "hundred percenter," the "little Englander," and the "jingo" all rolled into one. And despite the suggestion of gentleness conveyed by his name (Jonah means dove) he was an aggressive type that was likely to get in the way of God's beneficent purpose for the world. That suggests to us the historical background and the approximate date of the book.

HISTORICAL BACKGROUND

Why the writer should desire to represent Jonah in such fashion is easily enough understood. When the Jews returned from Babylon about 538 B.C. they experienced a great feeling of release which expressed itself in twofold fashion. On the one hand we have the glowing oracles of Deutero-Isaiah uttered under the immediate impact of the great redemptive act of Israel's God. The prophet sees the deliverance under Cyrus as the outworking of God's redemptive might, and finds therein a challenge and call to missionary enterprise. Israel has been saved, and it has been saved to serve. Israel redeemed is called to be a missionary people and to serve as God's messenger to the ends of the earth. They are to become "polished shafts" in the quiver of God, his agents and instruments for the establishment of his kingdom. This missionary idea of Israel's going forth in evangelising zeal is most completely represented in the well-known *Servant Songs,*[1] and whether those songs proceed from the hand of the prophet or are incorporated from another source matters little, for they coincide with the view of the prophet expressed throughout Isaiah 40–55.

But the prophets are lonely souls who stand on heights which lesser men dare not, or will not, climb, and such a view

[1] Isaiah 42:1-4; 49:1-6; 50:4-9; 52:13-53:12.

as that expressed by Deutero-Isaiah did not find general acceptance. It may well be that a succession of untoward circumstances militated against this wider view and its popular acceptance. The life of the returned exiles was drab and dreary, and a period of disillusionment supervened upon the high hopes and glowing expectations that had filled the hearts of those leaving Babylon. The ideal faded in the light of common day. The group that had remained in Jerusalem looked askance on the returning exiles and did not welcome them heartily. There was much internal jealousy and strife. It could not be otherwise, for any community settled on its lees is bound to feel disturbed when new and energetic men enter to upset the *status quo*. Suspicious neighbors without and unkindly brethren within the city created a sense of frustration and defeat. A succession of bad harvests and futile efforts to rebuild the temple combined to depress the spirit of the people and make them lose heart. Missionary zeal is not likely to flourish in such circumstances, though it would be true to say that the infusion of such a spirit might well prove an invigorating tonic in precisely these conditions. It is not surprising, therefore, that we find here an embittered mood of deep hostility against the enemies of Judaism. The Jew set himself to cultivate a national exclusiveness and withdrew more and more into himself. Instead of praying for Babylon and his other enemies he proceeded to curse them in no measured terms. Between him and them there was a great gulf fixed, and the passage of the years only deepened that gulf and set Jew more and more apart from Gentile. This, too, came out of the exile, and we can trace it right down the centuries until it culminates in Nehemiah and Ezra with their rigorous legalism and emphasis on Jewish separation from the world. The conflict runs down into the Christian era and is finally settled at Antioch when "the wall of partition" was finally cast down by the expansive force of Christianity (Acts 15).

It is against such a background that the book of Jonah

is to be read. Its purpose was to re-iterate the challenge of Deutero-Isaiah, and show that:

> There's a wideness in God's mercy
> Like the wideness of the sea;
> There's a kindness in his justice,
> Which is more than liberty.
>
> But we make his love too narrow
> By false limits of our own;
> And we magnify his strictness,
> With a zeal he will not own.[2]

All that the book contends for is simply this, that it is possible for human beings to repent and turn to God, and that, too, independently of the question whether those human beings are Jews or Gentiles, black or white, brown or yellow, bond or free. That is the thesis of the writer. God, he holds, is too big to be imprisoned within the walls of any particular sect or church; the divine grace and the human heart fit each other like lock and key. We are dealing with something universal here, and the book may well be defined as the finest missionary tract ever published. It needed to be published to the Jews of that time, and it needs to be published to us. For it rings with "the sound of a grand 'Amen'" to the missionary call of Deutero-Isaiah.

DATE OF THE BOOK

There is fairly general agreement among scholars as to the date of this writing. Obviously the story speaks of Nineveh as a city that once was but now is no more. The very name of the reigning king is unknown. The whole impression given by the story is of something that happened long ago. The evidence of literary style and the large flavoring of Aramaic points to a late date in the history of Israel. The style, gener-

[2] Hymn by F. W. Faber.

ally, reminds us of such books as Esther and Daniel, and we may place it at a time near the close of the fourth century B.C. It will thus be one of the latest writings of the Old Testament.

THE MESSAGE OF THE BOOK

Thus we can understand how the writer chose Jonah, the prophet of nationalism, to represent the selfish recalcitrant Israel that refused to engage in its missionary vocation. To Israel, according to the Talmud, the Gentiles were "as the spittle that falleth from a man's mouth," and we catch echoes of this feeling in the Gospel of Matthew, which is the most Jewish of the Gospels (Matt. 14:21 ff.). "Salvation is of the Jews" might be only a selfish slogan. All that selfish feeling of superiority and special privilege is reflected in Jonah as he boards the ship to flee to Tartessus (1:3). Ordered to go east, he flees to the utmost bounds of the west—to Gibraltar. One might remark in passing that Jonah was the first man to discover that the earth was round, for when he runs as far as possible from God he finds himself finally back in the place he started from—the presence of God.

But we are anticipating the sequence of events. We can here return to the story, for the story takes time, and the time is filled with thrilling incidents. In his inimitable fashion the writer allows us to see the lordly Jonah paying his fare, boarding the ship, and going down "into the sides of the ship" (1:5). This does not necessarily imply that he sought an outside cabin, but there is a quiet lambent humor pervading the story, and it is not pushing matters too far if we interpret the story with a touch of Semitic humor. For the book of Jonah is an illustration of Hebrew humor. The Hebrews could really laugh, and what the writer wanted here was to laugh a ridiculous attitude out of court. Some abuses may be remedied by the saving grace of humor, and some evil spirits may be expelled by laughter.

It may be that Jonah thought discretion the better part

of valor, and accordingly he went straight to bed. Soon he was fast asleep. The Greek version does not hesitate to say "he snored" (1:5). The word used in Hebrew is the same as is applied to the "deep sleep" into which God cast Adam when he formed Eve from his rib (Gen. 2:21). Jonah must have been sublimely unconscious even though he was not sleeping the sleep of the just. Unlike the Greek, the Hebrew took rather unkindly to the sea, and it is the measure of Jonah's extreme dislike for Foreign Missions that he undertook this long and hazardous sea journey. Thus we see Jonah fast asleep and snoring.

The pious Psalmist had expressed himself on this matter of a distant journey:

> If I take the wings of the morning
> And dwell in the uttermost parts of the sea,
> Even there shall thy hand lead me,
> And thy right hand hold me. (Ps. 139:9, 10)

But Jonah was not as the pious Psalmist, and the issue was untoward.

> "And Jehovah hurled a great wind upon the sea, and there was a mighty tempest upon the sea, so that the ship thought she was going to be smashed to bits." (1:4)

Strange it is how sailors in all ages speak endearingly of their ships as "she," even though those ships be men-of-war, and strange, too, the vivid manner in which "she" is portrayed as an animate creature capable of thought! But stranger still is the picture of those heathen sailors working with a will and praying with a purpose. And Jonah slept. Those men Jonah despised, the hated *Gōyīm* (Gentiles), "the lesser breeds without the Law." How skilfully the writer sets it all before our eyes until we see both passenger and crew only as men, men in need, face to face with imminent death, men in their naked humanity. Though these sailors are heathen they are faithful to the light they have, which is more than can be said of Jonah, and they reveal a native courtesy and a deep respect for human life, even for the life of a self-confessed recreant prophet. Jonah's statement of his creed—favorite text of Jewish preachers—

"I am an Hebrew and I revere the God who made the sea and the dry land," (1:9)

had a startling effect on those heathen sailors. For they were immediately overawed and proceeded to call upon the name of Jehovah. The very thing that Jonah feared was coming to pass before his eyes: Gentiles were proving capable of repentance. One can almost imagine Jonah taking kindly to the sea as they

"took up Jonah and hurled him into the sea, and the sea ceased from its raging." (1:15)

These men had shown themselves capable of receiving an impression and forming a judgment:

"Then the men feared with a great fear, and they sacrificed unto Jehovah and made vows." (1:16)

Those who dwelt in darkness had seen a great light. The divine grace had triumphed over Jewish pride and Jewish selfishness.

THE GREAT FISH

It is at this point in the story we meet with that incident which has been a stumbling-block to the faithful and has afforded ample scope for the ribald scorn of the unbeliever—the great fish. It is to be noted that the Bible does not call it a whale, though we generally think of it as such. The writer was not concerned with any exact definition of the marine monster, and if he had foreseen how dumb and wooden and devoid of humor men living in a machine age might become he would doubtless have tugged his Semitic whiskers and laughed uproariously. For it is the tragedy of life that we must forever be turning poetry into prose, and have lost entirely the habit of running back "through the crystal doors of childhood" to the never-never land. But we may leave this matter aside for the moment—though Jonah may not like his cramped quarters for the time being—and return to it when we consider the interpretation of the story. Meantime we will proceed with the tale.

THE MISSION TO NINEVEH

Again Jonah stands in the presence of God (chap. 3), and receives his commission to preach to that great city. This time he goes, but with laggard foot and grudging spirit, for he is secretly afraid of what is likely to happen. One can imagine the savage gusto with which he cried,

"Yet forty days and Nineveh shall be destroyed." (3:4)

But all prophecy is conditional and contingent, and this book was written to prove that fact. Prophecy depends upon the reaction of men to the word of God declared by the prophet. All that the writer contends for is that heathen are capable of such reaction and may repent. And here the very thing that Jonah dreaded comes to pass. Fear and trembling laid hold of all in Nineveh, and the people humbled themselves before God in sackcloth and ashes, both man and beast. And

> "God saw their works that they turned from their evil way; and God changed his mind concerning the evil which he had said he would do: and he did it not." (3:10)

Here we begin to move towards the dénouement. Jonah, still recalcitrant, stands in the presence of God, from whom he fled at first to avoid his mission. Now he is petulant and peevish, and Jehovah deals with him as a father might deal with a spoiled child. Humor will help here, and God will try it so. Let no one think this is a forced interpretation, for the Old Testament well knows *le Dieu qui rit* (the God who laughs).

> He that sitteth in the heavens shall laugh,
> Jehovah will have them in derision. (Ps. 2:5)

It is not, as some scholars have maintained, that Jonah's anger is due to his being proved a false prophet—he was that in a wider sense—although that might easily enough be understood. Jonah's grievance is plainly against the goodness of God. God is bigger than Jonah's thoughts and his greatness leaves all poor Jonah's faint imagination far behind. Jonah's speech here would be sheer blasphemy if we did not understand the writer's motive, which is to laugh the narrow ideas of "the hundred percenter" clean out of court.

> "And he prayed unto Jehovah, and said, I pray thee, Jehovah, was not this just what I said. . . . I knew that thou art a God of grace and mercy, slow to anger and full of lovingkindness, and ready to change thy mind regarding punishment. And so now, Jehovah, I beseech thee, take my life from me: for I would rather die than live." (4:2, 3)

Jonah would rather be dead than see heathen going into the kingdom of God! But God will reason with him as one might reason with a stubborn, wilful child:

> "Do you think you are right in getting so hot about this?" (4:4)

But Jonah just sulks and pouts, and we should note where he pouts and sulks. For Jonah had gone right through the city and is sitting outwith its bounds on the far side, waiting for the thunderbolts to fall. There he sits in proud isolation, thinking only of his own comfort with never a thought for the thousands whose doom he has pronounced. To ensure his comfort,

> "he made himself a booth, and sat under it in the shade until he might see what would become of the city." (4:5)

One might as well be comfortable during the time of waiting! There is no doubt as to what Jonah wanted to happen to that city, and here we have the tragedy of the closed mind. Only a gentle humor will avail to drive a new and larger idea into the lockfast cranium of Jonah. But God will do it.

> "But Jehovah God prepared a gourd and made it to come up over the head of Jonah to give shade, to deliver him from his sad case. And Jonah was very glad for that gourd. But God also prepared a worm at sunrise of the next day, and it struck the gourd so that it withered away.

> And when the sun shone forth God prepared a blasting east wind, and the sun struck on Jonah's head so that he was exhausted." (4:6–8)

What a combination of evil circumstances to accumulate on this holy man's bald pate! It would seem as if the very stars in their courses were fighting against poor Jonah. Nature itself seems unsympathetic with his poor peeved soul. And so,

> "He asked for his life to die, and said, death is better than life." (4:8)

This is assuredly a sorry case. There are times when we feel pushed to such extremities, but they are usually times of agony and desperation when our pain has sharpened itself to a veritable point of intolerableness. "I do well to be angry at times," said George Matheson, "but I have often mistaken the times." Jonah does not know his mistake—not yet.

> "And God said to Jonah, are you right in being so angry about the gourd?
>
> And he said, I am so very angry that I could die." (4:9)

Here God stops to reason more closely and show clearly the childish folly and petulance of Jonah. Does it not seem just ridiculous and absurd that a man should worry about a vegetable plant, and fail to show any concern for the fate of human beings? Or can it really be that it is "better to be Caesar's dog than to be Caesar's wife"? Not if we are going to live in a moral world where personal and spiritual values are maintained.

> "And Jehovah said, you have worried about the gourd, which was not due to any work of yours; you did not make it grow: it just came in a night (the son of a night) and it passed away in a night." (4:10)

We feel the next clause should begin with a "How much more—" but it does not. The Hebrew way is just to put two things side by side and leave the rest to common sense. That is what happens here. It may not finish the argument from a logical or historical viewpoint but it leaves nothing more to be said from the dramatic point of view.

> "And should not I worry about Nineveh, that great metropolis, where more than twelve times ten thousand people dwell who are morally incompetent?" (4:11)

That is the last word, the final argument. Did it move Jonah? There is no record of the result as concerns him, but one would like to think that Jonah found the larger light, and that when he returned he was singing that song which has found its place in chapter 2:1 ff. If it was not that song, then it must have been one like it, and its final word must have been Jonah's great discovery that

> "Salvation is of Jehovah." (2:10)

INTERPRETATION OF THE BOOK

Here we may return to that matter of the great fish, and consider what we are to make of the monster. How may we deal with this in a way that will not offend reason and still satisfy faith? Many scholars here find traces of a myth that has wandered far and appears in many forms, for myths are notorious travellers. It may have originated in India [3] and subsequently found its way to Asia Minor and Greece. In that case it is merely a literary expedient of the author, and as such would be recognised by all. The whole tale, as already indicated, is of an imaginative character, and there is no ground in history or reason to regard it otherwise. The description of the beasts in sackcloth and observing the proclaimed fast (3:7, 8) and the mass conversion of Nineveh do not suggest a real world but rather an imaginative flight. The Jews call it a Midrash, meaning a fanciful tale, and we call it a didactic story. For the writer is not concerned with *truth of fact* but with *truth of idea,* and such truth of idea is independent of truth of fact.

But the present writer feels drawn to the older allegorical intepretation as represented by Kleinert, Cheyne, and George

[3] Sellin, Ernst, *op. cit.,* Vol. I, pp. 286–288.

Adam Smith.[4] This interprets Scripture by Scripture, gives a more satisfying interpretation, and is in accord with Hebrew literary practice.

In this connection it is to be noted that the Hebrew word for "swallow" used in reference to Jonah's engulfment in the great fish is the same word as is used by Jeremiah (Jer. 51:44) with reference to the engulfment of Israel in the Babylonian captivity.

> "I will execute judgment upon Bel in Babylon, and I will bring forth out of his mouth that which he hath swallowed." (Heb. *bala*)

The same word is used with similar reference in Psalm 124.

> Then certainly
> they had devour'd us all
> And *swallow'd* quick,
> for ought that we could deem;
> Such was their rage,
> as we might well esteem.
> And as fierce floods
> before them all things drown,
> So had they brought
> our soul to death quite down.
> (Ps. 124:3, 4; Scots metrical version)

As Israel, recalcitrant to its missionary duty, must suffer the discipline of the exile and engulfment in the unclean land, so Jonah, type and representative of Israel, is subjected to the drastic remedial discipline of God. Nor is it pressing the allegory too far to say that most Jews returned from the iron discipline of the exile uncomprehending the purpose of God and the ultimate intention of the divine heart. But the writer of this story had seen to the center of things, and knew that judgment was God's "strange work," while mercy was his delight. He had entered into the vision of Deutero-Isaiah, and comprehended the deeper meaning of the Servant Songs, and

[4] *Book of the Twelve Prophets, op. cit.,* Vol. I, pp. 511 ff.

he sets it forth anew in this striking fashion. "The whole creation groaneth and travaileth waiting for the manifestation of the sons of God." God's redemptive purpose is of cosmic dimensions, and missionary expansion is a vital necessity to any church that would live.

APPRECIATION

And thus we can understand the oft-quoted words of Cornill:

> I have read the book of Jonah at least a hundred times, and I will publicly avow, for I am not ashamed of my weakness, that I cannot even now take up this marvelous book, nay, nor even speak of it, without the tears rising to my eyes, and my heart beating higher. This apparently trivial book is one of the deepest and grandest that was ever written, and I should like to say to every one who approaches it, Take off thy shoes, for the place whereon thou standest is holy ground. In this book Israelite prophecy quits the scene of battle as victor, and as victor in its severest struggle—that against self. In it, as Jeremiah expresses it in a well-known passage, the prophecy of Israel succeeded in freeing the precious from the vile and in finding its better self again.[5]

[5] Cornill, C. H., *The Prophets of Israel,* 1895, pp. 170–171.

20

CHRIST: THE GOAL OF PROPHECY

THE position of the prophets in the Hebrew Bible differs from that of our English versions. In the Hebrew Bible the prophets occupy the central area, and the "Writings" (*Kethūbim*) come last. In the Hebrew, the Law (*Tōrah*), consisting of the first five books of our Bible, is first, and is followed by what we call the historical books (Joshua–II Kings). These books the Hebrew looked upon as prophetical books, being composed by prophets, and these were called *the early prophets.* What we call the canonical prophets, Isaiah–Malachi, followed and these were known as *the later prophets.* The term 'later" or "latter" may mean that they were regarded as later in time, or that they appeared later in the volume. The "Writings" follow the prophets, and, beginning with Psalms, they include everything not included in the Law and the Prophets.

It was a sound instinct that led the Protestant Reformers to place the prophetic books, that is Isaiah–Malachi, at the end of the Old Testament and in close proximity to the Gospels of the New Testament. For those prophets seem to be standing on the tiptoe of expectation, waiting for "Him who is to come." The physical proximity of those prophetic books corresponds to an inward affinity, which is expressed in the New Testament word,

"The testimony of Jesus is the spirit of prophecy."
(Rev. 19:10)

For there is a profound organic connection between the Old

Testament and the New, and nowhere more than in the prophets do we feel the truth of Augustine's word:

> *In Vetere Testamento Novum latet,*
> *In Novo Testamento Vetus patet.*[1]

This can be expressed in many ways and amply illustrated. The New Testament would be unintelligible without the Old, and the Old would be a shapeless torso without its consummation in the New. "The teaching of the Old Testament as a whole," says Bishop Westcott,[2] "is a perpetual looking forward." The Old Testament is the story of a long search; the New is the glad tidings of a great find. The Old Testament represents religion in the interrogative mood, while the New Testament gives us religion in its glorious final affirmations. Here exclamations take the place of previous interrogations, for men rejoice in the full light of complete discovery.

The words of Christ himself support such an interpretation of the Old Testament:

> "Think not that I came to destroy the law or the prophets: I came not to destroy but to fulfil." (Matt. 5:17)

Christ is not only the goal of prophecy but of the whole Old Testament. In him the age-long search finds its end and full reward, and God is revealed and made known to the children of men.

> "God, having of old time spoken unto the fathers in the prophets by divers portions and in divers manners, hath at the end of these days spoken unto us in *his* Son."
> (Heb. 1:1, 2)

Here we interpret Scripture by Scripture, and to do so we may turn the word of the writer around and read thus:

> "God, who hath at the end of these days spoken unto us in his Son, of olden time spoke unto the fathers in the prophets by divers portions and in divers manners."

[1] In the Old Testament the New lies concealed:
In the New Testament the Old lies revealed.

[2] Westcott, B. F., *The Epistle to the Hebrews,* 1889, p. 485.

The writer here is declaring the fact that the full revelation that has come in Christ was preceded by partial revelations given to the fathers. The difference is of degree, not of kind. The first thing he says about those revelations is that they were 'by divers portions.' The Greek word *polymerōs* is not easily rendered into English, but it can best be understood by contrast with its opposite term, *a-merōs,* which signifies singly or undividedly. The earlier revelation, if we may say so, was not concentrated in a single volume, but distributed through many channels and mediated by a series of different agents. In that sense it was *fragmentary;* the divine self-disclosure was partial, given by different stages. The New Testament writer here recognises the full revelation as originating in the older dispensation, and it recognises that each stage was a preparation for the next. At no point was there completeness, but the fragments pointed forward to fulfilment, *teleiōsis,* which comes in Christ. In him those distant points of light come to full-orbed radiance.

For the creative element in Old Testament religion was a real and continuous self-disclosure of God to men. The divine spirit was always working, enabling inspired men to anticipate the purpose of God, and to interpret that purpose for mankind.

> "There is not one New Testament idea that cannot be conclusively shown to be a healthy and natural product of some Old Testament germ, nor any early Old Testament idea which did not press instinctively towards its New Testament fulfilment." [3]

"In divers manners": again the New Testament writer contrasts the variety of methods by which God disclosed himself to the fathers. He spoke 'in divers manners,' *polytropōs,* through dreams, visions, oracles, angels, and various other agencies and instruments. In his self-communication God seemed to accommodate and adapt himself to the varying types of mind and the various stages of moral development. Amos, Hosea,

[3] Schultz, H., *Old Testament Theology,* translated by J. A. Paterson, Vol. I, p. 54.

Jeremiah, Isaiah, Ezekiel—to all these it comes in varying form, but there is unity through all the variety. This manifold and multiform disclosure of God is contrasted with the final single and supreme revelation in One who was no subordinate minister but 'a Son.' Christ is the end of prophecy and its fulfilment in the sense that he completes what was imperfect, realises all that was but shadowy; in him we have the full development of what was but rudimentary, the full outgrowth of the original germ. Thus Westcott can say:

> "The Old Testament does not simply contain prophecies, but is one vast prophecy. Israel in its history, in its ritual, in its ideal, is a unique enigma among the peoples of the world, of which Christ is the complete solution."[4]

The bewildered question of Isaac, "Where is the Lamb?" (Gen. 22:7) may be construed as the question of the whole Jewish ritual which finds no answer until John the Baptist speaks the solving word, "Behold the Lamb" (John 1:29). The history is full of promises and hopes but all the hopes of all the years find their consummation in Him. "Mine eyes," says Simeon, "have seen thy salvation." For that men watched "more than they that watch for the morning." All the promises are "Yea and Amen" in Christ. The dreams and visions of the prophets are realised in him and surpassed in the light of his full-orbed splendor and perfection. In that sense Christ is the goal and end of prophecy.

To view the matter in this fashion saves us from the mechanical interpretation of prophecy that finds its strength in proof-texts, and regards the Old Testament as the New Testament in hieroglyphics. It is not to be denied that on certain occasions our Lord did set himself deliberately in line with the letter of Old Testament prophecy, as in the case of his entry into the Holy City on Palm Sunday (Luke 19:29 ff.). But this was exceptional procedure and adopted for a particular purpose. A right view of the person of Christ will convince any unprejudiced reader of the records that Jesus in all

[4] Westcott, B. F., *op. cit.*, p. 491.

his words and actions was free and spontaneous. He upon whom the spirit had come was free from all statute and ordinance, and moved with full and complete freedom. The picture of our Lord presented in the Gospels is the picture of a vital person directed wholly from within and not regulated from without. He is the inspired Son of God, not the slave of tradition. To think otherwise is to regard the Bible as a book of conundrums, or as a jigsaw puzzle whose pieces have to be laboriously fitted together. The writer of Matthew's Gospel tried to fit the pieces, and did not have much success, and neither will we succeed.

That which is spiritual cannot be thus bound with fetters. Prophecy is vital and living. It is organic, not mechanic. Its beginnings are obscure and small, but like the seed it grows to a tree full of strength and beauty. Some branches must be lopped off in the process of growth, and some buds may fail to develop, but in due time it yields its fruit, and the fruit-laden tree is the fulfilment of the tiny seed. Much is shed in the process of development, but at last its potentialities are revealed. To use the words of Westcott:

> "Christ and the Christian dispensation are . . . the consummation in life of that which was prepared in life." [5]

Thus we can say with Peter, though with a profounder meaning:

> "To Him bear all the prophets witness." (Acts 10:43)

To understand how Christ is the consummation of prophecy we consider briefly his teaching, his person, and his kingdom.

It is clear from his teaching. The prophetic emphasis on moral and spiritual values receives a new strength in the teaching of Jesus. The demand for righteousness in Amos, the revelation of the divine love in Hosea, the thought of the divine holiness in Isaiah—are all gathered up here, and in many a lovely parable and tender similitude the divine fulness is unveiled. The inward communion of the soul with God, as we

[5] *Ibid.*, p. 480.

see it in a choice spirit like Jeremiah, is here shown as a possibility for all, and the great God, who will not suffer a sparrow to fall to the ground, is here seen as the Father of all mankind. Every element of prophetic truth, every solemn sense of duty is here transfigured and set in a new light. The old obligations are not abolished; they are spiritualised. The eternal principles are extricated from their temporary form, and God's ultimate requirement is seen to be holiness of a heart purified by love towards God and towards man. The Christian law of love exhausts the teaching of both law and prophets.

With reference to the person of Christ we see a like fulfilment and completion. The dream of an ideal king occupies the minds of most of the Old Testament prophets, but the dream when realised exceeds all expectations. The various features of the portrait in the Old Testament are not easily harmonised, for here particularly the divine spirit seemed to speak in many forms. Isaiah's portrait of the ideal king, Micah's thought of the lowly peasant, the mysterious Suffering Servant of Deutero-Isaiah—all these are here and many more. In Christ we see all these broken lights gathered up in one who is the effulgence of the Father's glory and the complete revelation of God.

> "Surely, if slowly, the Church of the First Days, as under the guidance of the Holy Ghost it pondered on the Person and Work of the Lord, recognised in Him the union of the various elements which had been foreshadowed in many fragments and in many fashions, welcomed Him as her Priest, her Prophet, her Example, her King, her God; and worshipped in adoring love and wonder." [6]

When we consider the kingdom that Christ founded we see again the fulfilment of prophecy. The range and sphere of that kingdom are extended and removed from the material to the spiritual realm. But the theocratic principle that inspired the prophets is the central principle of Christ's kingdom. Though the prophets seem to narrow the bounds of the divine

[6] Kirkpatrick, A. F., *Doctrine of the Prophets,* 1912, p. 523.

kingdom to the bounds of contemporary Judaism the wider hope and ampler view shines forth consistently in the Old Testament. True, it was a kingdom of this world that they envisaged, for the Hebrew is concrete, and salvation in the Old Testament is always marked by a strong material content. The Hebrew rarely forsakes this concrete basis of experience, and seldom soars to the empyrean. There are times when they do leave the material and feel the spell and pressure of the spiritual ideal. Isaiah, Jeremiah, Ezekiel, and Deutero-Isaiah make us conscious of the inadequacy of speech to set forth thought. They see "the land of far distances," and they think long, long thoughts. But not until Christ came could men understand the significance of a kingdom that was wholly spiritual, a kingdom not of this world. The prophetic utterances then took on a fuller meaning, and a more adequate interpretation was given them. The conception of an empire, universal and eternal, entered into men's minds, and the outpouring of the divine spirit on men's hearts made its realisation possible.

We see not yet all enemies put under His feet, but we shall see them. "Jesus shall reign." The efforts of the prophets to bring the unredeemed tracts of life under the divine sway will be crowned finally. Like those prophets we must grasp the fundamental principles of theocracy and match them with our own time. The historical setting of those ancient oracles is temporary and accidental, but the principles with which they operate are eternal. The spirit that inspired those prophets and rested in fulness upon Him shall guide us into all truth "The letter killeth, but the spirit giveth life."

SELECTED BIBLIOGRAPHY

INTRODUCTION

Volumes on Old Testament Introduction deal with questions of literary criticism such as the date, composition, and authorship of the books. On the basis of the style and contents of the document they form a judgment as to its genuineness. Most of the works cited here are in English but it has seemed wise to cite representatives of Continental scholarship which has been particularly effective in this department.

Bewer, J. A., *Literature of the Old Testament,* revised edition, New York, 1944 (this volume is written from the historical viewpoint).

Cornill, C. H., *Introduction to the Canonical Books of the Old Testament;* translated by G. H. Box, New York, 1907.

Driver, S. R., *Introduction to the Literature of the Old Testament,* 8th edition, New York, 1909.

Eissfeldt, Otto, *Einleitung in das Alte Testament,* Tübingen, 1934.

Gray, G. B., *A Critical Introduction to the Old Testament,* New York, 1919.

MacFadyen, J. E., *Introduction to the Old Testament,* New York, 1933.

Oesterley, W. O. E., and Robinson, T. H., *Introduction to the Books of the Old Testament,* London, 1934.

Pfeiffer, R. H., *Introduction to the Old Testament,* New York, 1941.

Robinson, H. W., *The Old Testament: Its Making and Meaning,* New York, 1937.

Sellin, Ernst, *Einleitung in das Alte Testament,* 7th edition, Leipzig, 1935.

GENERAL: OLD TESTAMENT BACKGROUND

The volumes listed here are such as will give a view of the general background of culture and history in which the prophetic ministry was carried on.

SELECTED BIBLIOGRAPHY

ARCHAEOLOGY

Albright, W. F., *Archaeology and the Religion of the Bible,* Baltimore, 1942.
——, *Archaeology of Palestine and the Bible,* New York, 1933.
——, *From the Stone Age to Christianity,* Baltimore, 1940.
Burrows, M., *What Mean These Stones?* New Haven, 1941.
Glueck, N., *The Other Side of Jordan,* New Haven, 1940.
——, *The River Jordan,* Philadelphia, 1946.

HISTORY AND CULTURE

Cowley, A., *Aramaic Papyri of the Fifth Century B.C.,* Oxford, 1923
Finkelstein, L., *The Pharisees,* Philadelphia, 1938.
Jirku, A., *Geschichte des Volkes Israel,* Leipzig, 1931.
Lods, A., *Israel,* New York, 1932.
——, *The Prophets and the Rise of Judaism,* New York, 1937.
Oesterley, W. O. E., and Robinson, T. H., *History of Israel,* 2 vols., London, 1934.
Olmstead, A. T., *History of Palestine and Syria,* New York, 1931.
Robinson, H. W., *The History of Israel,* New York, 1938.
Rogers, R. W., *Cuneiform Parallels to the O. T.,* New York, 1912.
Schrader, E., *The Cuneiform Inscriptions and the O. T.;* translated by O. C. Whitehouse, London, 1885.
Smith, G. A., *Historical Geography of the Holy Land,* New York, 1932.
Welch, A. C., *Post-Exilic Judaism,* London, 1935.

CRITICAL AND INTERPRETIVE

Cook, S. A., *The Old Testament: a Re-interpretation,* London, 1936.
——, *The "Truth" of the Bible,* London, 1938.
Robinson, H. W., edited by, *Record and Revelation,* Oxford, 1938.

RELIGION

Abrahams, I., *Some Permanent Values in Judaism,* Oxford, 1924.
Knudson, A. C., *Religious Teaching of the O. T.,* New York, 1918.
Oesterley, W. O. E., and Robinson, T. H., *Religion of Israel,* 2nd edition, New York, 1937.
Robinson, H. W., *Religious Ideas of the O. T.,* New York, 1913.
Sellin, Ernst, *Israelitisch-jüdische Religionsgeschichte,* Leipzig, 1933.

SELECTED BIBLIOGRAPHY

THEOLOGY

Davidson, A. B., *Theology of the O. T.*, Edinburgh, 1904.
Eichrodt, W., *Theologie des Alten Testament,* Vol. I, Leipzig, 1933; Vol. II, 1935; Vol. III, 1939.
Köhler, L., *Theologie des Alten Testaments,* Tübingen, 1936.
Sellin, E., *Theologie des Alten Testaments,* Leipzig, 1933.

(A good work on Old Testament theology in English is greatly to be desired, but Continental scholars have been active recently in this field.)

WORKS OF REFERENCE

Hastings, J., edited by, *Dictionary of the Bible,* 5 vols., Edinburgh, 1898–1904.
Manson, T. W., edited by, *A Companion to the Bible,* New York, 1939.

PROPHECY AND THE PROPHETS

(Historical, Critical, Expository)

Batten, L. W., *The Hebrew Prophet,* London, 1905.
Cadman, S. Parkes, *The Prophets of Israel.*
Calkins, Raymond, *The Modern Message of the Minor Prophets,* New York, 1947.
Causse, A., *Les Prophètes d'Israël,* Paris, 1913.
Clausen, B. C., *Pen Portraits of the Prophets.*
Cornill, C. H., *The Prophets of Israel,* Chicago, 1897.
Driver, S. R., *The Ideals of the Prophets.*
Eiselen, F. C., *Prophetic Books of the O. T.*, New York, 1923.
——, *Prophecy and the Prophets in their Historical Relations,* New York, 1909.
——, *The Minor Prophets,* New York, 1907.
Gordon, A. R., *The Prophets of the O. T.*, New York, 1916.
Graham, W. C., *The Prophets and Israel's Culture,* Chicago, 1935.
Guillaume, A., *Prophecy and Divination among the Hebrews and Other Semites,* New York, 1938.
Knudson, A. C., *Beacon Lights of Prophecy,* New York, 1914.
——, *The Prophetic Movement in Israel,* New York, 1918.
Leslie, E. A., *The Prophets Tell Their Own Story,* New York, 1939.
Porter, F. C., *Messages of the Apocalyptical Writers,* New York, 1905.
Robinson, T. H., *Prophecy and the Prophets in Ancient Israel,* London, 1923.
Scott, R. B. Y., *The Relevance of the Prophets,* New York, 1947.

Smith, J. M. P., *The Prophet and His Problems,* New York, 1914.
——, *The Prophets and Their Times,* Chicago, 1925; 2nd edn. by W. A. Irwin, 1941.
Smith, W. R., *The Prophets of Israel,* new edn., London, 1912.
Welch, A. C., *Prophet and Priest in Old Israel,* London, 1936.

THEOLOGY

Duhm, B., *Die Theologie der Propheten,* Bonn, 1875.
Kirkpatrick, A. F., *Doctrine of the Prophets,* London, 1912.

WORKS ON INDIVIDUAL PROPHETS

ISAIAH

Duhm, B., *Das Buch Jesaia,* Göttingen, 4th edn., 1923. This is an outstanding work and reveals Duhm at his best. It was first published in 1892 and for quality it is unsurpassed.
Smith, G. A., *The Book of Isaiah, Expositor's Bible,* 2 vols., 2nd edn., 1927.

Smith's volumes on Isaiah and the Twelve Prophets represent the high-water mark of exposition. There is nothing like them.

The quality of Isaiah imparts itself to his commentators, and valuable and more accessible volumes can be found in the *Cambridge Bible* series by John Skinner, and in the *Century Bible* series by O. C. Whitehouse. S. R. Driver on *Isaiah: His Life and Times* is a valuable handbook. The Sellin series is well represented by Procksch (Vol. I, 1930) and Volz (Vol. II, 1932).

JEREMIAH

Jeremiah also has been fortunate in his interpreters. The commentary of C. H. Cornill, *Das Buch Jeremia,* Leipzig, 1905, does for the "impassioned man of Anathoth" what Duhm did for the regal Isaiah. For those who cannot read German, A. S. Peake's *Century Bible* (2 vols.) will convey much of the insight of Cornill's great work. Peake had profound spiritual insight and this commentary is most valuable. In the Sellin series Jeremiah is well represented by Paul Volz (Leipzig, 1928).

John Skinner's volume on *Prophecy and Religion* is worthy to stand beside Cornill. It was published in 1922 and is of unique value. A. C. Welch's *Jeremiah: His Time and His Work* is as useful as Driver on Isaiah.

SELECTED BIBLIOGRAPHY

EZEKIEL

G. A. Cooke's two volumes in the *International Critical Commentary* (Scribners, 1937), are the best we can get here. Ezekiel is still a problem to the interpreter. John Skinner in the *Expositor's Bible* did good work, but perhaps none were better qualified to interpret this bizarre personality than the quaint and peculiarly competent A. B. Davidson, who wrote the volume in the *Cambridge* series, revised in 1916 by A. W. Streane. W. A. Irwin's volume, *The Problem of Ezekiel,* Chicago, 1943, shows the problem still awaits solution.

THE BOOK OF THE TWELVE

The very title suggests G. A. Smith's great exposition, *The Book of the Twelve Prophets.* Here is exposition *in excelsis.* Smith had the capacity to make the past live, and in his hands these minor prophets become of major interest. None should fail to read these matchless volumes.

Das Zwolfprophetenbuch by Ernst Sellin has proved valuable in the composition of these studies. This series of commentaries (KAT) gives careful attention to religious values and does not allow these to be obscured by critical discussion, though full justice is done to critical questions.

Commentaries on the individual books of this group are not lacking. The *International Critical Commentary* with three volumes by W. R. Harper, J. M. P. Smith, W. H. Ward, H. G. Mitchell and J. A. Bewer, deal on a complete scale with all questions. S. R. Driver has the volume on *Joel and Amos* in the *Cambridge Bible* and his volume in the *Century Bible* on the last six of the Minor Prophets is of great value. G. W. Wade deals with *Micah, Obadiah, Joel, and Jonah* in the *Westminster* series of commentaries; in the same series *Hosea* is competently treated by S. L. Brown (London, 1932). Julian Morgenstern's stimulating researches on Amos will be found in *Amos Studies,* Vol. I (Cincinnati, 1941), and J. E. MacFadyen's *A Cry for Justice* (a Study in Amos), reprinted Edinburgh, 1927, will acquaint us with the social and religious passion of these spokesmen for God.

INDEX OF SCRIPTURE REFERENCES

INDEX OF SCRIPTURE REFERENCES

JEREMIAH—*Cont'd*

EZEKIEL

HOSEA

HOSEA—*Cont'd*

JOEL

AMOS

INDEX OF SCRIPTURE REFERENCES

HABAKKUK

ZEPHANIAH

HAGGAI

ZECHARIAH

MALACHI

INDEX OF SCRIPTURE REFERENCES

HEBREWS

JAMES

REVELATION

INDEX OF NAMES AND SUBJECTS

INDEX OF NAMES AND SUBJECTS

INDEX OF NAMES AND SUBJECTS